Children picking up our bones

Will never know that these were once

As quick as foxes on the hill

A Postcard from the Volcano
Wallace Stevens

For the grandchildren:

English, Emily, Ashley, T.R., Lindsey, Cate, Carly, Brooks, Natalie, Bronwynne, Aidan, Malcolm

Contents

Family Trees

LILLIS, 1923–2000

Her brothers and sisters:
Newell, **Lillis**, Earl, Lois (Hirschi), Don, Cleo (Atkin), Fuller "Ted"

Her parents:
Fuller Remington 1891–1982   +   Edith Leoma Hadlock 1897–1982

Her grandparents:
Joseph Fuller Remington 1859–1899   +   Amanda Alfreda Rasmussen 1871–1955
Erskine Curtis Hadlock 1855–1936   +   Edith Ann Hobbs 1861–1939

GEORGE, 1926–1990

His sisters and brother:
Beverly (Walker), **George,** Barbara Dean (Merrill), Samuel Jr.

His parents:
Samuel Brooks 1886–1962   +   Winnifred Parry 1892–1977

His grandparents:
George Brooks 1845–1930   +   Emma Cornelia Branch 1855–1929
Edward Thomas Parry 1859–1938   +   Charlotte Ann Edmunds 1862–1945

The Source Materials

LILLIS

Lillis wrote many long letters. Even during her 10 years as a quadriplegic, she easily wrote more than 1,000 letters. Thankfully, her mother, Edith, saved many of Lillis's letters and inculcated the practice of saving letters. Thus, many letters survive.

Lillis kept diaries from 1960 until her death. Her diaries are usually a mere catalog of mundane daily tasks, but they give a rhythm of life, they preserve names, and they fix dates of important events.

Lillis also kept scrapbooks for herself and on behalf of George and their children. These include summary write-ups of some important events, such as her courtship and marriage, or the summary of her employment in Hawaii.

Scrapbooking was an unschooled hobby. She used cheap binders and pages. She saved news clippings of births, deaths, marriages, and other important events, but usually cut off the dates, and used glue that bled through the newsprint. She cropped photographs to fit. Nevertheless, these scrapbooks were invaluable for fixing dates and for prioritizing what she viewed as important.

In the 1980s Lillis started to write fragments of her life story and she continued to make random and unorganized notes of memories through the 1990s. These are more like notes than a rough draft. The pages were not numbered, bound, or even kept in the same place. And they were written on mismatched paper. The dates that the notes were created can sometimes be extrapolated from references to known events. There are examples of her writing variants of the same events several times. This random clutter of notes was a gift for creating a memoir of her life while preserving her voice and priorities.

In all her writing, Lillis had a tendency to put a soft filter on troublesome events while emphasizing pleasant memories. She idealized growing up in a cabin without electricity or running water in an isolated mining camp. She could not bring herself to say that her aunt had committed suicide, even though her grandmother spoke of it openly. And she never spoke truthfully of the fire in her father's house. As with any source, it is important to understand its limitations.

At her death her papers—letters, scrapbooks, manuscripts—were in disarray. Pages were torn loose or were crumbling, the binders needed to be stabilized. Today there still has been no extraordinary effort to remount artifacts on acid-free paper or preserve them for the long term.

GEORGE

George's early life is more difficult to tease out because there are fewer written documents. The absence of primary sources makes his story shorter. He had only a dozen or so photographs of himself before the war; most were undated. His mother saved very little beyond such things as certificates of birth and baptism.

George's mother, Winnifred Parry Brooks, wrote a short autobiography that documents some important dates such as births, marriages, and improvements to their home. And she kept diaries (which are in the possession of Renae Walker of Salt Lake City), but those are little more than abbreviated notes or lists of errands and chores.

George's father, Samuel, wrote a much longer, rambling autobiography that failed to mention the births of his children. It offers no insight into George's day-to-day childhood and family life.

Most of George's contemporaries were dead or unreliable by the time these fragments were collected. George's brother, Samuel Jr., was 8 years younger than George. He freely acknowledged, "I have no detailed memory of him living at home." When George left home—first to war, then on a mission, then marriage—the paths of George and Samuel Jr. separated until the 1960s. By then, George's children were old enough to have their own reliable memories. Most of what is known today about George's childhood is what his children remember him telling them.

George started two journals during the Second World War, but neither is complete. He wrote about his combat experience after the fact. George probably wrote letters home from his military service in Europe but only two letters survive—both addressed to his younger sister, Barbara Dean, and both written after the end of hostilities. Apparently his parents did not save his letters. George saved some of his mother's letters and these give a bit of insight into his life as they reference and respond to his letters.

In the 1970s and 1980s George wrote randomly and infrequently about his "reflections, feelings, and values." Sometimes months would pass between his lengthy, essay-like entries. He wrote less than 40 pages over 10 years. These pages give valuable nuance to his opinions and motivations.

Some of the quotations and stories of George and Lillis preserved here are based on their children's memories: G. Remington, Dean, Leslie, and Nyman. No doubt those memories come with a bias.

Memory and preference determine which stories survive and which are told. No doubt it is so with all histories, and on all occasions. There will always be incidental truths revealed by what we choose to tell and what we forget.

I

Lillis
Earliest Memories
1923–1929

The Rector mining camp no longer exists. It seems to have vanished without a trace. Even when Lillis lived there it was insignificant and very remote, near the Colorado border south of the White River.

BIRTH

Lillis was actually born in Naples, Utah, a village on the eastern frontier of Mormondom, October 17, 1923. Rector was a half-day's drive to the south over rough roads. Her parents, Fuller and Edith Remington, traveled to Naples so that Lillis could be born in her Grandmother Amanda Remington's house, and be nearer to a doctor who lived in nearby Vernal. Lillis was a healthy baby, weighing 7 pounds 8 ounces at birth. She had reddish or brown hair and green eyes. She was the second child, 14 months younger than her brother Newell. The two children spent their first years at the Rector mining camp, one of several Gilsonite mines in the area. Gilsonite is a black asphalt resin. Her father and her Uncle Milo Hadlock had opened the mine a year earlier.

The Remingtons lived in the "foreman's house"—a rustic cabin without running water and without electricity. The house had four rooms: two bedrooms, a kitchen, and a parlor. Lillis idealized it in her memory, commenting on the beautiful green enamel-and-chrome cast-iron kitchen range, and the china shades on the oil lamps. She said the house was pleasant. No doubt her mother's attention to homemaking and her father's warmth and humor helped make her childhood memories what they were.

Even without electricity her mother could use a treadle sewing machine, and the family enjoyed listening to music on a wind-up Victrola phonograph. They had a pair of "Talking Machine" toy boxers who would stand above the record and box while the record went around.

To the west of the house there was a tent with a wooden floor. It was furnished with a cot, a potbellied stove, and a washing machine that ran on some sort of fuel. Guests sometimes slept there, and Lillis's mother, Edith, would dry clothes there in the winter. There were washtubs and a washboard in there also. Beyond the tent and up the path a ways was a privy. Ashes from the stove were dumped daily into the outhouse pit. There was also a root cellar under a mound of earth; storing or preserving food was a very common if not essential home industry. The door into the cellar was sloped and set into the mound. This door became an improvised sliding board for the children, who had few toys.

Rain gutters and rain barrels collected water to be used for bathing and cleaning. Drinking water was hauled in by truck. The house was heated with a small wood stove in the parlor, and the wood-burning kitchen range. The range also had a reservoir or water heater built in, and since the range was usually warm, so too was the water. Bathing would be done in the kitchen in a tub; when the tub was not in use, it hung on a nail outside.

Lillis remembered violent electrical storms and flash floods. Thunder claps and brilliant streaks of lightning rolled and crashed across the narrow valley, filling the streambeds with foaming, muddy water. The water would run in torrents off the roof, fill the rain barrels, run under the woodpile, and form rivulets rushing down the hills. On one such night, lightning struck the stovepipe and left a small crack in the kitchen range.

The "Foreman's House" at the Rector mining camp (center foreground) was Lillis's first home. It had no electricity. Drinking water was delivered by truck. Additional water was collected in a rain barrel. Newell and Lillis were given much freedom to play in the hills around the camp.

Playing Outdoors with Newell

Newell and Lillis were given much freedom to play in the hills around the camp. Some seasons they might have been the only children in the camp and they became close friends. Newell was only about 7 years old when the family left the camp forever. Yet his parents gave him the responsibility for looking after Lillis. She recalled:

> He was watchful over me and I felt safe when I was with him. There was only 14 months' difference in our age but he seemed years older to me. He never seemed afraid of anything, and I was fearful of many things. He had a strong sense of right and wrong. He was honest and obedient, alert, he was sensitive, he learned quickly, he was generous, and a perfectionist. He was an unusual child by most standards. He was tall and agile for his age. He could throw rocks swiftly and accurately. The miners used to challenge him to throw at things and were amazed at his ability. Sometimes he would stand beyond the root cellar and throw pebbles through the kitchen window to the stove where Mother was working to tease her. He never struck the glass or Mother. Though he died young, just 39 years old in 1961, I continue to hold the deep admiration and love for him that I had in childhood.

Among the few strict rules, they were not allowed to go in the miners' bunkhouse or in the boarding house. The desert landscape became their playground. They especially liked the large, flat formation of rocks that lay in the streambed and they like to climb the cliffs above it. There was usually enough water in the stream that they could float their homemade boats. Moss and wildflowers grew on a shadowy bank of the stream.

It was not unusual to hear the howl of a wolf or the bark of coyotes. There were porcupines, raccoons, rabbits, deer, rodents, snakes, feral cattle, and wild horses. The children would watch them from the ground, lying in the dirt among the piñon cones. Lillis could be fearful, but not when she was with Newell. One day Newell killed a large rattlesnake by stoning it to death. It upset Lillis to watch it die, swishing, curling, and coiling as it tried to protect itself. Newell finally picked it up with a long stick and dropped it over a ledge. On rare occasions they would see a

Lillis and Newell, c. 1928.

cougar watching them, and when discovered it would slink away. One time, while in the car in the mountains with their father, they saw a bear.

The winters were harsh. The clothes froze on the clothesline as stiff as boards, to be carried into the house to finish drying. Cars had no defrosters or heaters. Winter brought deep snow, covering hills and valleys. The snow would thaw and freeze so it was possible to walk on it without sinking in. Winter had its rewards. They improvised games of fox and geese or they built snow caves and forts. It was excellent for snow sculpturing. Fuller sculptured in the snow; once he made an open-top car big enough to sit in. He made snowmen with scarfs, hats, broom-handle arms, and Gilsonite eyes. He would take the children sledding. Sometimes he would ride down the hill with them; other times he would give them a shove, shouting instructions as they sped away. Sometimes he hitched the sleds to horses, their nostrils steaming in the cold crisp air.

Despite her idyllic memories, Lillis admitted to being lonely.

> I believe I was more restless than most children. It bothered my parents. They would ask me why I was sad and I would tell them I was lonesome and wanted to go somewhere but I had no idea where. Maybe it was because of this loneliness I developed an imaginary friend by the name of Janereen. Whenever I was alone I pretended to play with her. I talked aloud to her and sometimes brought her to the table with me at meal time. Both of my parents were aware of her. My mother seemed to accept it as being normal but I believe it caused my father some concern. My playmate was never so real to me that I didn't recognize her as a fantasy.

Lillis stopped pretending sometime after the family moved to Vernal when she started school. "My mother asked me if I ever saw or played with Janereen anymore. I told her she had gone away. Several years later my mother and I laughed about it."

DRAGON AND WATSON

The children were always excited on the days they drove to Dragon or Watson—both are now ghost towns. Earl and Alta Wardle, friends of Fuller, lived in Dragon; they would always visit with them. Dragon had a doctor's office, a one-room schoolhouse, and a couple of stores. Fuller and Edith would buy two or three weeks' worth of groceries at Heath's store. Finnicum's store would have candy. There was a warehouse in Dragon where Lillis saw her first movie. That was a big event. It was silent, and she was too young to read the intertitles. She remembered the jerky images, and a woman playing the piano to provide a soundtrack.

There was an old man named Oliver in Dragon who gave the children nickels. He later moved to Vernal and lived in a boarding house about the time Lillis started school in Vernal. Edith instructed Lillis not to visit him. But one day on her way home from school she did stop to talk to him. He called her and she went into his room. He gave her a dime and he put his hand on her leg.

> It frightened me so I ran out and never went near him or the boarding house again. Quite a long time later I told my mother about that experience. He was so old and shaky I can't believe he could have done more than feel my leg. I could have pushed him over and probably would have done it if I hadn't run away.

They would also buy gas in Dragon before returning home in the late afternoon. Quite often Fuller would have to stop to change a tire. Tires were not reliable, and motorists often carried more than one spare, as well as patching tools. The ride was bumpy. They would bounce around in the ruts of hardened mud. Fuller had a big black four-door Buick with pull-down shades on the windows. The back doors opened from the front so if ever a door was opened while the car was going, it was difficult to close until the car was stopped because of the air pressure against it.

SOCIAL LIFE

There was a boarding house in Rector that was also used as a public gathering place for parties, plays, and dances. People always took their children and babies to the socials with them. Fuller loved to dance. Sometimes when they square danced he would be the caller. Edith was more shy and didn't enjoy dancing so much, but she liked to visit with people. She would dance a few dances; Fuller would dance all of them. There were always some who simply tended their babies and watched the others dance.

Some of the men had good singing voices and they would go carol-
ing at Christmastime. The brothers Ross and Porter Merrell were among
those who sang. The children went with their father in the deep snow to
cut the Christmas tree, and they brought it home on a sled. They decorated it with twisted white wax candles in little tin holders that clamped
onto the tree. They threaded garlands of popcorn and hung tinsel. Edith
also had some glass ornaments. They would often receive a box of pome-
granates from Grandmother Amanda Remington who wintered in St.
George. The children would receive a stocking full of candy and nuts,
maybe a pack of gum, and an orange in the toe—all rare treats, but the
orange was the most rare.

MOTHER AND FATHER

Edith was a good cook and a good housekeeper. She did her own
baking and preserved many of the foods the family ate. She set the table
with a cloth and napkins for every meal. She never allowed anyone to
walk around while eating. The family sat together at the table to eat. The
family knelt by their chairs in prayer before breakfast. The children took
their turns in prayer. In these ways their culture and civilization were
expressed while living on the periphery near poverty.

Mining was dangerous; there were many opportunities for injury
and it was acknowledged that at any moment a life could be altered. The
ore was lifted from the mines in buckets on steel cables and pulleys. Once
Fuller was standing near the opening of the mine when a bucket slipped
loose from the pulley. It could have fallen with great force on the men
below had he not grabbed the cable with his bare hand. The cable rushing through his hand shredded the flesh, exposing tendons and bones.
Few had cars and Edith couldn't drive, but she went with him as he drove
his own car with one hand to the doctor. Fuller was lucky and his hand
healed without any impairment and very little scarring.

Fuller did not dig in the mines, but he did go into them often to
inspect the work. The miners would be covered with black Gilsonite dust.
Fuller would get dirty, but not as dirty as the miners. Lillis and Newell
would wait for him at the end of the day to come home, up the path,
carrying his lunch box, arms outstretched to greet the children.

The mining job paid well, but Edith wanted to move the family into
town so that the children could attend school and church. Also, Edith

was worried that Fuller had developed a chronic cough, probably from breathing dust in the mine; that's how Fuller's father had died. Lillis was almost 6 when they moved. Her younger brother Earl was about 4 and her sister Lois was just newly born. But Lillis only had memories of Newell from her days at Rector.

II

Lillis
Vernal Years
1929–1941

THE NEW HOUSE AND YARD

Lillis's father bought a white frame bungalow in Vernal in 1929. The new house had indoor plumbing, electricity, a gas refrigerator, a real bathtub, an electric washing machine, a long wide cement driveway and garage, green lawns, a small orchard, shrubs, trees, flowers, and a white picket fence. Now the family had neighbors, dozens of children to play with, and a city park only two blocks away. The youngest of the seven Remington children, Ted, was born in 1936. There were many Hadlock cousins living close by and going to the same schools.

The house was small but the lot was ¾ of an acre, big enough to plant a garden. Lillis recalled how happy she was with the new house, and enumerated the many flowers and trees in the yard:

> Our orchard had apple, cherry, plum, pear, and apricot trees. Our garden had raspberries, strawberries, and gooseberries. Dad built a large sandbox, swings, and teeter-totters for us to play with. The previous owner, Mr. Niles Huel, had planted many flowers and had won blue ribbons at the fair for his dahlias. So the yard had many beautiful flowers. There were exquisite roses climbing

on arbors. There were bleeding hearts, chrysanthemums, daisies, tiger lilies, irises, peonies, sweet williams, phlox, lily of the valley, white baby's-breath, coral bells, and many others I have forgotten. There was a hedge of lilac bushes that formed a perfect playhouse for me. Mock orange bushes would bloom all spring. Forsythia, potentilla, and brilliant crimson flag bloomed in late summer. Fuchsia, goldenrod, and many others filled the edges and corners of our yard. The roses were my favorite. We picked large bouquets twice each week; it seemed they were always on the tables or dressers in our house.

On the north edge of the property they had a stable where they sometimes kept a cow. Sometimes they also kept chickens or pigs. There was another one-room house in the back with a wood stove. That became a bedroom for the boys as the family grew.

Primary School

Lillis and Newell started first grade the same day in the same class at Central Elementary School. From the first day of school, in Miss Eleanor Parker's class, Newell was at the top of the class. He would remain at the top of his class even through his university studies. He was in the first reading group while Lillis was in the second. Lillis said she had a speech impediment and would mispronounce some words. But she took pride knowing that her brother was a better reader than anyone in the school.

There was a bell on the top of the building that signaled the start or end of school, lunch, and recess. The bell rope hung from the bell loft down in the middle of the hall. Iris White, one of the fourth-grade teachers, would assign children in turn to ring the bell. The children looked forward to their turn, and Lillis clearly remembered the day she was asked to ring it. It was wonderful to hold the big rope, hear the tone above, and feel the tug of the swinging bell. The bell was heavy enough that it could lift a child with a firm grip. But the children were cautioned not to swing the bell too hard.

It was also a memorable day when one of the larger and more irreverent boys was given the assignment. He jumped and swung on the rope, turning the bell upside down and leaving himself dangling far off the floor, swinging in midair, and fearing to let go of the rope. Miss White in her most firm voice reminded him of the broken rule and the slim chance he would ever be given that assignment again.

One terrible day in first grade, Miss Parker had a group stand in front of the class to sing. Lillis was never able to hear pitch or sing well, even as an adult. The teacher singled her out and tried to get her to hum or whistle or otherwise find the pitch, but without success. Unintentionally, the teacher humiliated Lillis. On her walk home, Newell told her, "Lots of people can't sing and it isn't that important. Nobody cares anyway." But it was important to Lillis and an example of her self-consciousness. That episode was also an example of her mutually supportive relationship with Newell.

All in all, Lillis had a good experience in school.

Fortunately I had good teachers in all elementary grades. I liked my teachers and had no reason to feel they didn't like me. For the most part I liked school, had many friends, and felt quite secure in my social relationships, even though red hair was not the most desirable color, nor were the freckles that came with it. Some of the more bold boys called me "carrot top" and "red-headed gingerbread." I discovered quite young I was physically stronger than most of my friends. I was underweight for my age, but average height, agile, and quick in most games. I could out-run, out-jump, out-perform most of the girls and boys my age, Newell being the exception.

NEWELL'S GLASSES

Newell had limited vision without his glasses. He was always afraid of having his glasses broken. They were expensive and had to be replaced in Salt Lake City. He was tall, strong, and athletic, but not terribly aggressive. So he became the target of two bullies who were smaller and younger than he was. As Lillis told the story,

They would wait until he was alone then pounce on him and beat him up. They would take his glasses off and make his nose bleed. For whatever reason Newell would not fight them. One of them, Harold Winward, was a short, stocky, loudmouth boy, and a poor student. His whole family was loud and when walking past his house you could hear them yelling or cursing at each other. They used very bad language. The other boy was seldom even in school. His name has long since escaped me. Most kids at school stayed out of their way. Newell was the one they chose to pick on. Newell was frightened of them. He would cry to Dad and Mother holding his bent glasses and wiping his bleeding nose. Dad would tell Newell that Harold was smaller, not as smart, not as strong. But Newell would run to get out of his way.

Lillis was about 10 or 11. She had a friend named Wanda Blank. Wanda liked Newell and they both felt sorry about Newell being harassed and humiliated.

One cold winter day Wanda and I decided to do something to stop the miserable situation. We knew the route Harold took to go home. We hid in the alcove of the courthouse and when he passed, we jumped out and grabbed him. We knocked him down and pounded him until he screamed and yelled. The more he called us bad names the more we hit him. We pulled his hair, bit, and kicked him. We stuffed snow inside his shirt and washed his face with snow. A large crowd of kids gathered round. We let him up and chased him half way home. Never again did he bother Newell or any other of our friends. At the time we felt we had achieved a great victory but in looking back I'm not so sure. We had robbed him of his only recognition and soon he was forgotten.

In the 6 years at Central Elementary School I began to notice that some were rich and others were poor; some were kind and others were not. I enjoyed a nice house, nice family, and many friends. But life was not always fair for everyone.

HER BICYCLE

Lillis had a cousin 5 years older named Leah Cook. Leah's mother had died in the Spanish flu pandemic, and was neglected by her father. So Leah was often in the Remington home and was like an older sister to the Remington children. Fuller bought Newell and Leah matching bicycles one year. It was during the Great Depression, and a substantial expense, so Lillis worried that she would never get one of her own. Lillis loved Leah but spent a year being jealous of that bicycle. The next year, when Lillis was about 12, Fuller bought a bicycle for her as well. It brought Lillis great pleasure and freedom for the next several years, even through high school, until she left Vernal. She was the first among her friends to get a bike, a subtle indication of the family's financial freedom. Soon Edna Colton and other friends got bikes. They would sometimes ride together, 10 or 12 miles. But it was also an activity she could enjoy alone; she usually hated being alone. She would get up early at sunrise and ride for miles.

> I felt such freedom riding country lanes, through the park, uptown, on streets that were unfamiliar until then, places I would never go on foot. The air was fresh and cool, the wind blowing through my hair and in my face. I could go to any of my friends' homes in a matter of minutes.

The Great Depression

The Great Depression affected everyone, but affected everyone differently. For people in rural Utah who had grown up with a pioneer subsistence economy, the impact may have been muted. And the concerns of the adults are not always the concerns of the children. The Remingtons may have been a bit better off than some. Fuller had a gregarious and enterprising personality which allowed him to attempt any job, such as opening the mine in Rector. Their house in Vernal was small but adequate. Lillis commented that her mother "never seemed to feel secure financially even though we always had enough. A lot of work was required to care for a big family like ours. Her planning, efficiency, and industry improved our standard of living."

Edith was industrious and frugal, even into old age. Her grandchildren, for example, remember her saving animal fat to make lye soap, just one example of her many home industries. She preserved food. She made clothes, quilts, rugs, and many useful things from recycled fabrics. She worked long, fast, steadily, and methodically. She took the children on walks to Ashley Creek. There they would wade and play, gather watercress, pick asparagus along the stream bank, and dig dandelion greens to serve at home.

The older children helped Edith earn extra money. Newell and Lillis grew horseradish, put vinegar on it, and sold it for 25¢ a pint. They sold milk for 10¢ a quart, eggs 20¢ a dozen, and also fruits and vegetables— all produced on their city lot.

On rare occasions Edith would do housekeeping for others at $1.50 per day. She and Newell also became custodians of the First Ward chapel. Newell did most of the work. People got their money's worth when Newell or Edith cleaned. Sometimes Lillis would help by washing and polishing the sacrament [communion] trays and the miniature sacrament glasses or silver cups. Newell kept that job through high school. It was a large building and took a lot of work.

Edith kept both Newell and Lillis close to her several hours a day in summer to help pick the fruit, peel and can it, weed the garden, pick the berries, peas, beans, dig the potatoes, pull the carrots, husk the corn, gather the eggs, catch a chicken to be killed. On laundry day Newell and Lillis took the clothes through their rinses—one with bluing, one through clear water. They had an electric washer, but not an automatic washer, so laundry required a lot of water changes and wringing.

The Telephone, and Other Quirks of Daily Life

And while on the subject of appliances, their telephone shared a line with others; it was called a "party line." It should have been called a "multi-party line." When a party's number was dialed, only that phone would ring. But anyone else who shared the party line might lift the receiver in their house and listen in on a conversation. If someone needed to make a call, they could lift their receiver and ask their neighbor to end their conversation and free up the line. So there was no privacy. Everyone knew everyone's business and took pleasure in talking about it. There would be several customers using each party line. If someone *could* listen in on a conversation, no doubt they often did, trying to be discreet and undetected.

Homes were rarely locked. And if one were locked, chances are the hardware store had skeleton keys to open just about any lock, except the bank or jail. The doctor made house calls. The butcher knew how much meat you needed, how large to cut your roast and steaks.

"Permanent" hair styling was a bit frightening. They used a huge electric contraption that would fasten hot clips to the hair. At least one of these would invariably burn you. The beauticians would forever be fastening and refastening the clips. They smelled terrible and were very fatiguing. Many times hair would be cooked frizzy and dry. Lillis usually wore her hair in a short pageboy with a pompadour in front that she could comb on the run. Mirror time in her big family was limited.

Beginning about 1935, Fuller worked for the city to help supervise and direct the work of the Civilian Conservation Corps (CCC), President Roosevelt's public work relief program for young unmarried men. There was a large camp in Vernal, and boys from different states would come to town to work. For nothing better to do, some would attend church and some were converted. Some dated local girls and some married them; others left them pregnant. There was another CCC camp on the Ute reservation about 30 miles from Vernal. One day Fuller was driving from Roosevelt and saw a young man walking along the road toward Vernal. He seemed ill so Fuller stopped to see if he could help him. The fellow was in pain and quite ill. Fuller took him to the hospital in Vernal where they removed his appendix. Fuller stayed with him the first night because he had no family. Fuller or the family would visit him each day, and they took him flowers and magazines to read. He was about 19 years old, and very polite. He was especially appreciative of Fuller and kept in touch with him for many years after.

Despite the many household chores, Lillis enjoyed a happy social life with her friends. From their earliest days in Vernal it seemed that the Remington house became a gathering place for friends from school and church. And Edith was good about welcoming the friends of her children into her house.

Lillis enjoyed a bit of her own money. When she was younger she tended neighbor children for 25¢ an evening. Many times that 25¢ included doing their dishes and putting their children to bed. She liked the children, but hated tending them with a passion. "The evenings were so long and I was fearful of being alone." After the children were asleep it was difficult staying awake and she was afraid of the unfamiliar noises in other peoples' houses. There were no TVs in those days, and some didn't even have a radio. She hated walking home alone in the dark even if it were only a block. As she got older she took various other jobs, a chambermaid at a motel, a sales clerk, and office clerk for a dentist.

HIGH SCHOOL

Grades seven through twelve were all on one campus known as Uintah High School. The combined junior high and high school had about 1,000 students. There were three buildings on the campus, and an LDS seminary building across the street. Many Utah school districts allowed "release time" so the Mormon students could to attend seminary during the school day while maintaining a separation of church and state. Those buildings became the hub of Lillis's life for 6 years. She usually preferred to walk the mile to school, joining friends along the way.

She ran in a crowd of fellows and girls whom she had known from elementary school. She went on to college with some of them, and remained close to others all her life. She went to church with some, and some were cousins. The "crowd," as she called it, used any excuse to party. They ate lunch together at school, met at each other's houses, and called on each other for rides. Not every family had a car during the Depression, but Newell could sometimes borrow Fuller's car. Sometimes they would meet at the drugstore where there was a soda fountain.

The Mormon youth auxiliary, the Mutual Improvement Association, met weekly one evening mid-week. On most "Mutual" nights the crowd would linger and talk on the grass of the church or at the Remington house. The boys would follow Newell and the girls would follow Lillis. Sometimes they would drink hot soups or chocolate, and eat crackers. The church youth group was large. Besides studying the gospel, they also learned to dance, cook, or sew. In the summer the Mutual girls went camping in the High Uintas or in the Ashley National Forest.

Her high school years were happy and successful. She kept up on her schoolwork and her grades were good. She won the Declamation, a seminary speech competition of about 300 students, while a sophomore. (Newell won as a freshman, and in a different year Earl also won this contest.) She played on the girls' basketball team; she was president of the Home Economics Club; she was in the Girls' Pep Club; she was on the yearbook staff and was a yearbook sales winner; she was Business Manager (a student body officer), and on the Board of Control (a council of students and faculty); she was on the typewriter team; and served on many other committees and in leadership positions. That being said, it was "the crowd" and her friendships that she remembered most fondly.

III

Lillis
Her Tribe

The Hadlock Family

Lillis moved to Vernal near her mother's family, the Hadlocks, when she was 5. By then her Grandfather Hadlock was in his 70s. The Hadlock family was a noisy, fast-talking, laughing, close-knit family. It was not unusual for several to be laughing and talking at the same time. When they were together they would often sing in part harmony. Most drank beer, some drank coffee, Grandmother drank tea. These vices were forbidden in the Remington house, yet somehow tolerated at the grandparents' house.

Food was abundant when they would celebrate holidays together around the large dining table at Grandfather's house. At family get-togethers, the men (cousins and uncles) would gather in the kitchen to drink Grandfather's home-brewed beer, aging in a crock behind the kitchen stove. Lillis's father, Fuller, and Jess Haws (who also married into the Hadlock family), would not drink with their Hadlock in-laws but would remain with the women in the front parlor.

Grandparents' House

The Hadlock grandparents had a large yard and many interesting places for children to run, hide, and play. Vases lined both sides of the path leading to the front gate. Lombardy poplars lined the outside of the front yard. The front yard and porch could be filled with cousins playing hide-and-seek. There was an orchard to the south of the home. The back yard had a pasture, stable, granary, outhouse, a field to the west where wheat was grown, a buggy shed, a car garage, a root cellar, and a coal house. A stream ran from the hills in the north, down through the pasture. Sometimes the Remingtons would keep a cow or two in the Hadlock pasture. The children might sleep overnight at the grandparents' house. Lillis liked to climb a ladder and sleep on top of the haystack. The desert air was clear and the stars were bright. She would also play in the barn and jump from the loft into the hay below.

The kitchen had a sink with cold running water. There was also a flour bin so large that children had a hard time reaching the cookies or crackers at the bottom. The kitchen had a polished wood-burning range. The pantry often had heads of lettuce in cold pans of water, and cream rising to the top of pans of milk in the cooler. The icebox had a pan to catch the melting ice. The iceman would bring large blocks of ice packed in sawdust in his mule-drawn wagon. He would chisel out a piece of ice and bring it into the house on his back with ice tongs, and a leather shawl on his back to keep him dry. They would sometimes dry corn on the kitchen roof with mosquito netting over it to protect it from flies.

A hand-carved clock with chimes hung over the player piano in the parlor. An oval picture frame held a photograph of Lillis's mother, Edith, and Lena (Edith's niece and playmate). As young girls, about 6 or 7 years old, Edith and Lena had sat for an itinerant photographer without permission and then charged it to Grandfather. There were bookcases with glass doors that covered Grandfather's many books: biographies, history, poetry, and some church books. A coal or wood stove warmed the room. Sometimes Grandmother would sit near it in her rocking chair with her feet on a small footstool.

Their bedroom had a large beautifully carved bed where Grandmother slept. The cousins were asked not to play on it, but they did anyway. Then they would anxiously try to fluff up her feather bedding to make it look like nobody had been there. There was another smaller bed in the room where Grandfather slept. They had a washstand with a large white pitcher and porcelain basin, also a closet with a full-length mirror with drawers and a shelf for a dresser set and a chair. They had a large walk-in closet between the bedroom and kitchen where children could hide or pass from one room to the other.

GRANDFATHER ERSKINE CURTIS HADLOCK
Born November 6, 1855, Danville, Vermont
Married Edith Ann Hobbs, November 24, 1879, Logan, Utah
Died January 14, 1936, Vernal, Utah

Curtis was a rather quiet man with steel-gray hair, not tall, but strong. He worked as a blacksmith until his death. He wore glasses. He had a mustache. He was serious, not real playful, but kind and generous. He always seemed to have hard, white peppermints in his pockets and lots of nickels and dimes which he passed out freely. He and his family were converted to the church and came west during the big migration of the Saints. They settled first in Idaho.

His father (Lillis's great-grandfather) was also a blacksmith; he moved to Vernal when the church asked him to help settle the valley. Curtis remained in Idaho. He was a railroad engineer and drove a train from Blackfoot, Idaho, to Ogden, Utah. His parents wanted him to come to Vernal and work in the blacksmith shop. But he had met Edith Ann in Franklin, Idaho, and they were raising four children there. Family lore has it that one day a cow came onto the railroad tracks and Curtis's train hit it. The hot water from the boiler on the train splashed, apparently, on his legs and scalded him. After that he moved his family from Blackfoot to Vernal. Four more children were born in Vernal, including Lillis's mother, Edith Leoma, the youngest of the eight children.

Curtis opened his own blacksmith shop in Vernal and Lillis would walk past it on the way home from school. It was very interesting there but she felt a bit out of place. She said:

> Men were always there visiting—only men. Had I been a boy I would have spent more time there. Grandfather always would give me a nickel and ask how my day was. He never told me not to come but I felt he rushed me on my way by telling me to hurry on home. I don't think anyone else noticed me or paid any attention to me. Uncle Carl worked there. He and Grandfather wore big leather aprons. Quite often horses were being shod. These big animals would lean on Grandfather when he lifted

Lillis's Grandfather Curtis Hadlock (left) in his blacksmith shop, with his son Carl, center, and an unidentified man. Curtis was in his 70s when Lillis knew him.

their foot to fit a shoe. And he was an old man. You could smell the leather and the sweat of the horses. There would be wagon wheels and farm machinery to repair. There were always hot embers glowing in the forge.

Curtis seldom ever attended church. He remained home with his wife who was crippled from polio and unable to attend. He sat at the kitchen table to eat his meals as she sat near him in a rocking chair. He prayed aloud over his food.

Grandfather built his own home. He had a kiln on his property where many of the bricks for his home were made. He used to sing in a quartet. He also played the tuba in a band when he was younger. Grandfather had a sister, Libby Weeks, who lived in Vernal. He was loyal and kind to Grandmother.

One remarkable story that should be remembered concerns Curtis and his eldest daughter, Lucilla. Aunt Lucilla found herself pregnant and about to marry a man she did not love; the bridegroom was in fact abusive. On her wedding day Grandfather spoke to her and discovered her anxiety and confusion. Grandfather offered to tell the guests and the groom that the wedding was cancelled. He persuaded Lucilla that it would be alright. The wedding was cancelled, and Lucilla had her baby out of wedlock. It is remarkable that Curtis was so sympathetic and courageous against the backdrop of frontier sensibilities and social pressures before the turn of the century.

GRANDMOTHER EDITH ANN HOBBS HADLOCK
Born April 25, 1861, Cheltenham, England
Married Erskine Curtis Hadlock, November 24, 1879, Logan, Utah
Died January 26, 1939, Vernal, Utah

Edith Ann (not to be confused with her daughter, Edith Leoma) was a paraplegic, most probably from a bout with polio. While still a young woman about thirty years old she had an undiagnosed illness lasting 3 weeks which left her paralyzed from the waist down. She spent the next 48 years of her life in a rocking chair. She could move herself in that chair from one room to another, doing her housework. While sitting in her rocking chair she would wash dishes, polish her kitchen range, mop the floor, and cook. Like many women of her era, she also did handicrafts, such as knitting rag rugs. She kept an immaculate house and was a good cook. If she couldn't reach something she was not shy about directing someone to help her or to complete a task. She had a quick wit and a caustic tongue. In her later years she was partially deaf but nevertheless seemed to know where the children were and what they were doing.

Grandmother's oldest daughter, Aunt Lucilla, helped raise the younger brothers and sisters while she was raising her own children. Lucilla's daughter Lena was the same age as Lucilla's sister Edith Leoma. Thus Lillis had cousins whom she referred to as *aunt*; Lillis always called her cousin Lena *Aunt Lena*.

As Lillis grew older it became her responsibility to go to Grandmother's house, help her prepare for bed, and stay with her until Grandfather came home. Lillis would pull her grandmother in her chair into the parlor to be near the potbelly stove. She would remove her shoes and sometimes rub her feet. Edith Ann had feeling in her feet but could not move them. Grandfather would lift her into bed when he returned home in the late evening.

Grandfather Curtis Hadlock died of pneumonia and of a bowel obstruction, possibly cancer, when Lillis was 12. He was 79. Grandmother had been so dependent on him for so many years his death was difficult for her. Grandmother Hadlock moved into the Remington house after Grandfather died, and shared a room with Lillis. Lillis attended to her at night. Grandmother praised and appreciated Lillis. Sometimes she would cry because she felt she was a burden. But only moments later she would see some humor in it and the two of them would laugh.

Grandmother Edith Ann Hadlock was a widow for 3 years, and died when she was 75, leaving forty-one grandchildren and six living children. Lillis read a poem at her funeral called "The Old Rocking Chair." Lillis was 15 years old at the time.

THE HADLOCK AUNTS AND UNCLES

The eight Hadlock children—including Lillis's mother, aunts, and uncles—were:

1. Lucilla, who married Byron Eaton. Lucilla had five children. Lena, the eldest daughter, also had five children. Those children were about the same age as Lillis, and close friends while growing up. Cousin Mable [correct spelling] was 17 years older than Lillis; Lillis was close to Mable, and to

her only child, Colleen Young Slagle, who was Lillis's age. Lucilla's youngest was Barbara, who was the same year at school with Lillis, and a bit of a rival.

2. Milo was the oldest uncle; he and Fuller opened the mine in Rector. He and his wife, Rosanna, had five children. They lived nearby the Remingtons in Vernal.

3. Mary married Walter "Dwight" Dow; they had eight children. It seems Mary committed suicide by poison while she was pregnant. Lillis's cousin, Walter John Dow, paid hospital bills for Edith Remington and employed Lillis's brother Earl in 1942 when the Remington family was broke and suffering a run of bad luck.

4. Charles, who died in infancy.

5. Richard married Eloise (also known as Lois) Bravo. She was a Catholic woman of California Spanish descent whom he had met while stationed in California after serving in World War I. They had only one daughter, Carmel, who was the same age as Lillis.

Aunt Eloise isolated herself and Carmel from the Hadlocks and from Mormons in general; she did not want Carmel to be enticed away from the Catholic church. Eloise would not bow her head during mealtime prayers with the Hadlock family, and would even walk out of the room during prayers. Carmel was not allowed to talk about religion with Lillis, though Aunt Eloise would sometimes try to talk to Lillis about Catholicism. When Carmel was a little older she was sent off to Catholic boarding school in California. Lillis would stay with Aunt Eloise because Eloise was so lonely and isolated and Lillis's mother felt sorry for her. Aunt Eloise may have felt closer to Lillis than to anyone else in the Hadlock family.

Uncle Richard was seldom at home. He was always herding sheep and when he was in town he would spend his time with his parents at the Hadlock home or with his brothers or sisters. So Eloise lived quite a lonely life. Lillis went to Mass and became acquainted with the nuns and priests. But it always seemed exotic to her. Lillis had a loving and respectful relationship with her aunt, made awkward only by religion. When Eloise died, Lillis had the vicarious Mormon rites performed for her. No doubt Eloise would have seen that as a betrayal and an indignity.

6. Carl was next, married to Aunt Minerva. He worked as a blacksmith with Grandfather. Carl and Minerva had eight children. Cousin Verna used to wave Lillis's hair on Saturday mornings. Cousins Curtis

and LeGrand would bring their guitars and sing at the Remington house. They were excellent basketball players and played on the 1939 Utah state championship team at Uintah High School.

7. Uncle Ferry was born after his mother's bout with polio; she became sick during her pregnancy. Ferry was a little man with a tremendous sense of humor. He was small enough that he would sometimes sit on his wife's lap to be silly. He was very generous and would often leave a silver dollar at the Remington house when he would visit. And he would give a nickel and a peppermint to the children. He suffered all his adult life from emphysema and asthma because he was gassed in Siberia during the First World War. That condition disturbed his sleep and ultimately killed him in old age. He married Jennie Steel, a good wife and mother, but not a good housekeeper. It was a small flaw, but difficult for the Hadlocks to overlook. Uncle Ferry was a close friend to Fuller into old age, and often visited him in Sugar House to play checkers or to talk.

Cousin Hattie was Uncle Ferry's daughter; she was about Lillis's age. The family lived in Salt Lake City and thus Hattie always seemed a bit sophisticated. She knew how to swim, she acted in plays, she could dance, and she took music lessons. She taught Lillis how to ride the buses and streetcars, how to go through revolving doors, how to ride elevators. Lillis observed Hattie and her friends very carefully and tried to behave as they did, to act nonchalant and self-assured.

8. Edith (September 25, 1897–January 1, 1982), was eighth of the Hadlock children, and Lillis's mother. She went by her middle name, *Leoma*, to avoid confusion with her mother who was also named Edith. Fuller insisted on calling her *Edith* and so that became her name again when they were married. Edith was very outgoing and talkative around her family but rather quiet and shy in public. Once she remarked that there were so few eligible bachelors in Vernal that she could only have married Fuller or Jess Haws. And those men could only have married either her or Cousin Lena. As it turns out Fuller married Edith, and Jess married Lena. The four remained lifelong friends, though some have suggested that Jess was jealous of Fuller's marriage to Edith.

GRANDFATHER JOSEPH FULLER REMINGTON

Born October 11, 1859, Salt Lake City, Utah
Married Amanda Rasmussen, October 3, 1888, Logan, Utah
Died November 28, 1899, Vernal, Utah

There were not so many Remingtons. Lillis's grandfather Joseph Remington died of a respiratory disease some 24 years before she was born. He was 40 when he died and Fuller was not yet 9 years old. Joseph operated a limekiln on his property, and his illness and death were likely the result of inhaling ash. He and Grandmother had three children: Amy, Fuller (Lillis's father), and Agnes. Amy married Mark Cook. She died young, during the flu pandemic of 1918, leaving two children, Morris and Leah Cook. So there were only two Remington cousins. Aunt Agnes died of tuberculosis when she was 28; she did not marry.

GRANDMOTHER AMANDA ALFREDA [OR ELFREDA] RASMUSSEN REMINGTON

Born November 15, 1871, Montpelier, Idaho
Married Joseph Remington, October 2, 1888
Died August 17, 1955, Naples, Utah

Lillis and even Lillis's older children knew Amanda. She had a house in Naples, where Newell and Lillis were born, and a winter house in St. George, Utah. The 400-mile drive from Vernal to St. George was long and exciting. Fuller seemed to know people in every town along the way. And he knew where all the roads led. When he would drive his family to visit Grandmother in St. George, he would often take side trips to visit points of interest such as Cedar Breaks, Zion Canyon, Bryce Canyon, or Cove Fort.

Grandmother was widowed in her twenties, left with Fuller and the young girls to raise. When the girls died, Fuller remained as her only child and means of support. She was dependent on him and quite directive and even demanding. Fuller, in his autobiography, characterizes his mother this way:

> My mother and I didn't understand each other. Our work and needs were very different. She had a very sharp tongue and was always ready with a whip to keep me in line. She was severe

in her discipline of me. She was a woman of great faith who loved her children very much. She had a strong testimony of the gospel and an unbending will. She was strong in character and immovable when her mind was made up. Her homemaking came as a natural art. She was very talented at creating a lovely and attractive home with the most limited materials to work with and the humblest house.

Lillis said, "She was a proud, strong-willed woman, firm in her belief of the gospel, and quite unbending in her opinions. She could be critical and quite severe in her reprimands but never did I doubt her love for me."

From the time Lillis was old enough to write, she corresponded with her grandmother. Some of those letters survive. Amanda died at the age of 85, soon after Lillis's third child, Leslie, was born.

REES JONES WILLIAMS
Born June 17, 1851, Little Keg Creek, Iowa
Married Amanda Remington, June 22, 1928
Died February 10, 1933, St. George, Utah

Amanda remarried in her later years to Rees Williams. He died when Lillis was in fourth grade. Lillis remembered him as a kind, playful, and tolerant "grandfather."

LEAH COOK
Born August 2, 1918, Vernal, Utah
Died November 13, 2012, St. George, Utah

Cousin Leah Cook was the child of Fuller's sister, Amy Remington Cook. When Leah's mother died, her father, Uncle Mark Cook, was disinclined and poorly equipped to care for a baby girl. Mark abandoned Leah to the care of her grandmother Amanda and to Fuller, who was not married at the time. Fuller and Amanda cared for Leah exclusively for 5 years. Fuller even brought baby Leah along as he was courting Edith. Leah often stayed or lived in Fuller's house, so Lillis remembered Leah almost as a sister.

Uncle Mark kept his son, Morris, but did not contribute to Leah's support. Mark married again. The new wife, Ada, bonded with Morris

Leah Cook in high school, c. 1933. Leah was one of only two Remington cousins, and was frequently at the Remington house.

but not with Leah. Some have said that Ada was an example of an evil stepmother. After Fuller married and had children of his own, Mark and Ada took Leah back. But Fuller continued to worry about Leah. He bought her clothes and toys, and continued to invite Leah to stay with his family. Mark and Ada continued to be indifferent and negligent.

Lillis remembered Ada as, "a large, tall, slow-moving woman, easy-going and cheerful. She was warm and cheerful with me. She and Mark seemed to enjoy and understand each other, and have fun together in a graceless way." But even as a child Lillis did not enjoy the Cooks.

> There was no beauty of any kind in Ada's house. She had no carpets and not one piece of nice furniture, no telephone, no radio, no electricity. Leah did have a piano. But the house was very small and Leah had no privacy. This lack of privacy worried my father.

Lillis remembered Uncle Mark as:

> . . . a handsome man, and kind to me. But he was gruff, he shouted, he was unrefined in his manner. He was rough with his animals and would shout at them, which upset me. He was also cross and irritable with Leah. I did not enjoy being around him. I was always a bit fearful of him.

Sometimes Lillis would visit the Cooks in the summer and stay at their house for a few days at a time. She had chores to do there. She would dip water out of the canal and bring it into the house for drinking and housekeeping. There were rocks on the canal bank which helped her avoid the mud, and made dipping water easier. She would feed the chickens and turkeys which ran freely in the yard, gather eggs, and weed the garden. The Cooks had sheep, pigs, cats, and a horse named Prince. At night when it grew dark they lit kerosene lamps and would sit around the kitchen table.

Lillis would stay maybe 3 or 4 days and would always feel homesick, suppressing tears and a lump in her throat. She would watch out the window for any sign of her father coming to take her home. Many times throughout Lillis's life, the sight of her father was the promise of salvation, the resolution of one difficulty or another. And so it was for Leah, as well.

Leah broke the bonds of her uncouth childhood and became a successful businesswoman. Lillis said she was optimistic, smart, and pretty.

IV

Lillis
Commencement and Catastrophe
1941–1942

HIGH SCHOOL GRADUATION

Lillis and Newell graduated from Uintah High School on May 23, 1941, when she was 17 and Newell was 3 months shy of turning 19. Lillis had done well in high school scholastically and socially. She had been a member of many clubs and served in student government. Newell had been student body president and captain of the basketball team. Lillis never had trouble finding part-time work and had always had extra spending money. Throughout her youth her father seemed to have enough money to buy bicycles, cars, clothes, and recently had even built a new house on the same lot next to their old house. Lillis lived in that new house the summer after graduating from high school. She was aware of the droughts in the Midwest, and that the world was 10 years into the Great Depression, and that many people were hungry or were losing their farms. Nevertheless, life was good for her and the family. The Depression and the war in Europe seemed a bit remote.

JOBS

As a teenager she worked many part-time jobs after school, during the summers, or over Christmas break. She tended babies, worked as a maid in private homes, was a maid at a motel, was a sales clerk at Kress 5 and 10 Cent, J.C. Penney's, and at ZCMI (Zion's Cooperative Mercantile Institution; a Utah department store). She worked as an office clerk for a dentist in Vernal, Dr. Stevens, and also for Dr. Hansen, MD, who shared the office building. Among her duties she vulcanized dentures and tended to patients recovering from minor surgeries such as tonsillectomies. She wore a white uniform, and it might have been there that she decided she wanted to be a nurse. She also worked at Calder's Creamery, mostly packaging butter. Her father offered to match her savings. She was able to save $150 before graduating from high school, and her father gave her another $150, the value of six quarters of tuition at the University of Utah. This was typical of her father's financial and moral support throughout her life.

NURSING SCHOOL APPLICATION

Lillis wanted very much to enter nursing school in the fall class of 1941, but her father opposed nursing as a profession for women. He felt it was hard and made women hard. But Lillis asked him to drive her to Salt Lake City to visit the four accredited schools there; after that he never again expressed opposition.

She liked LDS Hospital's nursing school best, but classes were full until January of 1943. A second choice was Holy Cross, where she applied and was accepted for the fall of 1941. Classes would be taught at Saint Mary-of-the-Wasatch, which was located about 14th South and about 2500 East. It is difficult to imagine now, but that location was very remote in those days, completely undeveloped, and did not even have public transportation service to Salt Lake City. Orientation was held on a rainy day, made more dreary by the austere monastic hallways of the school and the nuns in their black habits who seemed to her to be very aloof. She was reluctant to discuss her change of heart with her father, but she wrote Holy Cross and withdrew her application. A week later her father took her back to Salt Lake City to LDS Hospital for an interview.

LDS HOSPITAL INTERVIEW

Lillis interviewed with the Director of Nurses, Miss Maria Johnson. The decorum of this woman made a great impression on her. Miss

Johnson was tall, beautiful, articulate, precise in her remarks, and impersonal. She was dressed in a starched white uniform seemingly without a wrinkle. Her hair was also white, and not a hair out of place. She wore glasses and had steel blue eyes and looked directly at Lillis. Miss Johnson stood when Lillis entered the office and motioned for her to take a chair. She carefully reviewed Lillis's high school grades and other credentials and asked several questions. Then she said she had an opening in January of 1943. She talked about the costs of tuition, room, and board. But, she noted, Lillis lacked a geometry credit from high school and could not be admitted without that credit. She would hold the spot for Lillis but only until September to allow her time to fulfill the geometry requirement.

Lillis felt the interview went well, but she had no idea how to take a geometry class now that she had graduated, and school was out. On returning to Vernal she called Mr. Melvin Jorgensen, her high school chemistry and algebra teacher. He graciously offered to teach her geometry that summer while some teachers and staff were still in the building. They met a couple of times each week at his desk. Finally, he told Lillis that she was ready. Mr. Harold Lundell, her high school principal, administered the test. She passed, and the credit was transferred on to the school of nursing in Salt Lake.

Maybe that kindness was typical of small-town familiarity; maybe it was a measure of respect toward the Remington family, or toward Lillis in particular. Whatever the case, Lillis was grateful toward Mr. Jorgensen. Soon thereafter he moved his family away from Vernal and she never saw him again. But decades later while touring in Taiwan she met a young Mormon missionary with the name Jorgensen. She immediately made the connection with her old high school teacher and as it turned out, this young man was the grandson. She thanked the grandson as she could not thank again her teacher.

So Lillis had a year and a half to wait for nursing school to start—time to work and save money. She worked most of the summer in Vernal as a sales girl and recalls that she enjoyed being the first to see new merchandise and taking advantage of her small discount.

PEARL HARBOR, DECEMBER 1941

The war seemed abstract and not quite relevant until the attack on Pearl Harbor. Then things changed quickly. She recalled the streets and train stations in Salt Lake City became crowded with men in uniform. Young people rushed to get married, sometimes only days before being forced to separate. Small genteel services at hotels, restaurants, and shops disappeared. She had to stand in line for shoddy substitutes or empty store shelves. Soap would not lather, shoes came apart, and buttons would not hold up to washing. Girls would put makeup on their legs so that it would appear that they were wearing stockings, even painting a seam down the back of their legs. Numerous consumer items were rationed. Housing construction stopped. So, as people moved to the cities looking for work in the war plants, they had to double up in small apartments, sometimes with strangers. But there was a lot of new war construction; Fort Douglas, Camp Williams, Camp Kearns, Hill Field all expanded, and new plants and depots were built. The war was in every newsreel, on billboards, and constantly on the radio. Lillis saved newspaper clippings noting the boys from Vernal who were drafted, killed, or missing. For a very long time the news from the front was grim with one island after another falling to the Japanese.

SALT LAKE CITY

Lillis moved to Salt Lake City after Christmas, seeking to get established there and to wait for the war plants to open so she could earn higher pay. Employment and living conditions had already started to change. At first she lived with her cousin, Mable Young. But Mable's house was small and five adults were already living there. Lillis took a job at Paramount Laundry on State Street ironing shirts on a press. She made $8 for a 48-hour week of work, or about 17¢ per hour.

Soon she found work as a live-in housemaid for the Sheets family who lived in the upscale neighborhood of Harvard Avenue. The pay was the same, but it had room and board. She used the back door and lived in the basement with the hot water heater, furnace, and laundry room. But she had her own bathroom. She would clean, do laundry, shop, and prepare and serve the evening meal. It was a bit intimidating for an 18-year-old girl to shop and cook for this sophisticated family. In particular, she did not know how to make coffee. She was unfamiliar with cuts of meat. On one occasion she was told to cook artichokes and cut out the hearts; she had never seen an artichoke. Occasionally when guests were coming she was asked to set out glasses for wine or Champagne or highballs. So she had to learn the difference between the many glasses. Her parents had some friends in town, the Sainsburys, who were also wealthy and were friends of the Sheets. Lillis would often call Mrs. Sainsbury for advice and for clarification of the daily instructions which Mrs. Sheets had left her.

Lillis enjoyed the work, and soon gained the confidence that she was a better cook than Mrs. Sheets. She was also more efficient in the kitchen and with housekeeping; these were values she learned from mother growing up in Vernal. But work as a live-in housemaid made it difficult to attend church, there was no way to invite a friend over, and the evening work made it difficult even to read a newspaper or a book. On one of her days off, her father came to visit. He took her on a long drive, and told her about the Beehive House, the historic residence of Brigham Young which was then being used as a girls' boarding house. He came prepared with a bishop's recommendation, which was required for her application to live there. Also, typical of his support and involvement, he persuaded her to look for other work. She submitted an application to live at the Beehive House that very day. Soon she had a new job at the Utah Finance Co. in the Walker Bank Building. Mrs. Sheets offered her $9.50 per week and Sundays off if she would stay. But the decision to move had been made.

While waiting for an opening at the Beehive House, Lillis moved in with a high school friend, Winifred "Bing" Bingham. They shared a small room in the home of Winifred's married sister. They also shared a bed. Soon she found a new job at Safeway in accounting where she learned to use an electric adding machine. With each new job came a pay raise and new things to learn.

BEEHIVE HOUSE

Finally there was an opening to live at the Beehive House. It was a delightful place to live, right in the heart of downtown Salt Lake City. There were strict rules but the girls were well-behaved. The atmosphere in the beautiful home was warm and friendly. There were two reception rooms where the young women could entertain guests or dates. There was a baby grand piano and quite often girls would gather around it to sing. There were two prepared meals each day. The evening meal was served in a dining room, beautifully presented, and the meal always began with prayer. Breakfast was served cafeteria style. Some of the residents were Lillis's friends from high school, and she became acquainted with others who became lifelong friends. Winifred Bingham also applied and soon moved in. By late spring 1942 the arms plants were finished and hiring, so Lillis started looking there for a higher-paying job.

HOUSE FIRE OF 1942

The beautiful new Remington house caught fire in the very early morning hours of Thursday, May 21, 1942; it was damaged but not destroyed, and indeed, is still occupied today (2017). There was evidence of arson, including more than 50 gallons of gasoline placed in small containers throughout the house that had not ignited. Also, many of the furnishings had been removed from the house, indicating a foreknowledge of the fire. Furnishings that had been left in the house were sent to a lab and it was determined that they were tainted with gasoline. No one was home at the time of the fire; Lillis's father, Fuller Remington, was in Provo on business. Nevertheless, he was arrested, arraigned, and he pled guilty to arson. Fuller was sentenced on August 25 to at least 2 but no more than 20 years in the state penitentiary. Then, curiously, he was given a 90-day stay to put his affairs in order (*The Vernal Express*, vol. LI, no. 35, August 27, 1942, pp. 1 & 8). In the new year he was granted a parole, according to *The Vernal Express*, without serving a day of his sentence (vol. LII, no. 3, Thursday January 21, 1943, p. 1). It seems strange that a felony would be treated with such leniency. The firemen at the trial were livid for being exposed to the danger of so much gasoline, and had asked the court to enforce the full penalty for this offense.

Character witnesses for the defense noted that Fuller had worked as county road supervisor and okayed hundreds of dollars in wages for those working under him. In all these many transactions every cent had been accounted for. As a public servant and community worker Mr. Remington had done much good. Others testified of his fearless and selfless work with the sick and dead during the flu epidemic of 1919.

Fuller and Sheriff H. M. Snyder implicated another person, but not by name. Over the weeks this issue of accomplices, conspiracy, or coverup annoyed Judge Abe Turner, particularly when the defense asked for probation or a light sentence. Judge Turner admonished Fuller, saying, "It is your privilege to protect another at the expense of yourself being sent to state prison." He then recessed court to give Fuller 3 weeks to think it over.

The trial lasted from June through late August. In the last session before sentencing, William Stanley Dunford, the district attorney, tantalized the overflow crowd in court with a most bewildering and opaque assertion. He said the state had investigated the case and found certain elements that would make the defendant sacrifice all his past reputation to do this thing; some of these elements were quite powerful. "We find in the analysis that they are of such a nature that they would confound the average mind to some extent." And the case had ramifications, some of which the state was not at liberty to disclose. He believed that the best interests of the state would be served by probation, whether before or after judgment (*The Vernal Express*, August 27, 1942).

Those are the facts; the rest is hushed family rumor or speculation. To state the obvious, this was an apparent case of insurance fraud, or some other scheme to get out from under the debt of the new house during the Depression. Fuller did not start the fire but was willing to go to prison to protect someone. The gossip of at least two family members implicated Fuller's wife, Edith, along with her accomplices. One of the sources was Fuller's niece, Leah Cook, whom Fuller had protected and cared for in her childhood. The other source was Edith's sister-in-law who shall not be named.

It is difficult to imagine anyone beating a 2-to-20-year felony sentence without broad support in the community. In this case even the district attorney did not have heart for a stiff sentence, saying, "the best interests of the state would be served by probation." The reader is left to consider how a man can accumulate such a reservoir of reputation and good will. One may also wonder what conditions would motivate him to expend it all at once.

Years later, on the very rare occasions that Lillis spoke of the fire, she recited many implausible excuses, which maybe she believed. It was a topic that no one could talk about with her. The only important point for this narrative is actually quite simple: the fire was a catastrophe for the Remington family. It was a time of quick transition into profound disgrace and poverty. The parents and children who had enjoyed some status and esteem in the community soon moved away from Vernal where they had lived for generations, not to return.

CONSEQUENCES

Suddenly and briefly, at 18 years old, Lillis was the only wage earner in the family. In July she had to reconsider how to finance nursing school, or whether she could attend at all. She wrote to her mother that she was considering attending the Salt Lake County Hospital School of Nursing, which she had previously ruled out in favor of LDS Hospital. The advantage of County was school would start earlier, and she could save some money on room and board. She thought she could also count on a government grant, and suggested, "Newell can have my money and that will keep him" [on his mission]. "Gee whiz; I'm still up a stump," she writes as she comes to terms with the new financial realities and the expense of her schooling.

In the same letter of July 25, 1942, she comments, "You asked me so many questions but you told me to destroy the letter and I cannot remember what you asked." She states that she had met with her grandmother Amanda Remington.

> She said you had written to her. She is so terribly sad all the time. I just hate to go and see her too often. She cries and of course I can't cheer her up. I just don't know what to say. She is so worried over his [Fuller's] reputation. . . . I think it would help her a lot if she could see him. When is Dad coming [to visit his mother]?

It is apparent in these letters that Lillis was either naive or in denial about the facts of the trial and that her father had already pleaded guilty. She wrote of suing her father's accusers for slander.

In early August Lillis took a job at the arms plant, making 52¢ an hour, working 8 hours, 6 days a week. That would be almost $25 per week compared to $8 or $9 per week in her previous jobs. Lillis had an easy commute. The bus picked her up on Main Street and took her right to the factory door, regardless of which shift; the factory was always up and running. She worked in the Remington Small Arms plant making and packaging cartridges for the war. Thousands were employed there in many large buildings.

Newell was on a church mission when the fire occurred and wrote distraught letters home trying to learn the truth of what had happened. Lillis started to send him money regularly.

The family was further fragmented in August when her mother, Edith, moved from Vernal to Ogden to take work at Arsenal Depot in Clearfield. Edith rented a single room in a house with strangers; the room was so small that she only had space to bring 14-year-old Lois with her. Don (11), Cleo (8), and Ted (6) remained in Vernal, essentially becoming indentured servants to Uncle Mark Cook and Aunt Ada. That autumn Edith suffered a bowel obstruction that required emergency surgery. Lois took the initiative to get her mother to the hospital; she recalls that she did not even have a dime for the phone call. Edith was critically ill, and unconscious for several days. Lillis was called upon to transfuse blood. Edith's nephew, Walter John Dow, came forward to help pay medical expenses.

Lillis visited Vernal in October 1942. She saw her young siblings at Uncle Mark Cook's house. She wrote, "Don and Cleo both about cried when they saw me. Cleo's little arms were around me all the time I was to see her." Don was quiet but would not leave her side. Little Ted did most of the talking. She gave the Cooks $5 (a little more than a day's wage). She also visited the damaged house which was locked; only the basement was open. She was nervous alone in the dark basement and so she didn't stay long. She also visited her cousin, "Aunt" Lena, who "cried like her heart would break." Lillis commented, "I don't care whether I ever go back again."

Fuller fell from a boxcar in Provo while loading steel pipe, probably in October 1942. Sixteen-year-old Earl was working with him and saw his father fall. Both Earl and Fuller thought the injuries would be fatal; as Fuller was lying on the ground he instructed Earl to go through his pockets and remove his money and wallet. Fuller injured his back and neck and spent about 2 weeks in the hospital in Provo. Fuller lost that job. The exact dates were not recorded, but the accident approximately coincided with Edith's hospitalization.

While her parents were in different hospitals in different cities, Lillis completed a series of Red Cross courses in October to earn a certificate in the Nurses Aid Corps. She also performed clinical practice to earn her cap, which she completed at the end of November. So she was working part time at the hospital while working full time at the arms plant.

Around this time, Cousin Leah Cook visited the younger Remington children at her parents' home in Vernal. Because of her own difficult childhood, Leah wanted to take Cleo out of that house to protect her. Finally Cleo was moved out and went to live in the single room with her mother and sister in Ogden, but the boys stayed on with the Cooks.

During this difficult period, Lillis found respite in the pleasant social interactions she had in the Beehive House and neighboring Lion House. Occasionally the house would sponsor lectures or firesides, and she also enjoyed a very active social life outside the house. Many friends, boys and girls, would visit. They would go to movies, dances, football games, bowling, or go skating. Sometimes she would go out with soldiers who were in transit. Melvin Hodgkinson, a high school friend, came to see her at the Beehive House and caught her crying about the disintegration of her family. Melvin had taken her to the Junior Prom at Uintah High School when she was 16, and he continued to write and visit her in Salt Lake City. (Melvin went on to win the Silver Star as a PFC in Italy when he assaulted a machine gun nest alone, using hand grenades and a Browning Automatic Rifle, then continued to protect his patrol as they retreated under heavy fire.)

Ever conscious of her relative comfort at the Beehive House, Lillis worried about her mother's living conditions, and the number of shifts her mother was working. Lillis wrote to her mother sometimes three times in a week. In her letters she always asked about Lois, Cleo, and particularly about her father, with whom communication seemed to be infrequent or unreliable. Lillis would try to buoy her mother's spirits, often in religious terms, relating positive stories from church talks or good movies. She encouraged her mother and sisters to go to church. Lillis would visit her mother in Ogden when possible.

On one occasion Cleo showed up at the Beehive House unannounced.

I was supposed to have gone to work this morning at 6 but she [Cleo] looked so afraid among these hundred older girls and there was no one to comb her hair or take her to breakfast or wake her up so I decided to take today off. It's the first day I have missed so all I'll lose is the money.

In a letter dated December 16, Lillis worried how to budget for Christmas gifts, suggesting that buying gifts for only Don, Cleo, and Ted, and getting the family together would be enough. She had already bought a few gifts. She tried to encourage her mother not to worry about losing the Vernal house, and assured her that she would not be evicted from her rented room in Ogden (possibly because of Edith's illness or unemployment).

There was good news also. Lillis finally had secured a scholarship to nursing school and would move into Carlson Hall on the campus of the University of Utah. Additionally, her father had visited her in Salt Lake City. One of her friends had seen them together in the city and presumed he was her date; the friend had commented that Lillis's "man was nice looking." Her father, generous even in bad times, gave her a formal black dress which she sketched in her letter and described in some detail. She wore it to a ball at the Lion House and again when she was rushed by the Tri Delta sorority. "They don't know I'm a pauper," she commented. Indeed, she was a pauper. One might wonder why Fuller would prioritize such a gift for Lillis in such a time of austerity and family upheaval.

Earl spent some time working on a turkey farm in Fairview, Utah. He also worked for a while for his cousin Walter Dow. He moved to Ogden and enrolled in Weber High School, but for the next year, with his mother ill and in poverty, he felt like a drag on family resources. When he turned 17 in October of 1943 he dropped out of his junior year and escaped by enlisting in the Navy with his mother's signature. He did not resume his education until he was 20.

The family went from one crisis to another with no money and kids scattered. By December 1942 it seemed that the storm was passing. Fuller was recovering from his fall and Edith was recovering from her near-fatal bowel obstruction. Lillis had a path forward for nursing school and was even planning how she could finance Lois's education as soon as she could graduate and find work as a nurse. By January 1943 Fuller was granted a parole. He took a job at Hill Field, and moved the family into a small house in Washington Terrace near Ogden.

V

Lillis
Nursing School in Salt Lake City
and Albuquerque
1943–1946

CARLSON HALL, UNIVERSITY OF UTAH

LDS Hospital Nursing School held classes at the University of Utah. When school started in January 1943, Lillis moved into Carlson Hall on the corner of University Street and 4th South. This was, again, a very comfortable and dignified dormitory for women, maybe even better than the Beehive House. It had a solarium where the nursing students could relax and socialize, also a library, a living room, and a dining room where occasionally special programs or lectures would be presented during dinner. Dinner was served each evening on a linen tablecloth.

Her letters show an awareness that her living arrangements were more comfortable than where her younger brothers and sisters lived. The family was united again and settled in Washington Terrace, a new government housing project built to accommodate workers in the armament plants near Ogden. At that time it was the third largest town in Utah. Their house was a small, drab, frame duplex with three bedrooms, kitchen, dining area, living room, and bathroom with a cement bathtub. All rooms were miniature. Thousands of these little units looked so much alike that it was difficult to find your house, particularly after sundown. It sat on a sandy hill without shrub or tree or a blade of grass. The sand blew and drifted, filling the house with dust. But the Remingtons felt lucky to have one; so many did not and were crowded like sardines in with family or friends.

Her mother, Edith, was working at Arsenal Depot, the first time she had held a job in her married life. And she was continuing to recover from her surgery. Newell, still on his mission to the southern states, asked for daily updates on his mother's health. It seems like an impractical request, but it does illustrate how the family continued to worry about Edith; also, it was not unusual for Lillis to write Newell more than once in a week. Her father was the church branch president and was employed as the postmaster at Hill Field.

Winnifred Kennard was Lillis's roommate. They had been high school friends and "Kennard" in time would marry Newell and later divorce him. Across the hall were two Japanese-American students, Anna Kurata and Masako Miaso. These young women had not met each other prior to being assigned the same dorm room on the first day of school. Both had parents or families in the Japanese internment camps. One family was at Topaz near Delta, Utah; the other at Minidoka, Idaho. Anna also had a brother fighting in Italy. Anna and Lillis became lifelong friends.

The academic workload was heavy. Lillis carried 21 credit hours of required classes that first quarter, including several labs. Some students failed out. They used the same textbook that the medical students used, but nursing students finished the book in one quarter while medical students studied it for three quarters. Occasionally she would walk 2 blocks to study outdoors in the peace of Mount Olivet Cemetery on 5th South and about 14th East. She would sit by a waterfall.

Physical education was a required course, and Lillis was actually enrolled in two physical education classes; one was prescribed because of her scoliosis. The scoliosis was a recurring issue throughout her training and even later in life. In December 1943, some doctors at the U decided that she had suffered years earlier from poliomyelitis. It was at best an incomplete diagnosis because she did indeed have scoliosis. But they noted the muscles in her back were atrophied, and did not react to tests as normal muscles should. They prescribed physiotherapy and ultraviolet therapy every other day. Sometimes the therapy was so exhausting that she would find herself unable to move her arms or head, and would have no choice but to go to bed. Yet she felt lucky to receive such treatment supervised by the nursing school.

There was a little free time on weekends. It seems she had something going on every weekend; it could be tennis or ice skating or movies with her friends. There were few men on campus. Most of them were in uniform. In April, 350 university students were inducted into the military at a ceremony at Kingsbury Hall, and then taken away in trucks. Governor Herbert Maw spoke at the ceremony, and his son was the first to climb into the waiting trucks. A similar ceremony was held a couple of weeks later. The U was beginning to look like a girls' school.

Harvey Peterson was a medical student who dated Lillis quite a lot. They went to Delta Phi parties, canyon picnics, and the medical ball. They played tennis, went to church, and studied together. She even used some precious vacation time to go on a chaperoned, annual medical school retreat with Harvey at the Granddaddy Lakes in the Uintas, passing up an opportunity to visit her family at Washington Terrace. She described Harvey as the nicest fellow she had ever met and a gentleman. She described time with his friends as most comfortable, happy, and brotherly.

Most of Lillis's social life was preoccupied with war. Occasionally soldiers would be invited to Carlson Hall for dinner. They would eat and walk together, sing and converse at the piano, dance and play ping pong, and then never see each other again. Most often they were not Mormons. Lillis remarked on how much they smoked, but many of the nursing students in the house also smoked. Don Davis from Roosevelt, Utah, and an acquaintance of Newell's, visited Carlson Hall. He was serving as a gunner on a troop carrier. When asked if he had ever sunk a ship he became sullen and refused to answer.

One weekend Lillis was asked to put on a uniform and raise money for the Red Cross at the Uptown Theater before the main feature. A short newsreel-like film featured the World War I flying ace Eddie Rickenbacker; pictures of men dying on the battlefield; and "God Bless America" sung by Kate Smith. Then the lights came up, a giant red cross was projected on the screen, and Lillis and her friend passed baskets and collected $500. It was not surprising that several of Lillis's friends were in the audience that day; after all, Salt Lake City only had a population of about 150,000. Someone said "Remington! What are you doing here?

Didn't you pass English?" Others called her by name, "Lillis!" And someone called out, "Why is your cap white and your friend's is blue? Are you her commander?" Other soldiers teased her, but all gave money.

LDS HOSPITAL CAMPUS

After 6 months of classwork on the university campus, Lillis and her class moved into LDS Hospital student nurse housing on the Avenues. Then in August she passed her tests to earn her cap and become a probationer (similar to an intern). She continued at LDS Hospital for more than a year and a half to fill additional requirements in obstetrics, maternity, nursery, pediatrics, surgery, diet, psychotherapy, medical, communicable disease, formula lab, and other areas. These requirements took her into the middle of 1945.

Most of the lectures were good. In particular she looked forward to Dr. Louis Moench, who always ended his lectures with something uplifting to put the practice of medicine in perspective. Sometimes it was poetry, sometimes artful colored slides that he had photographed himself.

The lecturer in diet therapy however was so boring and her diction so poor that Lillis could not listen to her, and she made a habit of writing letters home during that class. Kennard actually skipped that class to visit her father in Logan before he shipped out. When the teacher called the roll that day, both Lillis and another girl answered, "Here" trying to cover for Kennard. The teacher suspected some sort of conspiracy and asked Kennard to stand. The other girl, Annette Nelson (the class vice president), stood but the teacher was still not convinced, so she gave the class a punitive pop quiz. Annette turned in two tests—one with Kennard's name on it. Kennard, Annette, and Lillis could have been kicked out of school for this offense, but Lillis shrugged it off, saying, "You have to take chances sometimes."

Maybe she was flippant because her workload was so heavy. In a letter of October 7, 1943, she describes a typical day at LDS Hospital in this way:

> I went to work this morning at 7:00 and worked until 11:00.
> Went to class till noon, ate dinner, and went to class till 3:30.
> Went to work 4:00 to 7:00. Now wouldn't you call my day pretty
> well filled up? I don't know when I'll get all my homework done.

Lillis and her childhood friend and future sister-in-law, Winnifred Kennard. They were probationer nurses in 1943. Here they pose in front of student housing at LDSH.

I'm getting farther behind all the time. I'm so tired after the day is over I couldn't study if I wanted to.

By the time she took her exams to become a probationer after 8 months of class, she had lost 13 pounds and was wondering if she had a thyroid problem. It's possible she was simply exhausted.

Given her workload and her social life, it is remarkable that she wrote as many letters as she did. It is quite apparent that she wrote several letters each week to family and friends and that only a fraction of her letters survive. The letters are long, usually four notebook pages, but sometimes twice that. There is an aspect to her letters that was not surprising given her context. Most letters have a very strong religious component. She often fairly gushes over church lessons or talks she has heard. Sometimes she quotes them. She would include inspirational clippings or poems. She also tried to encourage her parents, usually in religious terms. It is likely the family was still reeling from their string of bad luck and needed a little encouragement. On many occasions she expressed at length her love and gratitude toward her parents. This, by the way, is also typical of Newell's and Earl's letters. As an example, here is a passage Lillis wrote to her father, May 3, 1943:

> Dad you make me feel bad when you say the things you did in your last letter, about [being] sorry you have not done more for me. You and Mother have given us the greatest gifts that could be given to us. You have given us bodies so that we could come here on this earth as mortals and live and then you taught us the principles of the true and everlasting gospel. I'm sure no children have ever had more to be thankful for. No children have had better parents than we have got. I only hope we will be able to live worthy of your love and be as grand as parents as you have been. We have never really gone without anything that we really needed.

ALBUQUERQUE VETERANS ADMINISTRATION

When the class of probationers finished their coursework, they were divided into thirds. One third was chosen to affiliate with out-of-state hospitals; Lillis and three classmates went to the Veterans Hospital in

Albuquerque in July; they were Avon Sirrine, Viola Jeanne Paul, and Erna Neves.

The Albuquerque VA Hospital sat on the East Mesa, some distance from and overlooking the city. Decades earlier, World War I veterans had built houses on this site to recover in the clean dry air from respiratory injuries related to mustard gas. The VA hospital campus was designed to look like a Puebloan village, perhaps Taos. There were some 20 buildings on the campus connected with colonnaded pathways, and many buildings had rooftop terraces. The location and architecture were beautiful. At more than a mile above sea level, there was always a cool breeze in the evenings. The grounds had a fishpond with water lilies and hundreds of goldfish as big as trout. There was also a duck pond on the property, walking paths, and the occasional rattlesnake.

Not far away was the Kirtland Army Air Base. Lillis liked to sit on the veranda of the nurses' dormitory and watch the silver B-29s land and take off at all hours. She describes an occasion when six took off at the same moment with a thrilling rumble that shook the windows at the hospital. Sometimes they would fly so low that it was easy to imagine that you could touch them. Their wingspan, she said, was longer than the nurses' home. In contrast, the small, fast Kingcobra fighters looked like streaks.

> And there you sit with nothing to do but rest, think, and enjoy the beauty all around you and be happy; for already you have forgotten you were ever in training, and the fact that state board exams are coming up doesn't even matter.

So she was able to disassociate herself from the war to some degree.

Perhaps best of all, the workload was easier. She worked from 7:00 AM to 3:30 PM with Sundays off. There was spare time to attend basketball or football games at the University of New Mexico, time to attend church, to date, and even to read.

The only things she complained about were smoking and open intolerance to Mormons. That was her assertion; it is unclear what form the intolerance took. Everyone smoked everywhere. She and Erna Neves, her LDS Hospital classmate, were the only women on the hospital staff who did not smoke. Patients also smoked, passengers on the city buses smoked, people smoked in stores, at the lunch tables, while on duty in the hospital, and friends would even presume to smoke in Lillis's dorm room.

BOYFRIENDS

Lillis attended the small Mormon branch in Albuquerque. It was also attended by some Navy cadets from the Navy Academy at the U of NM, university students, and the occasional soldier. Many of the locals had never heard of Mormons but those who had, openly expressed antipathy. Lillis also found a Nazarene congregation and would go on their picnics and attend church with them. She liked them because they were polite about religion, and they did not smoke or drink. No doubt there was a thinly veiled hope to proselytize her. But one member of the congregation, Paul, took a romantic interest in her, and she strung him along (typical of the war years) all of September and October. Paul was an outstanding young man, and Lillis admired him. But as her rotation at the VA was winding down, she started to ignore his calls.

She also dated Robert "Bob" Bunker, who had grown up in Los Angeles and was a member of her Mormon branch. He was a Naval cadet studying at the U of NM. He took Lillis to the military functions, fraternity parties, and college football and basketball games. He was a graceful dancer and "just wonderful anyway you look at him. He isn't handsome," she wrote artlessly, "but . . . quite reserved and very nice." He took her to a "formal fraternity dance at the Hilton Hotel, the most beautiful hotel in Albuquerque." In a letter to her mother she described her dress and jewelry, her hair and the flower he gave her. Bob said she looked like a goddess. She wrote home:

> Mother, you just can't imagine how wonderful it was to see all their commanding officers in their stiff white uniforms and all those formals, and fellows who weren't in the service in their tuxedoes, and see and hear those fellows sing their [fraternity] song.

Before the evening was over he asked her on another date. In December, just weeks before Lillis was to return home, Bob gave her a silver bracelet and his fraternity pin; essentially they were engaged. She wore the pin for 2 days and returned it without explanation. She wrote home saying, "He is a fine fellow. . . . All the kids think I have lost my mind, and maybe I have."

Lillis also had a friend and pen pal named Jack Rencher who was a pilot in the Army Air Corps, and a bit of a character. He had sense of humor that could fix any predicament. He was stationed in Dallas, but pilots were given a lot of latitude. When they had leave and access to an airplane they could fly it, and he would occasionally show up in Albuquerque to see Lillis at convenient times—and at inconvenient times. He also visited her in Salt Lake City. Curiously, Jack Rencher showed up to visit Lillis in Salt Lake City in 1967, some 20 years later. By that time Lillis had four children, two in high school. George was on a business trip at the moment. She wrote in her diary:

> Jack Wrencher [*sic*], a fellow I went with while a girl (nursing training), came to see me and we spent a very pleasant evening of visiting and catching up on the news of 20 yrs. He invited me out to dinner but I declined.

Lt. Evan Woolley from Vernal also wrote to Lillis, and would visit when he could. He was a flight officer in the Army, but not a pilot so his flying in for a visit was less frequent. Evan was a faithful pen pal who also kept in touch with some of Lillis's friends from Vernal. He liked to complain about the senselessness of the Army administration and his several transfers; his letters were postmarked from Chicago; Lincoln, NE; and Phoenix.

There were several others who have gone without mention. She even dated a patient, Harry Ferguson, the son of a wealthy doctor from Atlanta. They shared 4 romantic months, then parted as friends who disagreed only on religion; he was a Methodist. It is easy to notice that her relationships with Harry, Paul, Bob, Jack, Evan, and to some extent, Harvey, all overlapped.

During her time in Albuquerque, Harvey Peterson, the University of Utah medical student, got married. Melvin Hodgkinson, her high school sweetheart and war hero, returned from Europe and quickly married. Jeanne, and several of her other close friends were married, and Lillis started to feel a little insecure about being single. She was 22 years old.

THE END OF THE WAR

Evan summed it up well. At the end of August, the Army was still surprised that the war was over, and did not know what to do with all the soldiers. "So we drift again on a sea of GI uncertainty." He was in Chicago on VJ-Day, August 15. "I never seen so many wild, happy, care-free people. Everyone kissing each other. Thousands and thousands of people jam-packed in the narrow street for block upon block. Paper covering the streets white as snow." Then he complains that the Army wanted to give him some more vaccinations.

The Trinity nuclear test was conducted at 5:30 in the morning of July 16, 1945, just days after Lillis arrived in Albuquerque. The test range was about 100 miles south, as the crow flies. People in Albuquerque who were paying attention could have seen the flash and felt the explosion if they had been up that early. Lillis writes that there "was a bright color and we felt a slight tremor." She does not say explicitly, "*I* saw the flash and *I* felt the tremor." The papers minimized the event, calling it an explosion at a munitions dump, and it was quickly forgotten. But on August 6 and 9, bombs were dropped on Japan and the secret was out. The war in Europe had ended in May. The war in the Pacific was over by August 15.

She wrote home on August 9 a letter that is somewhere between con-fused and rhapsodic. Everyone knew the war would be over in a matter of days if not hours. She tried to equate the news with a religious experience. "It sort of thrills me to hear and read all of these things. This helps me to believe our gospel more strongly." Reasoning that if such vast power could be hidden in such a small place, possibly "we, ourselves could be as powerful as that bomb and even more so because we are composed of more intelligence." She admitted, "This letter no doubt is one grand scramble. I just can't express myself on paper." She acknowledged that putting this power in the hands of man posed some risks. In fairness to her, the war had been a long slog for everyone; it took most of the world a long time to figure out the implications of atomic war; and her sentiment was not far removed from the words, "He has loosed the fateful lightning of His terrible swift sword."

Earl wrote in October from somewhere in the South Pacific that his ship was ordered to destroy its ammunition before returning home, which they accomplished by dumping it in the sea.

Lillis commented wistfully how odd it was that the B-29s were sitting quietly, side by side on the flight line; it had been such a pleasure to watch them fly just a few days before.

With the end of the war in Europe and the Pacific, veterans started pouring into the VA, many from prison camps. Lillis had one patient who was 15 years old and now a wounded veteran. Another veteran was a young woman, an RN who had served in a combat zone for three and a half years. She was a friend of Miss Martin, the nursing supervisor at the VA. The story goes that this RN was shell-shocked. Miss Martin took her to eat at the Albuquerque Hilton to celebrate her return, but she could not eat the sumptuous meal of steak and shrimp, and only wept at the dinner table. Lillis wrote home, "I'm so thankful that it didn't fall my lot to spend 3 ½ years in foxholes, coveralls, mud, and danger in some foreign land."

Tuberculosis, Syphilis, and Gonorrhea

A lot of men came home with tuberculosis. Lillis admitted one fellow from Denver who was suspected of having TB and was waiting for a sputum test result. He had been a prisoner of the Germans for 9 months. He was 26 years old and had two children, a girl 21 months, and a boy 8 months old. He lay in the receiving ward for a day, hoping against hope that his lab work would come back negative, in fact, acting like he could not go on if he should be diagnosed with TB. He lay there a day and a half saying, "I just know I haven't got it." But the test came back positive and he was moved to the TB building. "He really took it swell." He said, "I'm willing to do anything to be cured." Lillis commented, "We never know what is going on in their minds and what battle they are fighting within themselves."

The cadet nurses, such as Lillis, were assigned to the TB patients, alongside the hospital staff. Lillis and a couple other students in her cohort protested their assignments to the TB ward. They argued that the VA did not practice standard isolation technique, which required gowns, masks, and scrub bowls. They also argued that students were not required to serve in the TB ward. Lillis and another student from Oklahoma actually refused to work there, while Jeanne had submitted to work with active TB patients for a month without mask or gown.

Lillis was intimidated by the senior staff and worried that she had been too strident, invoking the law and saying they were under age and so on. But then the supervisor responded by ordering that isolation technique be implemented, and ordered that student nurses would only serve voluntarily in the TB building. Lillis wrote home on September 19:

> You can imagine how all this has upset things, to have four student nurses come in and change everything like we have, and tell the older graduates that they are still in the dark ages. I have been in surgery for the past month. They don't like me up there either but one of the doctors said I was a bright girl and an excellent surgical nurse. He doesn't like us either, but they all have to put up with us.

It wasn't just the issue of isolation technique; the young cadets were better educated on a variety subjects. Penicillin, as an example, though discovered in the 1920s, was not used or produced in quantity until 1944 or 1945. Doses had to be mixed, and the older nurses did not know how to do that—but the cadets did. She wrote:

> All the older nurses . . . think we are a bunch of smart alecks because we know all about the new drugs and treatments that they have never heard of and we do all the things here that the doctors have been doing, such as mixing our own penicillin etc. and none of them can answer any of our questions. . . . They look at us like they could choke us. We all sit together at meals and laugh and talk and they just sit and stare. All of them are white-headed either real skinny or real fat. They all cough and smoke and drink their coffee black.

As soon as isolation technique was instituted, Lillis volunteered to work on the TB ward. She felt it was a good opportunity to learn, and she felt there was little risk if proper protocol were followed. Besides, she reasoned, she was in good health, not run down, and "I weigh more now than when I came so there is nothing to worry about."

A week later on October 27, she wrote home about the ward and its patients, and about her anxiety related to TB.

Today one of our TB patients hemorrhaged, off and on, all day long. He was admitted yesterday and we haven't transferred him to the TB building yet. It really gives you a strange feeling to see these robust, healthy-looking fellows lying there in their beds coughing up glassfuls of blood at a time and some bleed quarts and die. They will be laughing and talking one hour, and the next they will start coughing and begin to hemorrhage. At times I feel panicky when I'm around these patients. I can just feel the bugs crawling on me (almost) other times I don't give it a thought.

By November 3 Lillis was ordered off the TB ward. It turns out that cadet nurses also needed parental consent to work with TB patients. Her letters home had rattled her mother so much that her mother intervened and asked for her to be reassigned.

The miracle of penicillin took everyone by surprise. She writes home that we are "curing syphilis and gonorrhea in 9 days with penicillin. It is a sure cure." She was treating patients in all stages. Some were blind, others had injury to their central nervous system and shuffled their feet when they walked. She treated two "innocent little children" who had the symptoms or deformities caused by congenital syphilis such as "saddle nose" (missing cartilage in the bridge of the nose), and Hutchinson's teeth (small, blunted or notched teeth).

Back Home

Her 6-month rotation at the VA ended before Christmas. Lillis packed her bags with mixed emotions. She had a lot of happy memories in Albuquerque, as well as stressful work experiences. She was leaving friends, but was eager to see her family. She was anxious over state board exams coming up in the new year. In a real sense her world was being remade.

She boarded a train on a Wednesday night that went through Pueblo and Grand Junction, and arrived in Salt Lake City early Friday morning, December 21. Her friend Jeanne Paul had already arrived in Salt Lake City. Jeanne picked her up and took her to another train at another station that carried her on to Ogden, near where her parents lived at Washington Terrace. This was the first Christmas she had spent with her family since 1941.

Lillis upon graduating from the LDSH Nursing School, 1946.

Lillis met and became involved with Keith Fernelius during the Christmas holidays. He was fond of books, music, and sports, and he was a student at Weber College. Despite the men-to-women ratio during and after the war, her social life never seemed to suffer.

GRADUATION; REGISTERED NURSE

Lillis graduated from nursing school on January 8, 1946. She received her state certificate as a registered nurse on February 4, 1946. She took a job at LDS Hospital as a supervisor of the Formula Lab. The job put her in close contact with student nurses and their problems; she enjoyed that assignment. She moved into a room in a private home across the street from the hospital. Against the headwinds of war, acute distress in her family, and financial uncertainty, she had achieved her aspiration, and largely alone.

VI

Lillis
Nursing in Hawaii
1946–1947

Lillis considered working at Thomas Dee Memorial Hospital in Ogden to be closer to her parents. But then a more intriguing suggestion came from her friend Ruth K. Needham who lived on the Big Island of Hawaii. (The *K* stood for Keali'iho'owaleolikelike.) Ruth had been in Lillis's nursing class of 1946. She invited Lillis and another classmate, Annette Nelson, to work at the hospital on a sugarcane plantation at Pahala, near Hilo, Hawaii. Annette was excited with the offer. Lillis was indifferent and would have stayed in Utah, but her father thought it would be a great adventure and persuaded her to go.

THE VOYAGE

Annette and Lillis flew to Oakland (diverted from San Francisco for weather) on April 23. They spent 2 days sightseeing in San Francisco, then boarded the Matson liner *Lurline*. They boarded in the early evening before supper while the sun was still high. They sailed under the Golden Gate Bridge, watched the mainland disappear, and watched the sunset over the Pacific. The voyage took 5 days. The first 2 days at sea were rough but Lillis and Annette were excellent sailors and never missed a meal or a party.

Of course there was a lot of entertainment on the ship—movies, games, dances. She reported:

> We've had one gay time since we left Salt Lake. . . . Last evening I played ping-pong until we knocked the ball overboard. However I played 15 games. . . . We are going to a dance tonight . . . and my face and arms are so sunburned it will be a tragedy if anyone tries to dance cheek-to-cheek.

They were surprised to attend a church service conducted by two Mormon missionaries who were also traveling to Hawaii. The elders commented, "We knew you were LDS when you got onboard."

The *Lurline* arrived at Honolulu on May Day, or as they say in Hawaii, Lei Day. A flotilla of small boats came out to sea to greet the *Lurline*. Passengers on the *Lurline* would throw coins and trinkets in the water and the locals would dive from their boats to retrieve them, a small indignity. The Royal Hawaiian Band in full dress uniform was playing, also there was a small women's chorus, and there were flowers to decorate the pier. Ruth's sister Leah came to meet Lillis and Annette, and gave them armfuls of leis.

Honolulu

They spent 5 days sightseeing in Honolulu, staying at the Edge Water Hotel on Waikiki Beach. Lillis swam every morning, and wrote home that it was too beautiful to describe. Lillis ran into Dr. Sax and Mr. Helms who had worked with her in Albuquerque, small world. These older men had a car and took the girls around to Pearl Harbor, Diamond Head, through the residential district, and took them to dinner at the Elks Club. The elegant dining room was glassed in so they could look out at the sun set or look down on the breakers coming in under the floor. They also went to see the tuna fishing schooners come in and then to a little Italian restaurant near the waterfront. Somehow Lillis found an officer in the Army Air Corps to take her to the Pago Pago nightclub. It was turning into the adventure her father had imagined.

THE BIG ISLAND AND THE PLANTATION

Lillis and Annette arrived at Hilo on the Big Island by plane on Sunday, May 5. Ruth Needham and Jean Langdorf (also a nurse of the class of 1946) met them at the airport and drove them about 100 miles sightseeing, and introduced them at the LDS mission home in Hilo. The streets and buildings near the coast still showed the terrible damage from the deadly April Fools' Day tidal wave. It was raining in Hilo, and continued to do so for 6 weeks.

Pahala was a company town owned by the Hawaiian Agricultural Company. The population was about 3,000—all employed by the plantation or family members of the workers. The plantation owned all the homes. Only the churches, the movie theater, and the stores were independently owned. Pahala had a post office, cafe, gas station, beer parlor, bank, high school, a social club, and a Caucasian Club, in addition to the sugar mill and plantation infrastructure. The plantation provided water and electricity and even owned a ranch and dairy farm of 1,000 acres all by itself. Skilled and unskilled laborers of all kinds answered to the same manager, who, like a feudal lord, was paid a fabulous salary. There were chemists, mechanics, engineers, accountants, timekeepers, electricians, veterinarians, truck drivers, welfare workers, and of course, physicians and nurses. All called at the same office for their checks. Forty-five of those 3,000 inhabitants were Caucasian. There were about 14 similar sugar plantations on the Big Island.

Lillis was spellbound by the beauty of Hawaii. The Big Island was paradise but with a lethal edge to it. She wrote about the beauty of the plantation, the sweet smell of the cane, the music, and the informality and kindness of the locals. But the locals could be violent; she often treated stabbing victims. The controlled burns at harvest could burn people to death; for example, the previous manager of Pahala, William Cushnie, was burned to death in 1944. Occasionally she would describe a high tide; there was a 50-foot tide in February that killed a 17-year-old boy. A similar storm surge originating many hundreds of miles away occurred in January 1947. The waves hammered the coast for 24 hours and were higher than those of the 1946 April Fools' tsunami.

Even normal tides could be dangerous. In July she described breakers at Punaluʻu as taller than a car—so possibly 6-foot seas. Nevertheless, she "rode the waves" (in her words) that day. The water was warm. Punaluʻu beach was not far from Naalehu—another plantation—where she and her friends often relaxed. In August she described a strong current that she thought might drag her to San Francisco. Then she tried to reassure her family that she always went with companions who knew the beaches and were good swimmers. Also in August she seemed unaware of the danger at Punalu'u when waves quickly put out a fire where they were roasting wieners. Then waves soaked their towels and clothes. Then Annette cut her foot when she was thrown on the rocks.

> The water was real ferocious—more so than I have seen it before. We had loads of fun and got a big bang out of all the surprise attacks of the waves. We rode the waves for about an hour and then it was a little too rough for us so we drove back to Naalehu.

Punalu'u could also be calm and beautiful. She went there in September at night after a dinner party, and watched the full moon rise.

> Needless to say it was beautiful. The tide was low and the breakers were especially beautiful in the moonlight. We then drove over to Naalehu just for the ride. The highway follows the shoreline. You can well imagine how lovely it was.

Once while walking to the library she fell through the surface of the ground into a lava tube, a hazard that a mainlander would not foresee. She struggled to climb out while refusing help from a farmer who had watched her disappear. Lillis knew there were lava tubes on the hospital campus. In fact, her cottage may have been built over one; sometimes while sitting in her house she could hear private conversations at some distance through the tubes.

In the fall and winter months there would be heavy rains and flooding. It could rain 6 inches in a day. Roads would wash away and sometimes people would be stranded. There were detours everywhere.

The Pahala Plantation was at the foot of Mauna Loa on the southern coast, about 50 miles from Hilo, above a beach of black volcanic sand. Mauna Loa is an active volcano that erupted in 1942 and again in 1950. There were between 40 and 200 earthquakes every month while Lillis lived on the plantation. Some were strong enough to wake her from her

Lillis on the black beach of Punaluʻu, 1947.

sleep at night. One knocked bottles off a shelf at the hospital, and when she stooped to pick them up, another tremor knocked her to the floor. By late June, fire, smoke, and steam could be seen coming out of the ground. So the mountain was in the back of people's minds, and a topic of speculation. Many of the locals expected the mountain to erupt at any moment.

THE HOSPITAL

The hospital had a 45-bed capacity, a surgery, delivery room, and nursery. It was all well equipped and modern. Nurses worked on rotating shifts. Two doctors lived on the campus and were always on call. There were also orderlies, aides, and nurse assistants.

The hospital was spread out over a large area, with many doors opening to the outside. When Lillis would finish an evening shift and walk to her cottage, she would invariably write home about the beauty of the moon reflecting off the ocean or shining through the coconut trees, the smell of flowers, fruit, or the cane fields. After finishing a night shift she would write home how beautiful the sunrise was. The "day is beautiful. Can't remember being more happy than I am these past months."

Nurses shared cottages near the hospital. Lillis and Annette were roommates in an "ultra-modern beach cottage . . . with six rooms, adorable electric fridge, radio, recording machine, completely furnished. Beautiful back yard with palm, banana, and cocoanut trees, lawn chairs and table." Annette was later reassigned to a different plantation.

LAURA DESHAZO

Her new roommate was Miss Laura DeShazo of Alabama, the Director of Nursing, a woman of about 60 years old. In a few places Lillis describes her as a staunch Baptist and contemptuous of Mormons. Lillis never substantiated that accusation, but she did write home that DeShazo "was a very lovely person and treated me as though I were her own daughter. She has traveled all over the world and is very fascinating to talk with." Miss DeShazo had a car and often drove Lillis to beaches or to dinner parties. She cooked well and Lillis remarked, "I always gain weight when she cooks for me." Just before Lillis returned to the states she wrote home:

DeShazo has done everything in her power to be kind to me. Even so, I don't think a young person should share a room with a 58- or 60-year-old roommate. Especially when their beliefs and backgrounds are so different. And a general staff nurse should not live with the director of nursing.

Months later Miss DeShazo wrote to Lillis in Utah and said, "You will never know how much we miss you here. . . . I hope our paths cross again."

THE WORK

The workload wasn't too heavy but there were rotating shifts. Lillis had days off and time after work. She played tennis with Ruth almost every day. They even hired a tennis coach. She was very active in local church work, and she had a busy social life. The work sometimes came in waves. Often she complained of sleeping only 5 hours between shifts. The hospital treated a wide variety of illnesses and accidents—scratched fingers, broken bones, or malaria. Lillis had many roles, from surgical nurse to midwife to primary care practitioner. So it was a great learning experience.

Lillis delivered a baby alone for the first time on her first day at work. "The experience was wonderful, but believe me . . . I felt like handing the baby back to the mother and running home." There were six new babies in the nursery that day. Months later she delivered a baby to a Filipina woman who named the child "Lillis Deogracias." Another time, Lillis delivered a baby to a woman who took her marriage vows on the delivery table. The minister had to stop talking when the mother moaned with contractions.

They had one patient who was thought to be more than 100 years old who lived in the hospital though he wasn't really sick. His name was Mr. Wong.

In November, Lillis wrote home:

I prepared a patient for the morgue last shift. She died of an active tuberculosis. Every time I went near her I could feel the bugs crawling down my throat. I'm glad I don't have to take care of her another day. She was also old with diabetes and a heart problem. I'm going to have a chest X-ray Saturday to make sure none of the stray bugs have made their new home in my lungs. I'm sure they haven't.

On another occasion she reported:

> We had two other deliveries and a terrific hemorrhage case. A young Filipino man came in with blood all over his hands. I examined him to discover a deep wound in his back. He had been stabbed with a kitchen knife by some woman's husband.

He survived and was released the next day. She treated other knife incidents:

> It's amazing how forgiving the wives are over here. One Filipino man became out of patience with his wife and sliced her 14 times with a knife across her face and head and neck, deep lacerations each one of them. The ones in the skull looked like they had gone clear through the bone and into the brain but she got well and now she is appealing to get him out of jail on parole. I could go on.

NURSE ASSISTANTS

The hospital employed "maids," or nurse assistants. It was their duty to sharpen needles (hypodermic needles were not disposable), autoclave instruments, refill alcohol or merthiolate bottles, and perform similar tasks. Lillis enjoyed and was amused by one maid in particular, even though she couldn't seem to learn these simple tasks. What she lacked in skill she made up for in personality. She was of Portuguese heritage and married to a Chinese-Hawaiian husband. While the husband was in Honolulu on business, the wife "had a different man every night." She fought with other women, smoked most of the night shift, cursed freely, and had a temper. But she told the "darnedest" stories, and then would laugh out loud when Lillis would look shocked.

On one occasion Lillis made a phone call home. A transoceanic phone call was such an unusual event that her polyglot staff gathered around to watch and listen, and whenever Lillis would shout into the phone, "I cannot hear you," their faces would drop and look worried.

DOCTOR SLATEN

The head doctor, Dr. Slaten, was eccentric, undiplomatic, even rude, both to patients and to hospital staff. His house, like Lillis's cottage, was just a few doors down from the hospital. At one point he got it in his head that Lillis should learn to play chess. She avoided him for weeks until he finally stopped inviting her to his house. Rumor was that Dr. Slaten was a very good chess player and had won tournaments. He almost flunked a semester of medical school because he was so distracted by the game. Dr. Slaten had a reclusive wife who rarely left her house. Lillis said, "I don't care for his wife, and I usually can't stand him either."

Regardless, Dr. Slaten was a good doctor and he was kind and supportive of Lillis, though he did not like Annette. Early on he had Annette reassigned to Naalehu, another plantation about 13 miles farther south. The move was good for Lillis, Ruth, Jean, and Annette (all of the class of 1946) because it expanded their social contacts; they were all very social and often invited each other to the beach, for tennis, or to parties. Sometimes on her days off Lillis would stay over at Naalehu. Nights were beautiful there. "Sometimes you hear a fruit fall from a tree, and soon you can smell it. . . . In those waves of fragrance roll unknown mysteries. . . . I have yet to distinguish them all." She could smell mango blossoms, the perfume of ylang ylang, lady of the night, and cup of gold. "With these and many more is mingled the night breath of leaves, the delicate distillation of earth and dew. Mother, it is just wonderful. I wish you could spend a night with me here."

THE PLANTATION MANAGERS

John Ramsay managed the Pahala Plantation. James Beatty managed Hutchinson Plantation down the road at Naalehu, where Annette worked.

Once, Ramsay summoned Lillis to a meeting or some other pretext. When she arrived it quickly dawned on her that she was alone with this older man who wanted to take her for a car ride in the mountains. With difficulty she suppressed her anger. He was probably near 50 years old, "almost as old as Dad," and married with children. In her letter she reflected on the irony of how much she had admired this man, probably because he was so wealthy, famous, and influential on the island, British-educated, and smart. This was the second time Ramsay had entangled her. She was furious and completely incredulous that she had not made herself clear the first time. On this second occasion they talked for a long while. Ramsay tried to explain why he was so unhappy, presumably with his monogamous life. He commented, "If I were only ten years younger."

Lillis asked him what he would do if he lived those 10 years again and then found himself back in the same spot with the very same problems. At length Lillis said, "I am tired and I have to get up early tomorrow." He looked astonished and got up, slowly realizing how much of her time he had wasted. He said, "Lillis, you don't know how much I've enjoyed this evening." She speculated in a letter to her mother that the gospel could help a man like Ramsay, but she had no illusions that she had persuaded him on any point.

Lillis successfully avoided any further contact with Mr. Ramsay until just before she was to return to the mainland.

> I went to a big party at the home of the Ramsays, plantation manager (the one who took me for a ride that time). First time I've been in their home. Needless to say it is a mansion. There were 80 guests and we were all seated at long tables outside in the lovely garden. While saying good night I had to ask Mr. Ramsay to let go of my hand. I don't think anyone noticed except [another guest and nurse] Mrs. Kempfer [noticed and] teased me about it on the way home.

Lillis and Annette had a better experience with the Beattys, maybe because they only spent time with Mrs. Beatty or her 19-year-old son, John. John was a lot of fun; he had a car and an airplane. He took Lillis and Annette into the mountains, to the movies, all around the old volcano craters, to Kona, Waiohinu, and Hilo. They were happy just to converse with John, and once stayed up late into the night talking in his library. John also took Lillis to the mill to watch the cane being processed, something she had not witnessed at Pahala. Lillis would stay over at the Naalehu plantation on her free days, and go to the beach at Honu'apo with Annette. Once they went swimming in mid-day and got sunburned and burned their feet on the black sand looking for shells. Then they played tennis in the afternoon. They stopped in to see Mrs. Beatty and she gave them prune cake and root beer. Then they went to bed, "lulled to sleep by an earthquake." So Mrs. Beatty could even make sunburns and earthquakes seem like a good time.

Mrs. Beatty loaned formal gowns to Annette and Lillis for a formal party they had been invited to on Oahu. They traveled to Oahu in

November, principally to visit the temple. But there was also some tourism, church administration, and a formal party at the Queen's Surf nightclub. The plane fare alone cost them $70 each, about half of a month's pay. Mrs. Beatty invited them into her bedroom to try on the gowns; she had many and she loaned one to each of them. "Mrs. Beatty is just wonderful, despite all her money." Lillis slept the night before in the Beatty's spare room. "It was the most beautiful and spacious bedroom you ever saw. It has a beautiful sunroom and sitting room off from it, and beautiful bamboo curtains."

THE STRIKE

There were rumors of a statewide sugar strike from the moment Lillis arrived in May of 1946. Wartime restrictions on labor unions were lifted in 1945. Martial law was lifted late in 1944, restoring *habeas corpus* and civilian courts. There had been wartime price and wage controls. All this had contributed to low wages and poor labor conditions. There had also been a plantation practice of isolating racial groups so when one group would strike, the plantation would hire from another, or even import new laborers. A variety of Pidgin languages, sometimes plantation-specific, were spoken late into the 20th century. This all began to change with the strike.

Negotiations broke down and the strike finally began on September 1 and lasted until mid-November. It was statewide, the unions integrated all races, they targeted most all plantations, and also included dockworkers, who refused to ship non-union sugar. It was largely successful and benefitted the workers. However, over the decades it also contributed to the decline of the sugar industry in Hawaii.

As an aside, Lillis had discovered that sugar and canned pineapple were so cheap in Hawaii that she could actually buy those commodities and mail them home cheaper than her parents could buy them in Ogden. She purchased sugar in 100-pound lots on probably three occasions and sent it home. She also sent canned pineapple home, and instructed her mother not to save it because she could send more. That scheme was interrupted for several weeks during the strike when all commodities were scarce, even rice. But she resumed in the new year.

The specter of the strike—the threat of violence, the shortages and austerity, the disruption of community and friendship—were frightening unknowns. The plantation nurses were among the few allowed to cross the picket line. Lillis expressed distrust for the unions even while she was sympathetic to a boatload of Filipino immigrants workers who came to Pahala just prior to the strike. In a June letter she tells her mother when to expect to receive 100 pounds of sugar; then she writes:

> A big boat from the Philippines loaded with women, children, and fellows to work the plantation arrived. All so tired and discouraged looking. Many were ill, some with pneumonia, measles, impetigo, malaria, etc. Reminds me of the Negro [slave trade], at the mercy of the plantation owners. They are treated well here, and given good medical care. It seems so unfair to see these Filipino fellows who used to be the leaders at home, university students, and some are very polished and from once-wealthy families, coming here to do unskilled work in the cane fields. Anything to get away from the Philippines. You can imagine how terrible it must be there. They will at least have enough to eat here. Some of them speak several languages fluently and others can only speak Filipino. We have had so many of them for patients.

The Philippines had suffered during the war. Her observation, "They are treated well here, and given good medical care," sounds like a Confederate apology, and it might have missed the point a bit. After all, the unions were trying to negotiate an end to perquisites on the plantations such as free electricity and free health care as a step toward clarifying fair wages. And certainly, the purpose of imported labor was to break the strike or drive down wages.

Mormons

There was no Mormon organization in Pahala when Lillis arrived. The nearest congregation was in Hilo, more than 50 miles away. But with her arrival there were four Mormon nurses in cottages next door to each other. One of the remarkable things Lillis and her cohort did was to establish a branch in Pahala. Of course, women did not have the institutional authority to do such things, but they pestered and persuaded the mission until missionaries were assigned and ultimately a branch was organized.

Beginning in about May, Lillis took it upon herself to organize "cottage meetings" (informal meetings where missionaries could meet people to proselytize in the home of a mutual acquaintance). As many as 25 would attend. Then she continued to press for missionaries to be assigned to the south part of the island, arguing that long-time Mormons in the area were asking for missionaries to return. There were about 20 missionaries on the island, and their numbers were increasing, so there were enough to go around.

The nurses canvassed the area to discover all the members who lived there. They found one who was an ordained elder, Brother John Kalua, and his 12-year-old son, who soon became a deacon. These two became the priesthood leadership in the new branch. The Kalua family had lived through the war years without close church affiliation.

Lillis attended and often spoke in the Sunday meetings in Hilo. In one of those meetings, possibly July 28, it was announced that the Pahala Sunday School Branch would be organized. The first Sunday school meeting was held at the Pahala Plantation Social Club on August 4. Annette played the piano, Ruth led the singing, Jean taught the Primary, and Lillis was the Gospel Doctrine teacher. She wrote home, "I've never been more happy than I am now. Eventually we will have a fine Sunday School, Primary, and Mutual." Indeed, before she had left the island, they had organized all auxiliaries including a Relief Society, and six missionaries were assigned to the area. In her letters home she invariably asked her parents to send her church books—usually specific titles, conference transcripts, and teaching materials—which she used to build a branch library.

In September, Lillis and Annette were set apart as part-time missionaries. They continued to speak at special meetings at Hilo. They also organized dances, a Halloween party, and a Christmas party. The Halloween party was a great success, with 200 locals in attendance. There was a spook alley and the nurses performed a fake surgery behind a shadow screen. At the climax they threw a real cow's heart over the screen. There was "much smoking and drinking on the premises, which made us feel bad, but nothing to do about that."

In the course of their missionary work, Lillis and Annette became very closely associated with the full-time missionaries, Elders Beardshall and Kolter. Annette drove them to appointments. They all worked together decorating for dances or parties. (Sometimes the mission leadership was also present.) They celebrated Christmas and New Year's together. They were all in Honolulu when Lillis and Annette went on a temple trip, and spent an evening together at a nightclub. Sometimes they would cook for the elders or send food home with them. Lillis remarked on a few occasions that she thought Annette was in love with Beardshall. Beardshall was from a wealthy family and a "collegiate" type, whereas Kolter was the son of an Idaho farmer. Lillis said, "They are both too young for me."

Mormon policy had one curious problem in Hawaii. The gospel was taught in English. The missionaries were not competent in Japanese, for example. To teach in Japanese they had to call on missionaries from the Central Pacific mission, a mission that included Japan. Mission rules did not allow elders to speak Pidgin, or *Hapa Haole* as Lillis termed it. "Of course at the hospital, that's all we speak."

ZEAL

This display of enthusiasm or ardor to organize a branch is not entirely surprising. From her earliest letters, Lillis often writes at length about religion, the spirit she feels in meetings, and she encourages and even admonishes her parents in a way that can only be described as a role reversal. To demonstrate a characteristic often present in her writing, here is one example passage—longer than some—from a letter she wrote on September 29:

> We are receiving reports from Utah telling us that many people are finding fault with the church's [welfare program] and some of the leaders of the church. . . . I do hope no member of our family is ever guilty of ever saying one negative word against any man holding a position in the church. . . . We will do well to judge ourselves. It seems that the day of judgment is near and the time when the great sifting will soon begin. Mother, don't let any of the children find fault with our leaders because that is a sign of apostasy.
>
> It is about time for all of us including Lois and Don to start to study and learn all we can about the gospel and begin to live it. . . . Men should serve missions. No fellow can realize the thrill, joy and satisfaction which can be obtained until he labors in the mission field. Lois should not talk Harvey out of going

on a mission. . . . [Lois married Harvey Hirschi; Harvey served a mission after they were married.]

Is Dad attending church every Sunday he is away from home? I would be so happy if I just knew for sure he was doing all he could to keep the commandments which we have been given. Why I should give this a second thought is beyond me because he has always been my ideal but lately I even wake up at night and find myself worrying about him. Why, I don't know.

You no doubt think I'm irrational but it's probably because I'm so far away from you all. . . . When I write it helps me.

THE CULTURAL EXPERIENCE

It was the informality of the place that Lillis found most charming. When it would rain hard, professionals would go barefoot around the hospital compound. Even teachers in the classrooms would be barefoot. Late in her tour, she wrote that she was eating with her hands, playing tennis barefoot, and learning to speak Pidgin so that her patients could understand her. Fearing that she was going native she enumerated her bad habits and then said, "I hope you don't put me in a cage when I get back."

Lillis wrote to her mother that she was too busy to date men she had met on the island, which was not entirely true. Race and its companion issue, social status, may have been a bit of a barrier. Most of the men on the plantation were unskilled or semi-skilled laborers. On another occasion she wrote that she was happy to go to a dance or spend an afternoon at the beach with the locals, but "I haven't gone out with one I really want to see again." But she acknowledged they were all good dancers.

In June she went to a dinner party at the home of Mr. and Mrs. Ito, an elderly Japanese couple. All of the 20 guests were Japanese except for a few nurses, including Miss DeShazo and Lillis. Some did not speak English.

We took our shoes off at the door, sat on little white cushions on the floor, ate from a table that stood no more than 8 inches high, and ate with chopsticks. They served every kind of fish you could think of, and each fixed in a different manner.

Rice servings were molded in small decorative shapes. There were many courses which were too strange for her to describe adequately. And of course there was tea and straight alcohol. The Japanese hostess had the insight to offer Lillis only fruit juice, a small but remarkable courtesy.

> The little dishes were just beautiful. . . . We broke all the rules and much to the surprise of our host and hostess we . . . helped them with the dishes. I'll be darned if we didn't end up doing them all and had a great time. Mrs. Ito brought out sandals for all of us and we wore them into the kitchen, and laughed and sang and had a gay time while we washed and dried the dishes.

The most singular acts of kindness came from the local residents. A Filipino patient with whom she could not even communicate gave her a nightgown after his stay in the hospital. Her Japanese maid gave her some glass fishes to decorate a whatnot shelf. Even Reverend Chikyoku Kikuchi, the Buddhist priest, gave her a Christmas gift, though he had been living in poverty since Pearl Harbor and his internment on the continent.

She ate at the home of Dr. Kurashige and his wife. He also worked at the hospital. In a letter home she enumerated about 20 courses that the Kurashiges served her that evening.

Annette and Lillis went touring on their days off. They went to Kona on occasion and even stayed overnight. The food was always good at the Kona Inn, as were the rooms and the floorshows. In September they visited the Hawaiian archeological site City of Refuge, then drove on to stay at the Kona Inn. "We took many detours and followed zigzagging highways around the curving shores. I'm sure many of the road-makers must have followed a mongoose when they made some of those roads, but it was loads of fun." There they saw an excellent Hawaiian floorshow and enjoyed the conversation of strangers.

There were frequent impromptu beach parties, sometimes with the nurses, sometimes with local boys, and particularly on nights with a moon. On the 4th of July, Lillis and Annette went to a luau, a rodeo, a carnival, and a dance. Annette was always up for a hike, and once the two of them hiked 7 miles through cane fields to the edge of a huge gorge with a narrow boardwalk along the edge. They explored a lava tube as far as they dared without lights. They often drove to view the various craters. Miss DeShazo took Lillis and Annette to visit the Kapapala Ranch at Christmas time. Miss DeShazo introduced them to the Sumner family who managed the property. The ranch was so high in the mountains that they had a fire in the fireplace to keep warm.

LIFE GOES ON AT HOME

Lillis had continued to correspond with Shirley Melvin Jeppson, who worked for the State Department and had duties in the White House; he was also studying at George Washington University. Both he and Lillis were aware that their career paths had isolated them from eligible Mormon partners. Shirley wrote frequent and long letters. In one he suggested he should visit Salt Lake in April or May of 1947, when Lillis was to return from Hawaii. "I did not want to get romantically involved with anyone during the war because of the indeterminate separation," he wrote. "You probably read this and think I am something of a mathematician when it comes to the emotional side of my life." When April 1947 rolled around she had planned a long vacation trip with her family, and had suggested that Shirley should consider a mission—advice she had given others.

She was still writing to Bob Bunker; she had been engaged briefly to him while in Albuquerque but now she was slow to answer his letters. She was still corresponding with Keith Fernelius and Jack Rencher. Jack suffered a perforated ulcer and almost died. Lillis believed that Jack had abruptly lost interest in her, until she started receiving letters from Jack's mother, who was at his bedside.

Lillis had a sense that the clock was ticking. Her younger sister, Lois (18 years old), graduated from high school and married while Lillis was in Hawaii. Her cousin Colleen had also married. Lillis had six friends who had babies, including Jeanne Paul.

Lillis's mother, Edith, was laid off in June when the war plants were winding down. The fact that Edith had continued to work is interesting because it says something about the family's finances in 1946. Lillis suggested that it was time for Mother to take an easier job or fewer hours.

Her dad's insurance business was picking up, and by August he was even in the competition to win a trip to Havana. He sold insurance to Lillis and Annette, which may seem exploitative, particularly when these young women had no dependents or beneficiaries. Most likely these young women were buying "whole life," which has since fallen out of fashion. But in those days it was difficult to invest small amounts, except in the bank. Whole life was seen as an investment opportunity for the common people. Regardless, both Lillis and Annette balked at Fuller's suggestion to save $100 each year; both offered $50. Lillis was already sending $25 each month to Earl on his mission, and she had other obligations.

Lillis learned in June that LDS Hospital was paying nurses $215 a month—more than she was making in Hawaii. Furthermore, she had already resolved to return to Utah at the end of her year obligation in April of 1947. So she reserved a seat on the modern, dolphin-shaped Constellation airliner for a 9-hour flight to San Francisco.

Her only souvenirs from Hawaii that remained among her possessions were a wooden Buddha small enough to fit in a closed hand, a green glass fishing float which she said had broken away from Japanese fishing nets and drifted to the beach, and the small glass fishes that her maid had given her. That green glass fishing float sat on her mantle in her house on Wilson Avenue into the 1960s.

VII

Lillis Returns to Utah
1947–1948

Lillis had a great time in Hawaii. She must have matured from her responsibility and autonomy at that small hospital, from her leadership in the fledgling church, from her social life, from the beauty of nature, and from the exposure to the cultures, languages, social strata, the strike, and all that went with it. She had played tennis frequently and was in good health. She weighed 130 pounds, the heaviest she had ever been, but still looked like a skinny girl. It must have been the adventure that her father had hoped for her. But she wanted to go home. She had always seen her assignment as a 1-year term. She was conscious of being single, like Miss DeShazo. She was tired of nursing and commented, "I don't want to be a nurse after I am married. It is not a normal life."

Back home her family was planning an extensive vacation trip through many states and touching on Canada and Mexico. She planned her return to the US, motivated in part by that trip. The members of the Mormon branch gave her a luau; the patients and friends from the hospital loaded her down with flowers. Mr. Ramsay gave her a $200 bonus which helped with travel expenses. She departed Hilo on April 4, and arrived in Utah on April 6, 1947.

With her departure from Hawaii, her detailed letters came to an end. She began a scrapbook, possibly in 1948. It holds postcards from New

York and Washington, D.C., and a few other clues to the several transitions over the next years.

Lillis went to live in Washington Terrace near Ogden, where her family had become established. She had been separated from them for 6 years since graduating from high school. She had never lived in that part of the state. Meanwhile, her younger sister Lois had graduated from Weber High School, married, and moved out. Her father was postmaster at Hill Field. He had canvassed the wartime boomtown of Washington Terrace while it was still being built to discover thousands of Mormons—enough to organize four wards—and he had served as a branch president, and served in the newly formed bishoprics. The family was starting to come together again and move beyond the stigma of the fire and the austerity of the war. A trip was planned, in fact, to meet Newell in New Orleans where he was being discharged from the army. They would travel in their new Frazer, one of the first new cars sold in Ogden after the war.

Lillis and her brother Don toured with their parents in the spring of 1947 through New Mexico; Texas; Juarez, Mexico; and on to New Orleans to pick up Newell. At that point there were seven in the car including Newell's wife, Winnifred Kennard, and their infant son, David. The ambitious road trip took them through Newell's old mission field, east to Washington and New York, the tourist sites of Mormon interest, Chicago, and home. It was a lot of miles on two-lane roads, decades before the interstate system. It was apparent early on that Newell's marriage to Lillis's childhood friend "Kennard" was under stress.

Back in Ogden, Lillis took employment at the newly opened St. Benedict's Hospital. She wore a starched white uniform, a starched white hat, white nylon stockings, and white shoes—the typical attire for all nurses. But a starched white uniform was impractical, even then. In the final days of steam locomotives, her uniform would not stay clean even one day. The railroads ran close to town and created a lot of particulate pollution. It wasn't just trains; even private homes heated with coal.

She continued to date the refined and thoughtful Keith Fernelius, whom she had met while on Christmas break from her assignment in Albuquerque. He was now at the University of Utah. He invited her to ballets, to hear Marian Anderson sing, and to hear Yehudi Menuhin play violin. He also took her on a chaperoned, 3-day geology excursion in the Uintas with his university class.

Possibly Lillis was reconsidering her career in nursing when she enrolled in classes at Brigham Young University for the fall quarter of 1947 and the winter quarter of 1948. Her studies included Hebrew. There she met and dated Eldin Ricks who later became a professor at BYU. The move to Provo, intentionally or unintentionally, put some distance between her and Keith. While she was living in Provo in 1948 her family bought a house at 2193 S. 10th East in Sugar House, as luck would have it, in Lincoln Ward where George Brooks lived. Lillis gave up school in the spring, moved into her parents' home in Salt Lake City, and took work at LDS Hospital. So there were many changes in quick succession for her and for her family. Important as these decisions and transitions were, there is very little written documentation.

VIII

George
Childhood
1926–1944

BIRTH

George's parents, Winnifred and Samuel, found themselves in financial straits in 1925. They had a 10-month-old baby girl, and Winnifred was pregnant again. They were indebted to their parents, and suddenly unemployed. Samuel needed money immediately. He moved the family to Park City where he took work as a mucker in a hard rock mine. Park City was a boomtown where jobs were available in the silver mines, though in hazardous conditions.

George was born in the Miners Hospital in Park City, Utah, on March 6, 1926. The hospital still stands in Park City, used today as a community center and meeting hall. The little family lived in Park City a bit more than 2 years; then Samuel took the civil service exam and was offered a job in Salt Lake City with the Post Office. They moved to Sugar House when George was 16 months old. George only knew one home growing up—1998 McClelland Street.

George would go away to war, then to serve a mission, then marry. Within a few years of marriage he returned to Sugar House and bought a home where he lived for another 30 years—not more than 3 blocks from where he grew up.

FAMILY AND HOME

By all accounts George had a pleasant upbringing; he never spoke anything but affection for his parents. He never doubted his parents' love for him. George had a sister, Beverly, 2 years his elder; she married Clarence Walker. He had another sister, Barbara "Bobby" Dean, who was 3 years younger than he. Barbara Dean married Carl Merrill. The youngest child, Samuel Jr., was 8 years younger than George. Samuel Jr. had no recollection of George's youth, but he did recall that his parents seemed to treat the girls better, while not involving themselves too much in the lives of the Brooks boys.

George said his father was a competent amateur boxer, and George said he always felt safe walking with his dad. During World War I, soldiers would occasionally spar in their leisure time, and it was possibly in the Army that Samuel became a proficient boxer. Samuel was a man who did not mind hard work, and in fact seemed skeptical of anything other than physical labor. George characterized his father as not entirely comfortable in the 20th century. Samuel almost never drove a car, deferring to his wife, Winnifred. He buried apples, potatoes, turnips, and carrots in a mound of sand in his backyard in Sugar House because the city lot was too small for a root cellar. He kept a small vegetable garden with fruit trees, gooseberries, raspberries, and rhubarb. Samuel was gregarious and had many acquaintances. He was a storyteller with a brain full of memorized poems, anecdotes, Shakespearean soliloquies, and scripture, always ready to recite at a moment's notice. Somehow he avoided all positions of authority or leadership both in his profession and at church.

George's mother, Winnifred Parry, was gentry if only in her native hamlet of Manti, Utah. Some would say she bore that arrogant demeanor all her life. Her grandfather, Edward Lloyd Parry, was a stonecutter and quarry owner. In pioneer days he helped engineer and build the LDS temples in Manti and St. George. Winnifred hobnobbed with church leaders who were famous in Mormon frontier society. Many lodged in her father's house as they traveled up and down the territory. Her family's stone ended up in landmarks such as the Park Building at the University of Utah, the Hearst Castle at San Simeon, California, and the Manti Temple.

Winnifred was emotional—exultant over good things such as her family or a kindness that someone had done to her. Likewise, she may have experienced periods of sadness or anger. There is an unsubstantiated

George at about 2 years old, c. 1928.

rumor that when her children were young she became "tired" at one point and took rest for several days in a convalescence home. She could take offense, hold a grudge, and speak sharply. She suffered episodes of gout most of her life.

Winnifred was 27 and Samuel was 33 when they married in 1919, older than some of that era. Consequently, Samuel was 39 when George was born, and 48 when Samuel Jr. was born. George's two grandfathers were foster brothers, so Samuel and Winnifred were like first cousins. But Samuel grew up in St. George, and Winnifred grew up in Manti, and they were not acquainted until a few months before their marriage. Both attended some college; both taught school for a while.

THE GREAT DEPRESSION

It should be noted that the Great Depression nominally started in 1929 when George was 3 years old, and lasted more than a decade, until World War II. The Depression was one of the defining issues of that generation. Even though Samuel had a government job and secure income, people, including George's parents, were frugal and conscious of money for the rest of their lives. A letter that Winnifred wrote George while he was stationed with the Army at Fort Meade, Maryland, reveals that George's parents struggled financially throughout the depression. And as prosperity returned, Winnifred continued to worry that Samuel might lose his job to returning servicemen. Samuel would have been 59 years old at the time this letter was written.

Tuesday, Dec 18, 1945

Dear George

I hope this money order reaches you in time. I haven't been able to get to the bank since receiving your request for this $25 so am sending this out of what Daddy gave me for groceries. You know Jack sold his store to Sheffields and they are cash-and-carry. I guess we will do most of our shopping at Safeway because they are close and we like them. But we have to have the cash now and I think it will work out better.

George, I am afraid you are too extravagant. Maybe we all spend more freely than we should at Christmas time. I hope you haven't done too much. But really I think you should try to save a certain amount every month. Your money is coming pretty easy now, but there will probably come a time when you need a little extra badly. Now is the time to save. When you think of getting your board, room and clothes, I think you should be able to bank $40 or $50 every month. Other boys do it and have a neat little bank account. You have been in the service a little over or under 1 ½ years and have only about $100 in the bank. Why don't you set a goal and then stick to it? I do not want you to think I am scolding you. I am not. But I am advising you. Maybe I wouldn't think so much about it if we hadn't had such a hard time to try to get along for 20 years. This is the first time since we were married 26 years ago that we feel like we could pay a doctor bill or go out to dinner or a show or do the least little extra without having to go without something else or feeling the pinch of it. And we don't know how long this little spurt of prosperity will last. When I showed Daddy my bank book the other day he was surely surprised to think I had that much and you know he has acted different ever since. I believe it is such a relief to him to know we have that little to fall back on that it has given him a new lease on life. He isn't as young as he was and they are retiring the men whether they want to be or not. I think as soon as the boys come home from the army they will retire all the older men. We wish we could do more for you children but I do not know whether it would be good for you or not. I guess it is just as well that you hustle for yourselves. But we do love you.

And now I guess I'll do a little complaining. I haven't been well since I did the painting in the front rooms. My legs give me an awful lot of pain. After having the family out to dinner when Ed and Marie were here I went to bed for a day. Yesterday I felt pretty good so I did the ironing and then took the curtains down in the three front rooms. Today I can hardly move from the hips down and my knees hurt so. I guess I'm thru doing heavy work and I just love to work.

So George dear, you can't depend on us for very much financial aid any more, and we feel worse about it than you do. Bobby started working in the Post Office Saturday. She puts in 8 hours after school. She gets pretty tired but it will do her good. Daddy says everybody up there thinks she is pretty cute. She is so quick with an answer it tickles them.

Sammy is in a play in Primary Wednesday. I hope I can go over to see him.

We will miss you these holidays as we miss you all the time, but we are glad it is now instead of last year at this time. There is always something to be thankful for. I am glad the swelling in my knees is not on my nose. (So there, too.)

With love, Mom

Food preservation and home industries were important activities in George's childhood home, as in most homes. Pickling watermelon rinds was one of the things Winnifred did to optimize their home economy. She would also candy grapefruit peels. Winnifred had a hand-cranked meat grinder to make sausages or ground beef. She had a ricer with a long wooden pestle, a cold packer, cherry pitter, hand coffee grinder, and many other widgets that are not ordinarily found in kitchens today.

Everything was old or old-fashioned in the house George grew up in. The things that were in the house as late as the 1960s included: a collection of 78-rpm records and a phonograph with a clockwork motor. It didn't actually have a "morning glory" horn but it had internal baffles and channels for sound amplification, and finally, shutters on the front of the cabinet to dampen the sound. Of course, electric high-fidelity stereo was available and affordable at that time. Winnifred had a reed organ that had been in the home of her grandfather, Edward Lloyd Parry, in the 1880s. The organist would pump the bellows with foot pedals or with knee levers. Winnifred had a set of silver combs, hairbrushes, a hand mirror, and perfume bottles, essential possessions for women of her generation. They had a radio console that was as tall as a child, at a time when transistor radios were available and cheap. The silver was worn off the back of their silver-plate spoons and forks. Their furniture reflected turn-of-the-century tastes—Renaissance Revival, Victorian, Arts and Crafts—and was never updated.

The house George grew up in had a coal-burning furnace that was retrofitted with gas in 1931. Many houses continued to use coal for heat and thus the air in the city was sooty, particularly in winter. It was necessary to clean walls and furniture in the spring. Wallpaper could be cleaned by rubbing it with a cleaning substance the consistency of bread dough. It took strong arms and hands, and Winnifred mentions in her diaries that George would help her with such heavy housework.

George's house only had one bedroom; his parents slept there. George slept on a sleeping porch for years. The porch was essentially open to the air, with three sides screened in. He said the screens were effective for keeping out insects in the summer, and leaves in the fall, but did nothing to inhibit driven rain or winter cold. Samuel hung canvas over the screens in the winter, which did little to keep out the cold. The children said their prayers inside the warm house and were allowed to put their pillows against the heat registers before they made the dash across the sleeping porch. George said that running from the door to the bed in winter was a special thrill and it always took some time to warm the sheets and blankets with only his body heat. Once warm, however, sleeping was a wonderful experience, weighted down with several quilts, and his cherry nose to remind him all night how good it was to be warm. This porch was framed in and enclosed sometime after 1940; so finally as a teenager George had a proper room upstairs. Over time Samuel also excavated a basement, throwing bucket after bucket of dirt out a window. They built an apartment down there that they rented out.

Family Vacations

Though money was tight during the Depression, Samuel and Winnifred were able to go to the World's Fair in Chicago in 1934, leaving their children with relatives.

The family bought their first car in 1936. They used it to vacation in Manti to visit the Parry grandparents. The drive to Manti seemed interminable. Sometimes George's mother would actually get the car up to 40 mph, and she would announce it breathlessly, exciting everyone.

George and his sisters would play in Grandfather Edward Thomas Parry's barn. He recalled his grandfather telling them not to jump in the hay, saying, "That's the cow's breakfast; how would you like it if someone jumped in your ham and eggs?" This pleasant and often-repeated injunction was never enforced. They all did a fair amount of jumping in the hay, which indeed would shake the leaves off the stems and degrade the nutritional value of the hay.

They used to play in the Manti Temple. Mormon temples are restricted and private these days, but when George was a child, very few doors were locked in Manti. George and his cousins would wander in and explore this underutilized and opulent building. There was a room in the temple where the sacred drama would play out and the words would be spoken, "Place cherubim and the flaming sword that man may not partake of the fruit." In this room there was a real sword hanging on the wall, possibly a cavalry saber from the Civil War. Its prominent place of display on the wall was surrounded with a neon tube that represented flames. Of course, this stage prop was irresistible to George, and he would take it down and have pretend sword fights in the temple with his cousins. George would have been about 12 when his grandfather Parry died.

The drive to St. George to visit the Brooks clan was even longer than the drive to Manti, maybe 3 days—there was no railroad. They didn't visit often; sometimes several years would pass without a visit. The car would often overheat, and they could count on several tire repairs en route. His grandfather Brooks, also named George, died when George was 4, so he had little or no memory of his grandfather. But his memories of St. George were clear. He helped his cousin mow the 6-acre lawn around the St. George Temple. They used a large, horse-drawn reel lawnmower. They played in the Virgin River, which everyone, with rustic humor, referred to as "the dirty Virgin." They climbed the sandstone cliffs just a block or so above his grandparent's house. That house had been built by his grandfather Brooks, also a stonemason, using stone left over from the St. George Tabernacle. Later in his life, George would look at the worn sandstone step into that house and say, "My father as a child helped wear down that step."

When cousins from St. George or Manti would visit Salt Lake City, it was like "Town Mouse, Country Mouse"; George was astonished at their lack of sophistication. There would have been no streetcars and few multistory buildings in either Manti or St. George.

The family also spent many summer days at Saltair, a resort on the shore of the Great Salt Lake, which was easily accessible by way of a dedicated rail line. George was also active in the Boy Scouts and would go camping in the nearby mountains, or spend longer periods at Camp Steiner in the Uintas. He never achieved First Class in Scouting because he had an injury to his ear and could not pass the swimming requirement.

Most of all, George spent his summers unsupervised, playing with friends, riding his bicycle, or wandering around Sugar House. He said that as a child he usually wore only a pair of bib overalls—nothing else.

SUGAR HOUSE

Sugar House was like a village on the distant southeast edge of Salt Lake City. Farther to the south or to the east the valley was unpopulated. There would have been small orchards if not wilderness, where it was even possible to hunt deer. But Sugar House was an important community with its own "tabernacle" built in a Romanesque revival style. The Granite Tabernacle with its balcony could seat well over 1,000, particularly if the shutters in the back wall of the chapel were opened up and overflow seating was set up in the adjoining "cultural hall." This rich building with its tile roof, pipe organ, fresco, and parquet floors was built during the Depression in 1930 when George was 4 years old. That's where he attended church until he left home. Irving Junior High School, built in 1926 in a late Tudor style, was another beautiful and imposing building. Many structures of the time—such as the Sprague Branch Library (1928) with its slate roof, the Federal style post office, and South High School with its marble and brass foyer—were expensive commitments to architecture, taking the long view of community. The Utah State Penitentiary was on the hill only a few blocks east, where Sugar House Park is now.

Sugar House was known for its many furniture stores. Prominent were Granite, Rockwood, and Southeast, all sitting near a railroad line. Several important enterprises were born in Sugar House. Snelgrove Ice Cream began in 1929; Dunford Bakery began in 1931. There were movie theaters, restaurants, an ice plant and cold locker company (in the days before home refrigeration), a car dealership, library, post office, and park. There was small manufacturing, yet the community was small enough that most everyone knew each other. It was a community where a curious boy could watch mechanics and journeymen ply their trades. George would wander in and out of the various shops with complete abandon. He enjoyed chatting with tradesmen as he watched them work. No doubt it all contributed to his later, seemingly endless comprehension of how things worked and how to fix things. In 1976 he reminisced in his journal:

George, 1939.

. . . I would watch for hours as they worked, usually building a friendship with the workmen although sometimes they found me pesky and would send me away. I learned to recognize many of their tools and to appreciate, though superficially, their hand-iwork. A Mr. Binnington was a tinsmith, working with sheet metal, making chimney extensions, rain gutters, flour boxes, etc. Otto Boone or Bone was a shoemaker. I couldn't get too close to his work because I was usually barefoot and he had nails all over the floor. Orrin Mortensen and Willard Brown were upholsterers for Granite Furniture. There was a watchmaker who used to let me watch while he cleaned and repaired watches. The Dalebouts were bakers. The Jacobs ran a planing mill; there were two or three planing mills in Sugar House. Snelgroves were making ice cream as long as I can remember. Murphy had a candy factory right across the street from my home.

In his teenage years George worked at Granite Furniture, unloading boxcars of incoming stock, binding and laying carpets, sanding furniture for painting, and driving delivery trucks. Older employees chose George to help with deliveries because he was strong and careful and rarely dam-aged furniture. Granite sold wood-burning stoves and ranges. These were quite heavy, but George, with the assistance of a coworker, could carry these. And he could install them and the stovepipe.

SCHOOL AND CHURCH

In many cases the bonds of childhood friendships that were created at church or school endured his entire life. As a mature man he still attended study groups or dinner parties with friends he had made in Cub Scouts or at school. Sugar House and even greater Salt Lake City were stable communities where people lived all their lives. The result was that George had many long-term relationships. When he served as bishop of Richards II Ward, stake president in Sugar House Stake, principal at Forest Elementary, and even when working at the Salt Lake School Board office, he was always bumping into people who, for better or worse, knew details from his childhood.

George went to elementary school at Forest Elementary on 9th East and 21st South; then to Irving Junior High on 21st South and 12th East;

then to South High School on State Street and 16th South. His grades were poor; he achieved as many Ds as Cs, with an occasional B in choral music, industrial arts, or Latin. He repeated a grade—possibly third. His parents were not too involved in his education, and he complained that in his home he could never find a sharp pencil to do his homework; they did not have a pencil sharpener in their house. When he needed to sharpen a pencil, his father would sharpen it for him with a penknife. Thus George always had blunt, misshaped points and was self-conscious of his ugly handwriting.

Late in 1987 George wrote that he always felt that there must be a better way for a child to spend his time than in school. He didn't accuse his teachers of being incompetent or unprepared. Only a few of them were punitive, petty, or sadistic. He said of one unnamed teacher who taught him in fifth grade, that she

> . . . still elicits in me a negative visceral reaction. Once in my adult life I saw her crossing the street in front of me in a pedestrian lane, and like Voltaire, who had to control himself from driving his carriage over the Paris clergy, I almost seriously considered . . .

And there he stopped his narrative, noting, "Nevertheless I did learn to read well, my handwriting was never tops but legible, spelling turned out okeh."

George was held back by Miss Charlotte Gallyer, who lived 2 or 3 blocks from George even during his adult life. Holding children back a grade was more common in those days than today, but was still humiliating. The kids who were held back ended up physically bigger and older than their classmates. George felt it was an unnecessary and a lasting shock to his ego. It always caused him some twinge of embarrassment, even into his 60s.

Years later, Miss Gallyer would also teach George's children—G. Remington and Dean. George was assigned to be principal at Forest Elementary in 1965, Miss Gallyer's last year before retirement. In her last days at work George put his arm on her shoulder and quipped, "You should have held me back another year," suggesting that in that case she would not have had to work on his staff. George's assignment to be principal of Forest Elementary was a small vindication for him. It would not be surprising if his success also made Miss Gallyer feel justified in her disciplinary techniques. As an old woman she was still notorious for being humorless and strict, and for meting out corporal punishment, and she was by no means unique in her generation and profession.

George did not excel in junior high or high school. He always seemed to have enough friends, but he was never able to get a place on a sports team or in student government, or break into the popular crowd. He attended high school with his "close neighborhood friends in a kind of encapsulated anonymity." Even his teachers were largely impersonal. He got a B in ROTC once but did not achieve the rank or recognition that he wished for; ROTC was a required course during the war. His happy memories and rich social life came from church—participating in stake plays and musical operettas, going to dances, camping with the scouts, singing in the choir.

All those schools are now closed. Forest was torn down and replaced with a grocery store. Irving burned down. Only one wing is standing today—the boys gymnasium, repurposed as a commercial building and incorporated into a more recent structure. The South High building is used today as a community college.

George took his spiritual life more seriously. He never missed the Mutual Improvement Association (a church youth program which met one evening mid-week; also called Mutual or MIA). He rarely missed sacrament meeting or priesthood meeting, though he often sluffed Sunday school. His scrapbook preserves all his certificates and letters, documenting his naming at birth, his baptism, his ordinations, his youth leadership callings, his patriarchal blessing, and so forth. Mutual was like a weekly party where he enjoyed association with his friends. He would often return home late and his parents would ride him for being late, but he never complied.

MISCHIEF

George admitted to being mischievous and speculated that his misbehavior at school may have been as much a factor in his third-grade retention as was his academic performance. He felt resentful of the institutional arrogance and impunity that held him back. Most of his pranks were playful; a few were a bit vengeful.

When singing hymns in Primary he and his friends would change the words to something silly or absurd. There was one church song, "In Our Lovely Deseret," which praised the children of the church. "Children's voices, oh, how sweet, / When in innocence and love, / Like the angels up above . . ." This song was sung to the tune of the Civil War song, "Tramp, Tramp, Tramp, the Boys Are Marching." In the chorus where the "tramp, tramp, tramp" should go, the Deseret version sang, "Hark, hark, hark, the children's voices." George and his buddies sang this as, "Bark, bark, bark, the children's voices." Of course, in a short time that morphed into actual barking during the song. Nothing too surprising there.

Nyman recalls that George told him that a teacher at Forest Elementary disciplined him once by locking him in a closet. George jammed the door from the inside and pretended to be suffocating and enjoyed the teacher's ensuing panic when she couldn't free him.

Nyman also recalls a story of George locking an elementary school teacher out of the room, then persuading his classmates to be silent and unresponsive to her knocking.

Don Remington, George's brother-in-law, told a similar story which may be a variant, or a separate episode. George angered a Sunday school teacher, who went to find a priesthood authority to discipline George. While the teacher was out of the class, George locked the door and took the pins out of the hinges. Then he and the rest of the kids escaped through a window. The teacher knocked on the door without response. When the teacher pressed on the door it fell to the floor. Then it was easy to get in, but class was over.

Presuming these stories are true, it is interesting that he was able to enlist other kids in the class to take part in his mischief, however passively.

This next story is more or less common knowledge and has been recalled by several people. When he had a job dipping ice cream cones at Snelgrove's he discovered that he could lower the cone a bit at the moment when he was handing it to the customer and the customer would invariably miss the cone and end up with a handful of ice cream. He said the customer would always apologize for being so inattentive and clumsy. Of course George would accept their apology most sincerely.

Once, after a Mutual meeting, he and some friends wandered around Sugar House in the night rather than going straight home. One of the boys accepted a dare to climb the flagpole by the monument to industry in the middle of 21st South and 11th East. This boy excelled at flagpole climbing, and when he reached the top he made the pole oscillate while he was shouting and showing off by holding on only with his thighs, arms outstretched.

George would sometimes catch rides on the outside of streetcars, which was not allowed. He might also sometimes pull the trolley off the overhead power line, which would disable the car and force the driver to get out and put it back on the wire.

He had a space between his front teeth into early adulthood. He was self-conscious about this space and he would purposefully push his teeth back and together with his thumbs. By the time he was about 30 years old the space was closed.

To sum up, George had a loving home, but his parents were not terribly motivated and had few ambitions for him. He was curious and perceptive but not a good student. He was social and playful, but could tease to distraction. He never ran with the popular crowd but had many friends that he kept for life.

IX

George
Army Service
1944–1946

George summed up his war experience in letters to his 16-year-old sister Barbara Dean. It was June 1945 when hostilities were over, the weather was warm, and he was stationed in a beautiful area near the German-Czechoslovak border that had escaped the worst part of the war. He said it was like a long picnic. The letters gossiped a bit about a girl, Valine Anderson, whom he had taken to the South High graduation dance just a year earlier, and they speculated about when his unit would be sent home. In one of these letters he enclosed a photograph taken in the dark days, in winter, when the 87th Infantry Division confronted the last bitter resistance in the Ardennes (January), then the Siegfried Line (February), then crossed the Rhine (March).

Germany
June 11, 1945
Dear Bobby Dean,

    You'll never know how much your regular letters mean to me. I hope that now that you are out of school you won't slacken up just because you don't have a study period.

"The only ones of us left are Lutterman, Perrotta, and myself. All the rest were either killed or wounded." Inspection formation near Auw, Germany, February 24, 1945. Left to right: Leonard Munson, Delbert Lutterman, Palmer Behler (killed in action), George Brooks, Edward Culhane (killed in action), Richard Barnes (wounded in action), Chester Wawrzyniak, John Manikowski, Geodo Perrotta.

Enclosed you'll find a snapshot taken about two days before we jumped off into the Siegfried Line. The name of the town is Auw (Ah) and is in Germany just on the border. The formation is an inspection. The day was cold and muddy. See the boots I'm wearing? They were the only size they could get to fit me, size 14, and were about 4 inches too long.

I don't recognize any [one in the photo] except on the front rank. The only ones of us left are Lutterman, Perrotta, and myself. All the rest were either killed or wounded. Behler and Culhane, on my left and right respectively were both killed within a few days after this picture was taken in the Siegfried. We were in the Siegfried on your birthday [February 27], Bobby. Barnes, 4th from right, is now in a psychiatric ward in a hospital with shell shock. Perrotta (extreme right) is my platoon sgt and Lutterman is platoon sgt of the 3rd Platoon. To look at the picture you'd think we scared the Jerries back rather than fought them.

I think today is the last day we can send letters home. The next you hear will probably be a phone call or telegram. I hope. So far it's just a rumor. Keep your letters coming though because I think we'll pick them up when we get there. If you don't hear from me you'll know.

I hope to see you soon, Bobby. Lots of love,
George

INDUCTION AND TRAINING

George turned 18 on March 6, 1944, and reported to the draft board that day. On June 8 he graduated from South High School, 2 days after the Normandy landings. His uncle Nat Parry gave him a silver identification bracelet as a graduation gift. It's hard to know what this gift meant among men in those days. But this masculine jewelry had roots in the previous war, when so many went missing and dog tags were not quite standard issue. George received a patriarchal blessing—a personalized Mormon sacrament. In somewhat *pro forma* language, his blessing stated that he had a mission and purpose on earth, but in a specific reference to the war, it instructed him how to pray in secret while surrounded by comrades. He went through the temple with his parents and his sister's future husband, Clarence Walker.

Some boys avoided the draft, but there was a general willingness or eagerness to go to war. George did not volunteer, but said he would have been disappointed if he had not been drafted or fit to serve. He reported for induction on June 10, only 2 days after high school graduation. He was processed at Fort Douglas in Salt Lake City, had physical examinations, received vaccinations, and was issued a uniform. On June 19,

> We were told to put all our clothing etc in our barracks bags. We were put on buses and taken to the D and RGW [Denver and Rio Grande Western] Railroad station where we were put on trains, not knowing where we were going. We did not find where we were going until we stepped off the train at Infantry Replacement Training Center, Camp Wolters, [near Mineral Wells] Texas. There were almost 400 Utah boys that came here (Camp Wolters) on the same train.

The portentous name "Infantry Replacement Training Center" seems to have escaped his scrutiny.

> Our training here started out slowly. At first we did such things as classes in first aid, map reading, etc. with short hikes and close-order drill. It gradually became tougher but so did we. It finally came to the point where we could hike 20 miles in 8 hrs, work 20 hrs per day for four days or more at a time. Most days it would hit the 100° F mark and still we would work. Even though we did get tougher there were still those who couldn't keep up with the rest and had to fall out. . . . I don't say this boastfully; I was able to keep up with them on all of our hikes. I never fell back because of lack of stamina. . . . I attribute this to the fact that I observed my "Word of Wisdom." At one time over a fifth of the personnel of my company fell back because of lack of stamina on a hike.

George, however, did suffer from a stress fracture in his right foot. He does not mention this in his journal, but his mother references it a couple of times in letters and in her diary. In Europe, both feet gave him trouble because of the cold and ill-fitting boots.

He trained on a variety of weapons at Camp Wolters. George qualified as a sharpshooter with the M1 rifle, which is better than marksman but below expert. Years later George would recall that bayonet training started by teaching men how to allow a rifle to swing like a pendulum. Of course the rifle had mass and would swing easily. Next they would swing their rifles and bayonets into bales of straw. And finally they would swing them into effigies as part of a larger exercise course. It became easy and thoughtless.

Gas mask training included taking off a mask inside a chamber filled with tear gas. He recalled that while receiving instructions on poison gas, the troops were sitting on the ground and were passing around a vial with some charcoal holding a bit of poison gas so they could all smell it and learn to recognize it. As a prank one soldier dropped the charcoal into the back of the pants of his buddy next to him, which caused the other soldier to blister. Such was the task of teaching teenagers to go to war.

Late in life he reflected on the urgency of putting troops quickly on the front line. "Admittedly we were tougher and I suppose smarter when we came out than when we went in but the 17 weeks of this training seemed to me to be far too little to make us really fighting men or seasoned soldiers."

Deployment

George wrote in December 1988: "By September most of the men I trained with were in foxholes in the Pacific; assumedly many of them were dead by Christmas." But because of his stress fracture George was delayed at Camp Wolters for several weeks while it healed.

George was given a 10-day furlough, which he spent in Salt Lake City with his family. While home he had his picture taken; he visited friends and relatives and gave them his photograph. He attended the wedding of his sister Beverly. He did not mention these things in his journal, writing only, "I think [it was] on the 11th day of December 1944 when I left home after having a ten-day furlough, to report to Fort George G. Meade, Maryland, a port of replacement." His mother's very brief journal entries likewise show how mundane life can appear. On December 4 she wrote, "George and I cleaned the wallpaper in the two front rooms. Beverly came over to put a few of her things away. We were glad to be together. Am I tired tonight." In fairness, his mother Winnifred was 52, in poor health, and some say she was emotionally fragile. On December 11 she wrote:

> George left today. It is pretty hard to have him go. I did not go to the train. Dean [Winnifred's sister, Edwardena Parry Cottam], Mrs. Rigby, and I tried to comfort each other. We all have boys in the service. Dean and I went to the Marlo to a show.

So it seems Winnifred went to a movie with her sister because she was too distraught to see George off at the train station.

He traveled by train through Chicago, stayed overnight in Baltimore, where he enjoyed a USO show, and arrived at Fort Meade on December 15. He stayed about a week at Fort Meade and another week at Camp Joyce Kilmer, New Jersey, which was part of the New York Port of Embarkation—an army command responsible for moving troops to Europe. Fort Meade and Camp Kilmer offered liberal leave while the men were checked, rechecked, issued new equipment (but not weapons), and given more physical examinations and immunizations.

It was possibly during this time that George had his combat boots replaced with a new pair that was size 14. Years later he conjectured that it was not necessary to replace his boots even though he was ordered to do so. He believed the new boots affected his combat readiness, and caused him pain for the rest of his life, particularly in cold weather.

He spent his days of leave touring Washington, D.C., and New York. He visited the Capitol, the Smithsonian, and the Tomb of the Unknown Soldier. He collected a photograph of the iconic Mormon meeting-house near the intersection of 16th Street and Columbia Road NW in Washington, D.C. He attended church there and passed the sacrament. At church he ran into friends from Salt Lake City—Ralph Blunt, who was stationed there in the navy, and Russell Cannon.

He spent Christmas alone in New York, and slept on a cot provided for servicemen in the basement of a Protestant church. Someone had provided Christmas stockings there for soldiers containing razor blades, soap, nuts and candy. He acquired free servicemen tickets to a Broadway show, a concert in Carnegie Hall, and the Rockettes.

I was given a three-day pass to New York City. It was my first Christmas away from home and a very lonely and unhappy one. I stood that night on Times Square in the crowds and had never felt so all alone in my life. While there I managed to see the Empire State Bldg., Radio City Music Hall, the Statue of Liberty etc. I also attended LDS services in the Steinway Bldg. and enjoyed it very much. [From his scrapbook.]

On the 31st of December in the early morning we boarded electric trains and rode to Jersey City. We crossed the River to New York on a ferry. We got off the ferry and on the pier where the Queen Mary and the Queen Elizabeth were both tied up. After coffee and doughnuts from the Red Cross we walked up the gangplank and onto the Queen Mary. We stayed on board her and she pulled out at 9:00 in the morning New Year's Day. [From his journal.]

The RMS *Queen Mary* and her younger sister RMS *Queen Elizabeth* were built as luxury liners during the Depression. The British called the *Queen Mary* the "ultimate ship" for her luxury and speed; she could sustain speeds in excess of 28 knots. Now both ships were gray troop carriers with blacked-out portholes. Every time they came into port they received some little modification to improve their armament or carrying capacity.

The *Queen Mary* was designed to carry 2,000 passengers but now she carried 15,000 troops on each crossing. Troops slept everywhere—even in the drained swimming pool. There was a movie theater on board and also a store. But it was impossible to take advantage of either because of the crowds. Like the old joke, the food was terrible and the servings were small; there were only two meals each day. He felt lucky at least that he had a stateroom with a latrine, which he shared with three other comrades.

When George sailed the troops were told that the ship would not stop for a man overboard. They sailed without lights and in radio silence. The unseen enemy was in the back of everyone's mind. There was an abandon ship drill every day. George was so seasick the first 2 days that once he lay on a hatch cover and refused to participate in the drill and would not stand to salute an officer—an offense with no consequence on that occasion. "We must have gone far south because the weather became quite mild."

The *Queen Mary* sailed alone because she was faster than any escort. She typically left port in secrecy, in fog or under cover of darkness to disappear in the expanse of the ocean. She would take a longer, southerly zig-zag route but still arrive in 5 or 6 days. (See Steve Harding, *Gray Ghost: The RMS Queen Mary at War*, 2007.)

She crossed without incident and pulled into the Firth of Clyde near Glasgow, Scotland, on January 6, 1945.

Within a short time George was transported by ferry and train to Southampton. On the train, they were issued a day's K-ration. The K-ration was the least desirable ration, designed for men in combat when cooking was simply impossible. It was a dry ration that always included crackers.

> In Southampton we boarded LSTs (landing ship, tank). An LST is a craft that is built especially for landing tanks on beaches. It has a large maw at the front which when the ship is beached, drops open and enables the tanks to drive out onto the beach. At this time, however, they were being used as personnel carriers. We loaded on to the LST #400 at 5:00 that evening and it took just 12 hours before we unloaded in Le Havre, France.
>
> Le Havre was in a very, very bad shape. It was the first time I had really seen the destruction of this war. Many of the streets were nothing more than piles of rubble and mere skeletons of apartment houses where maybe pictures were still on the walls even though three walls were blown away.
>
> We were marched with all our earthly possessions which included a full field pack and duffel bag, about 4 miles to a camp of pyramidal tents on the outskirts of Le Havre. We were given hot chow there and told that the tents were full so we would have to make the best of it on the ground. By this time it was pitch dark, the snow was about 8–9 inches deep and still falling, our feet were wet, it was thawing and I for one was miserably cold and angry at the world in general, and the Nazis in particular. . . .
>
> At 6:00 the following cold evening, Jan 10 we left our hospitable transient camp and marched through the streets of Le Havre to the very big, once beautiful, now cold, railroad station. We waited there until about 11:00 that evening when we boarded the luxurious "40 and 8s."

The term "40 and 8s" refers to boxcars which could carry either 40 men or 8 horses. It was a French narrow-gauge boxcar made of wood, without windows, heat, and maybe without seats or any amenities whatsoever. Unchanged from the time they carried troops in the First World War, this very uncomfortable and dehumanizing mode of transportation was probably better than walking in the snow. George rode in such a boxcar for 4 days. Half his meals were hot, half were C-rations. They passed through Reims and Sedan, France near the Belgian border—battlefields of previous wars. They got off the train in Thionville, France, south of Luxembourg. From there they marched, still cold and wet, to a barracks where they spent the night. The barracks was on an old French army camp that more recently had been used by the Germans as a concentration camp. It was crowded and cold, and the replacement troops were left to sleep on the floor. They were given C-rations. It was there that they were finally issued weapons. Their personal possessions, which they had carried in a duffel bag since New Jersey, were taken away at that point to be stored in a warehouse until after the war. But their duffels and personal things were never returned.

THE NATURE AND LIMITATIONS OF GEORGE'S JOURNALS

At this point—January 1945—the dates and events become cloudy. George wrote his combat experiences after the war was over, in May or June of 1945, before he left Germany. He does not always put dates with his locations or with events. Some of his combat experiences are on such a small tactical level that they are difficult to match up with the greater movement of the Third Army.

George started two journals during the war but only wrote briefly in each, totaling about 6,000 words. The first and shorter journal is in a small, bound ledger of about 300 pages, all blank except for six pages wherein he wrote about being drafted in Salt Lake City and training at Camp Wolters, Texas, and seven additional pages where he recorded the names and addresses of some 50 of the men he trained with.

The longer diary is titled *My Life in the E.T.O.* [European Theater of Operation]. It is written in a repurposed leatherbound volume with brass hinges and a broken clasp that he found in eastern Germany. It has a title embossed in gold on its cover: "*Männergesangverein zu Netzschkau 1886*" ("Men's Glee Club of Netzschkau 1886"). This indicates that he started writing about combat after he reached Netzschkau, near the German-Czechoslovak border, at the end of hostilities—about May or June 1945. He does not write about events that occurred after March 1945, even though he and his unit were in combat until the end of the war. He does not write about the dash across the German heartland to the eastern border, so there are 6 weeks that get no mention. Other things he leaves out include his three battlefield promotions from private to staff sergeant; he may have been promoted twice in the last few days of April. He was awarded the Bronze Star, but it gets no mention in his journal, nor is it listed in his discharge papers. (He was among those who earned the Combat Infantry Badge prior to September 2, 1945. All such men in the 87th Infantry Division also received the Bronze Star without written citation. His original ribbons are missing and it is supposed that his Bronze Star ribbon did not have a V, which would indicate a citation for a specific act of valor.) He does not mention his meritorious unit citation. There was a fire in 1973 in the National Personnel Records Center of the National Archive which destroyed military records of his era, so details of those citations may never be known. His journal mentions only briefly his lifelong friend Calvin Plitt of Baltimore, and does not mention his other close friend, Guy Conover of Gettysburg, Pennsylvania. There is no mention of heroics. He rarely mentions the dead or wounded even though his division's casualty rate was above 80 percent in the first 4 months of 1945. Sometimes his journal gives a sense that very little was happening. The reader will have to presume that he was often under fire and returning fire. Later in life he would minimize his combat experience, saying, "We were told which way to march and which way to fire, and when we arrived, the enemy would be gone or dead." There is no mention of his postwar assignment to Fort Meade. Besides his own handwriting, his journal also contains 25 pages of handwriting in German, mostly lists of names—likely members of the Men's Glee Club—and dates ranging from October 4, 1886, to October 1, 1936.

Decades later George also interpreted and reminisced in a third journal on various episodes in his life. In 1988 he wrote a few pages about the war.

Here is a best effort to locate George at key moments in 1945:

THE BATTLE OF THE BULGE

The day after he was issued his rifle, January 15, 1945, George was taken by truck into Luxembourg to a town that is not legible in his journal, but likely Biwer, north of Luxembourg City. At that point he was assigned to "Item" Company (I Company), 3rd Battalion, of the 346th Infantry Regiment, in the 87th Infantry "Golden Acorn" Division, part of General Patton's Third Army, which at that moment was engaged in the last 10 days of the Battle of the Bulge.

> . . . In sight of the Moselle River, a beautiful winter landscape setting of rolling hills, forests, the river, and heavy but gently falling snow. I shall always remember the beauty of that spot and other scenes in the winter of France, Belgium, Luxembourg, and Germany. Somehow the beauty of the groomed forests, classically situated villages, the clear air, quaint buildings all helped to mitigate the discomfort of the cold and the loneliness and anxiety of the war.

He was on the front line in the area between Wasserbillig, Wecker, and probably Biwer, all in Luxembourg, on the south edge of the "bulge," a part of the line that held fast against the German offensive. He remained there for about 10 days, possibly until January 25. Wasserbillig is on the Moselle River which forms the German border.

January and February of 1945 were among the coldest months in Europe of the 20th century. Even in March, temperatures were often well below freezing. George slept on the ground in a foxhole as soon as he joined I Company. Soldiers wore all the clothing they were issued, including a towel which they would wear as a scarf. About those first cold nights with I Company George wrote: "I have been cold before, but never like this."

> I dug in with my newly assigned squad leader, Sgt. [Brittenham]. We were each wearing only an overcoat, a raincoat, two pairs of pants, two [wool] shirts, two suits of [long] underwear, a knit wool sweater and a field jacket. We spent that night without blankets. It snowed almost all night. The cold wet weather really played hell with our weapons, causing them to rust, and

freezing the oil that is supposed to lubricate them. We didn't know whether they'd fire for us or not if we were to need them. [From his 1945 journal.]

The cold caused me to shiver sometimes violently for what seemed like hours. Sometimes we had to stand guard at a lonely post for hours on end at night, in rain, and wind. I know I often slept standing up, hallucinating about home, bed, warm weather, good food, faces of loved ones, and scenes of home passing vividly through my mind. On one such occasion I saw my father on a hot summer day, sweating, drinking cold water from a gallon jug while it spilled beautifully from the corners of his mouth. [From his 1978 journal.]

George very soon suffered from frozen feet. He took full responsibility in his journal for not taking proper care of himself. He didn't mention the ill-fitting boots or blame the extreme battlefield conditions. He did not mention that many men in his division were disabled with frozen feet. He seemed worried that he might be labeled a goldbrick.

There are certain things that a soldier must learn for himself. Most of these things he must learn by experience and the sooner he learns them the better. I was lax in taking care of my feet and I let them become exposed to the cold and it was more than they could take. As a result I was now suffering from either frozen feet or trench foot. At any rate I was suffering. I wasn't wise to army life overseas and I couldn't get the medicine to do much for me. At that time there were too many who were trying to get off the line by gold-bricking. This made it tough for the ones who really had something wrong with them. The medics gave me a jar of wool fat and told me to massage my feet as much as possible.

"There were too many who were trying to get off the line," is likely an understatement. During the Battle of the Bulge it was not uncommon to return the wounded to the front line, sometimes immediately and without treatment. The lanolin placebo was of no help. But in the bigger context of the battle, his feet were really a secondary issue.

CROSSING THE SIEGFRIED LINE, FEBRUARY 2 THROUGH MARCH 6

The Siegfried Line took its name from an older line constructed in World War I. The World War II line, also called the *West Wall*, was a network of defensive structures—tank traps, tunnels, pillboxes, and moats—just inside the western border of Germany. The line had a place in German propaganda and psyche, and many Germans regarded it as a line to defend to the death.

After the Battle of the Bulge, George rested for about 10 days in a house belonging to a civilian. Then they boarded trucks and were taken about 100 miles north to Bastogne to stage for the next engagement.

> Bastogne was in very bad shape. It had exchanged hands for the third time as a result of the Ardennes Breakthrough. We finally came to a halt in a small town about 10 miles northeast of Bastogne [possibly in the area of Houffalize, Belgium]. It was late at night when we got there and we spent the night in a barn. The next morning, because my feet had pained so much during the night, I went to the aid station and the medical officer there arranged it for me to be temporarily assigned to battalion headquarters company where I would not have to walk in the coming attack.

While attached to Headquarters Company, George and another soldier named Milewski were assigned to guard the battalion's ammunition, stored on the ground near a ruined house. They were left there alone for about a week in early February, living in another home nearby with the civilian owners. The ruined house was not habitable; nevertheless, at some point doughboys (George's word) had camped there and left an ember burning in wet hay. George was awakened at about 1 AM by the sound of popping, which he thought was small arms fire. He grabbed his rifle and ran out to discover the ruined house on fire, and discarded rifle rounds exploding in a fire. With the help of the civilians, they were able carry enough water in helmets and buckets to put out the fire.

I Company attacked the Siegfried Line at 3:00 AM possibly February 2. They advanced through St. Vith, Belgium; Auw bei Prüm, and Roth bei Prüm, Germany, over 3 days. That would be a 38-mile advance over 3 days if they started from Houffalize, Belgium. They were repulsed at the Siegfried Line and fell back to Roth, a hamlet just inside Germany, essentially on the line. So George avoided the march to Roth and also avoided the first assault on the line.

When he rejoined I Company at Auw, the falling snow was wet and heavy and quickly turned to slush and mud. The 87th was stalled at the line for about 3 weeks and exchanged artillery and small arms fire with the entrenched Germans. Over the weeks, small patrols would go out to look for breaks or blind spots in the line. George's platoon went a couple of miles forward of Auw, and forward of Roth and dug in. In later years, George would comment that the foxholes would have mud or ice in the bottom and sometimes also frozen blood. Americans might take foxholes that had been dug by Germans because the ground was frozen and difficult to dig. They dispersed along a line extending about 350 yards. There was a house on one end of the line and a draw or gully on the other.

> The hill was thickly wooded and the slope where we were was bare of everything except grass. The night was very dark and cold. It stopped raining about midnight and a cold sharp wind started blowing which blew all night. I had lost my raincoat and overcoat. My every stitch was wet. We dug our emplacements and stayed on our positions all night except for a one-hour period when each took our turn in the house to get as warm and dry as we could by the stove there. That night I fell asleep several times standing up. I didn't sit down because I would have fallen too deeply asleep. All night my teeth chattered and my knees shook until by morning my muscles ached and I was stiff all over. I had had diarrhea for two days and I still had it. I had been vomiting and was very nauseated. That, I think, was the most miserable night I spent in Europe. When morning came we found we were in sight of Ormont [Germany].

The Siegfried Line was possibly 2 miles wide in this area. Some maps show it as two lines with Ormont between them. The Germans and the Americans were so close that each could observe the other. Food and water had to be carried in to the men in the forward foxholes. Nightly "carrying parties" were organized for this purpose. They would walk a couple of miles back to Auw under cover of darkness for provisions. The

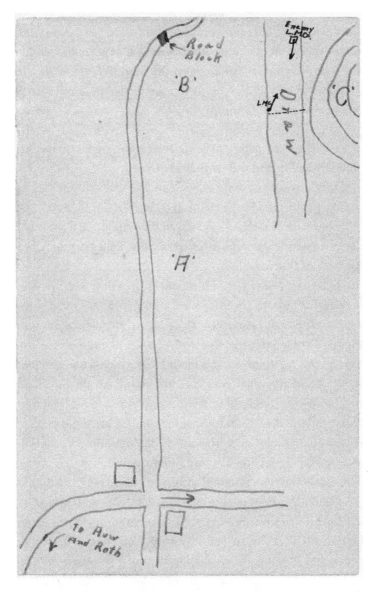

A drawing of the battlefield in George's diary. His unit was stalled in battle at the Siegfried Line during the month of February 1945, near Auw bei Prüm, and Roth bei Prüm, Germany. He notes an enemy light machinegun at the top right, confronted by his unit's light machinegun across the "draw"—possibly the streambed of the Rupbach. A dotted line shows where he crossed the draw. "C" possibly represents Ormont or Gold Hill. The "warming house" that was shelled may be one of the houses at the crossroads.

hill that George referred to was possibly Hill 649 or Gold B on American maps, and the key to breaking the Siegfried Line in that area. He also refers to a draw, which may have been the draw between Hills 648 and 649—Gold A and Gold B. Gold B was the higher and more strategic of the two, just outside of Ormont.

The house we had been using for a warming house had previously been hit and was partially destroyed.

The next day we were relieved by the 4th platoon and we moved to the thickly wooded hill where we dug in and made fairly permanent foxholes. We stayed there about 10 days. It was while we were here that I received my first mail from home on the 15th of February. . . .

From my [new] position on the hill I could see the farmhouse where we had been just a few days before. One day the Germans became suspicious of the house so they started shelling it. It was perfect the way they "bracketed" in with the two rounds and the third was a direct hit. The house was occupied by the 4th platoon and after the first round hit the house the skyline was alive with silhouettes of men running for their lives. Every time a shell would announce itself with the diabolical scream that always warns its victims, the men would promptly and obediently hit the dirt and offer a prayer that the missile would pass them by this time. A very horrible thing to behold.

Our foxholes were two-man foxholes with logs and cover overhead to protect us from shells bursting in the trees above. During the dark hours there had to be one man in each hole awake and listening. I was sharing the same foxhole with a fellow named Culhane from New York. We split the night into one-hour shifts. One would sleep while the other guarded for an hour listening for anything that might mean that Jerry was around, because it was much too dark to see for anything. Almost every morning we saw evidence of his presence but we stayed optimistic until one morning two men from a machine gun position were kidnapped not 150 yards from my hole. One fellow I knew. His name was Alvine. He came over on the boat with me and since the war ended I have heard that he was liberated from a prison camp.

From that night on we were more alert and we had barbed wire strung all around with tin cans to rattle, and trip flares that light up at the slightest disturbance of one of the small, fine, nearly-invisible wires attached. I spent my time in my foxhole with a grenade in my hand ready to pull the pin, roll it out of my hole, and duck should any Krauts decide to make an unwelcome call on Culhane and me. Fortunately they didn't. . . .

One afternoon when one of the officers was checking positions he discovered that mine and Plitt's were in such a position as to offer definitive advantages to two machine guns. So Plitt and I were told to dig elsewhere.

We had no sooner left than a barrage of artillery fire poured in. We immediately hit the ground and started hugging the low places to get the most protection we could. The shells came in so thick and fast that there was just a steady scream of the whistling shells with no let up. It seemed like it lasted for hours and at times it looked like they would never let up. There were only three sounds prevalent. First the horrible scream that seems to freeze your very blood as it grows louder and closer. That is followed by the crunching crash of the shell itself. Then the whine or zing or low buzz of the bits of shrapnel as they zip through the air only to stop when they've imbedded themselves in a tree or the flesh of some poor dogface.

Plitt and I were not in foxholes during that shelling. We were out lying on the flat ground. Every time a shell would whistle my whole body would writhe in anticipation of being hit. Neither Plitt nor I were hit although when the first shell came in as Plitt was dropping to the ground a piece of shell fragment cut an ammunition bandolier from his chest.

After the shelling was over I was detailed to gather up enough men to go on a carrying party. I went over to what I thought was a perfectly constructed shelter with plenty of overhead cover. I didn't know the man who occupied it who I thought at the time was asleep. When I tried to wake him I found him to be dead.

Somewhere, some way, a piece of shrapnel had found a way into the perfectly constructed shelter and found its mark.

Less than a mile away, there was a manned German road obstruction, and the road was mined. The mines had to be cleared before there could be another assault on the Siegfried. George drew a map in his journal possibly indicating that the obstruction and the mines were a half mile south of Ormont and north of the junction of modern Route 265, which runs between Schleiden and Prüm, and the L20, also known as Ormont Road.

One night our platoon was sent to cover an engineer squad while they swept a road clear of mines. We hadn't passed 200 yards from our own front lines when we were challenged with a guttural German voice not 25 yards away. Our platoon Sgt., Reiley [Riley], answered "hit the dirt" and emphasized it by punctuating what he said with a stream of .45 cal slugs from the Thompson sub that he carried as if it were just another limb and he used it with as much dexterity. He would stop firing long enough to ask them to surrender and then without time for them to do so he would give them another burst. Everyone was firing except me. . . . The two bandoliers I had picked up that afternoon were both of 5-round clips for the Springfield '03 rifle and were useless in the Garand M1 that I carried, which needed 8-round clips. At the same time that we were firing, the Krauts were firing over our heads with light machine guns. We all left one by one unhurt and we dispensed with mine sweeping that evening. We returned to our area.

The journal, written months after the fact, apparently does not to represent a strict chronology. At one point he interrupts his narrative to say:

In writing this story I find it very hard to remember exact dates in many instances. . . . Yet some dates are very vivid in my mind. Such as the day we crossed the Rhine or the day I joined the outfit or my birthday when we took that town. It's filling in between that makes it sound unbalanced sometimes.

And then he continues with his story:

> On Sunday on the 25th of February in the early morning we left Auw in an attack on the Siegfried. We went through the village of Roth and about 2 miles more to a forward assembly area where we waited until H hour. We were given two days K-rations.
>
> At H hour we left our forward assembly area and marched in a slow attack past the crossroads and about a mile more to about point B near Auw where we were stopped by the Germans because of a roadblock which they had very well covered with small arms and artillery. [This is a reference to the hand-drawn map in his journal, and not to Hill Gold B.]
>
> Item Company pulled up in a front reaching both to the left and right off of the road. There they [I Company] dug in and stayed, almost in sight of Jerry, for that day and the following night. At that time I was in Sgt. Smilowisz's [Smialowicz's] squad and we were attached . . . to a platoon of tanks to protect them from bazookas, etc.
>
> On the 2nd day six of us from my squad climbed a tank and rode down the road to just behind where our men were holding. The tank was to ride down the road to within sight of the roadblock, throw in a few rounds, see what it could see and then turn tail and run. We were to spread out on either side and protect it.
>
> We waited where we were for about 3 hours. While we waited, our men who were dug in took a horrible beating from the German artillery. The ambulances and jeeps shuttled unceasingly up and down the road from where the men were dug in to the crossroads where there was an aid station.
>
> At the appointed time the tank started its big aircraft engines and started to roll noisily down the road, slow enough that we could easily keep up with it. [Some American tanks used a Ford V8 aluminum engine which was developed but never used for aircraft.] As soon as the big medium tank came within sight of the roadblock, it started spitting machine gun bullets and throwing high-explosive 75 mm rounds at it [the road block]. At the same time they were shooting at us with small arms fire. God must have been with all six of us because we all came out of

it without a nick. After the tank threw about six rounds at it we turned and the tank backed out, our mission completed.

We stayed there until the following day about noon when we moved off the road to the right about a 90° angle with the road. We went about ½ mile when we came to a draw about 200 yards wide without any trees in it. Far to our left was a German light machine gun covering the draw and trying to keep anyone from crossing. [This is labeled "Enemy L.M.G." on his map. The dotted line seems to indicate where he crossed the draw.] As soon as it was discovered we set up a machine gun to keep them busy while we crossed which we did without much bother.

Over on the other side we went right up the side of a thickly wooded hill following a steep road or firebreak. We went right to the top and there we stopped and dug in. We were there until the 3rd of March during which time we lived on nothing but K-rations, and all the water we had was what we could carry in with our daily carrying parties that would have to come and go under cover of darkness. They would have to go back to the road where we left from nearly 2½ miles away.

As he said in his letter, George was in the Siegfried on February 27, Bobby Dean's birthday. But I Company remained under pressure from the retreating Germans even after breaching the line.

On the 3rd of March Sgt. Smilowisz [Smialowicz], Plitt, Broisman, Russell and I were sent back to the aid station because of our feet which were bothering us as a result of the early spring cold, wet weather. We received a little medical attention and then took a two-day rest, very much welcome. This we did in the town of Auw.

On the 5th of March we rejoined the company in the small town of Kerschenbach [5km east of Ormont] just on the inner [eastern] edge of the Siegfried Line.

Our lieutenant, "Stumpy" Watson had been hit and he was replaced with Lt Ian D. Brigham whom I met that evening. While we were back resting the company had attacked through the Siegfried.

From Kerschenbach on my birthday, March 6, we jumped off in the attack mostly to make contact with the enemy. We thought we were through the Siegfried, and we were. But we weren't sure. It was the first time Lt Brigham had been in combat and I for one was nervous about it.

All in all, their siege lasted about a month, and only in the last week were they able to advance, but only about 2 or 3 miles. I Company was not certain they had actually broken through the Siegfried, and continued to press forward against enemy resistance again on March 6.

We walked about 5 miles when we came to a small town on the outskirts of Junkerath. We approached the town in wide dispersion. We were fired on one or two times by what seemed to be a sniper. We found that the only way we could get into the village was to cross a stream. There was a bridge and it was intact but we were afraid it might be mined. We were just ready to wade when it looked like every civilian in town coming down to the bridge and crossing it, waving white flags. This made it look safe so we crossed the bridge dry and unhurt. Immediately we out posted the town and cleared the homes, hunting for soldiers.

That afternoon we left the small village and started to try to get into Junkerath but we were driven back because of intense mortar fire. We returned to the small village and stayed there until late that night. Lt. Brigham told us that we were to move quietly and quickly out of the village and down the road about a mile to the edge of Junkerath where we would clear and occupy two or three houses.

We moved out. The night was so dark that several times I thought I had lost contact with the man I was supposed to follow. We moved into the houses and the next morning before it got very light we were out clearing the town and not finding one soldier. They had all left. Conditions looked so good that we moved into the next town Glads, [location unknown, possibly a neighborhood on Glaadter Straße, near Junkerath] and cleared it without trouble.

CROSSING THE MOSELLE AND THE RHINE (MARCH)

After I Company crossed the Siegfried, they rested for 2 weeks at Glads. Then they went 60 miles by truck to Rubenach, near the confluence of the Moselle and the Rhine. They stayed there one night.

Their platoon then entered the town of Güls, on the bank of the Moselle. They were the first GIs to enter Güls, and they had no problem with the citizens. But there was sniper fire. Occasionally in the war, there was German-on-German fire, particularly if it looked like someone was going to surrender or collaborate. It seems this was going on in Güls. Snipers from across the river killed some civilians who were trying to come out of a shelter.

> We stayed in this town for about four days during which time we had to patrol the streets 24 hours a day. Part of the town was under observation and sniper fire from across the Moselle. When we marched into the town several of the people went down into a cellar on the banks of the river and every time they tried to leave they were fired at by the Germans from across the river. There were three killed; two were a brother and sister. After it quieted down I was sent as a guard over the civilians while they buried them. The mother of the two was there and the husband of the daughter. It was very touching. At times the mother would come to me and cry on my shoulder, muttering to me in German. Just a tiny incident in the game of war. Yes, war is hell.

They stayed 4 days in Güls, then moved a mile back from the river and camped there another 3 days and rested.

In later years George reminisced about crossing the Moselle into Koblenz with little resistance. The city had been bombed and shelled in the few days previous, and was in ruins by that time.

In stealth and in the darkness of night they left Koblenz. Their orders were to move 10 miles south to arrive in Boppard before sunup on March 26. They crossed the Rhine in the early hours of March 26. By that evening, they were on their way to take Dachsenhausen, spelled "Dauschausen" in his journal.

George, foreground, washes his face on a littered sidetrack, c. spring 1945. The wooden boxcars, "40 and 8s," were used for troop transport.

THE DASH ACROSS GERMANY (APRIL AND MAY)

George's writing stops with crossing the Rhine at Boppard, yet the war went on, and the Acorn Division continued to fight.

A broad-brush history can be pieced together from many sources easily available to the public. Among George's papers is a short chronology in *An Historical and Pictorial Record of the 87th Infantry Division in World War II 1942–1945, Golden Acorn* (Baton Rouge, LA: 346th Infantry 87th Division, Army and Navy Publishing Company, 1946). They took Saalfeld on April 13. They took Plauen on April 16, the day President Roosevelt was laid to rest.

The Acorn Division liberated some concentration camps, possibly to include Buchenwald, but this history is cloudy. George's mother responds to one of George's letters, saying, "We were so glad to get your letter of April 23rd. That was some experience you had helping liberate those Russian prisoners." Russians were held at Buchenwald. Buchenwald also had several "sub-camps," one of which was at Ohrdruf. That camp gets brief mention on page 43 of *An Historical and Pictorial Record of the 87th Infantry Division.* It says:

> All in all the duties of a combat infantryman were multiplied many times over when he became the liberator of the slaves of war. The concentration camp at Ordruff, which the men of the 87th Division captured was living testimony to the Nazi mentality.

Additionally, there are two photographs in that book with captions suggesting that units of the 87th liberated concentration camps. One caption reads: "Burgermeister of Saalburg, Germany, speaks to his citizens at a reburial ceremony for 56 victims of the SS troopers' March of Death from Buchenwald concentration camp." Another picture is captioned: "The taste of freedom: Russian slave labor liberated from Nazi yoke by 87th men at Plauen, cook a meal."

George was promoted to staff sergeant on April 25 and assigned as a squad leader; no doubt attrition was a factor in his promotions. Squads could number from 8 to 24 men, and could include two sections of 4 to 12 men.

The 87th Infantry Division's last battle was on May 6 near Falkenstein in Saxony, very near the German-Czechoslovak border, where they were

George and his two close friends, Calvin Plitt of Baltimore, and Guy Conover of Gettysburg.

ordered to stop their eastward march. The war in Europe ended officially on May 8, 1945. The 87th met up with the Soviet Army there near the border on May 12. At some later point, the 87th withdrew, ceding to the Soviets all the eastern heartland of Germany and some of the German prisoners of war who had surrendered to American forces in that area.

The Battle of the Bulge had lasted a month and a half in December and January; the battle to advance 3 miles through the Siegfried Line between Roth and Ormont had taken the month of February; the effort to take the whole of the heartland from the Rhine to the Czechoslovak border—advancing some 400 miles—took less than 6 weeks. Day by day, the fight became easier, weather improved, and enemy resistance diminished. In the end, units could advance great distances in trucks and could pass each other, and there was time to rest.

Only two of his letters from Europe survive, both addressed to his 16-year-old sister Barbara Dean, both dated after VE day. To read them is to wish more had been saved. Alas, the details, the ephemeral personal experiences, are lost. Only memories of memories remain.

He remembered the prisoners. They surrendered in the thousands, so fast that it was a problem to move them west. They often identified themselves, "Ich bin Schweizer" (I am Swiss), no doubt hoping to trade a transparent deceit for a bit of mercy. And indeed, George commented years later that there were men in his squad who would be happy to escort prisoners to some remote place behind the lines and shoot them; some men in his squad could not be trusted to guard prisoners.

He ended up in Netzschkau in Saxony. Now instead of sleeping in freezing, dispersed foxholes, they pitched their tents in the sun, in straight rows, and laid out streets between them. They held church meetings. They waited to be reassigned to the Pacific or sent home and discharged. It was a time to catch up on letters or journals, to trade war souvenirs, to take pictures. He acquired a camera and some film and started to send snapshots home. His scrapbook has pictures of his comrades posing with German uniform hats and otherwise mugging for the camera in a meadow.

PARIS

George visited Paris. Again, there is no documentation of this other than the souvenir postcards, which he pasted in his scrapbook without explanation; and a brief mention of the trip in a letter from an army buddy, Ray Broisman, who wrote to George's daughter, Leslie, after George's death. "We went to Paris together where we had 8 hours of freedom. Although [5 years] older than your father, I was no man of the world. But George's pristine naïveté was enchanting".

It is presumed that he took leave in Paris after the war in May, June, or July, possibly on his way home. Years later George said, "How could you see that great civilization of Paris and not be impressed?"

The whole division was sent back to the United States in July 1945. George arrived in Boston with the 346th Infantry Regiment on July 19, 1945, aboard the US Army Transport *Frederick Lykes*. The Golden Acorn Division was deactivated in September.

Fort Meade

George was soon assigned to Fort Meade. He worked there until the next spring. His Eisenhower jacket survives and bears the shoulder insignia of the Third Service Command. This is evidence that he was assigned to the Third Service Command after the war. Additionally, his mother addresses letters to Company G, 4 Bn, Separation Center. His duties are not known in detail, but he said he was involved with facilitating the discharge of the many soldiers returning home.

George spent some of his days off touring in Baltimore and in Washington, DC. There was a train stop on base, and he took the train to attend church in Washington. He dated a girl named Josephine from Baltimore. She was an employee at Fort Meade. He had a clear memory of Baltimore landmarks such as Fort McHenry, the Shot Tower, and the Washington Monument. He collected many picture postcards from Washington, DC. That's all that is known.

He was discharged on May 1, 1946, after 1 year, 4 months, and 3 days' military service, to return to Salt Lake City. Over the years, he kept in touch at least through Christmas cards with Calvin Plitt, Guy Conover, and possibly Josephine.

Statistics and Notes

The 87th Infantry Division had an assigned strength of about 15,000 men. In January, February, and March of 1945, the division suffered more than 1,000 killed, 4,000 wounded, 300 missing or captured, and 6,000 non-battle casualties, including illness, for a total of more than 11,000 casualties out of 15,000. This is according to the 87th Infantry Division Legacy Association and a study done by Mitchell Kaidy, "87th Infantry Division Lost 1,310 Killed, 4,000 Wounded in Three Months of World War II" (http://www.87thinfantrydivision.com/Commentary/000031.html).

The Division arrived on the front line on December 6, 1944, and by December 16 it was engaged in the Ardennes Offensive, "The Battle of the Bulge."

George arrived on the front line with replacement troops to restore the 87th, on January 15, 1945. He spent 113 days in combat, and spent 6 months 19 days overseas.

The men mentioned above are identified as:

Pfc. Edward F. **Alvine** of Cliffside, NJ, taken prisoner

Pfc. Richard **Barnes** of Houston, TX, wounded in action

Pfc. Palmer **Behler** of Phillipsburg, NJ, killed in action

S/Sgt. George **Brittenham** of Georgetown MN

Lt. Ian D. **Brigham,** possibly 2d Lt. Ivan **Brigham** of Cleveland, OH, Silver Star

Pfc. Raymond **Broisman** of Portland, ME

Pfc. Guy **Conover** of Gettysburg, PA, Bronze Star for Valor

Pvt. Edward **Culhane** of Waterbury CT, killed in action

T/Sgt. Delbert **Lutterman** of Alpha, MN, Silver Star

Pfc. John **Manikowski** of Milwaukee, WI

Pfc. Francis **Milewski** of Branford, CT

S/Sgt. Leonard **Munson** of St Paul, MN

T/Sgt. Geodo **Perrotta** of Brockton, MA

S/Sgt. Calvin **Plitt**, of Baltimore, MD, Bronze Star for Valor

T/Sgt. William **Riley** of Dorchester, MA, Bronze Star for Valor

Pfc. Philip **Russell** of Syracuse, NY

S/Sgt. Walter **Smialowicz** of Newark, NJ

Pfc. Chester **Wawrzyniak**, of South Bend, IN

T/Sgt. Wardlaw Mason "Stumpy" **Watson** of Birmingham, AL, wounded in action, Silver Star

X

Forgetting War
(Dean's Perspective)

My father, George Brooks offered to drive back to Maryland with me when I started a new job at Ft. Meade. It was January 1981 and very cold. I think we both looked forward to a road trip to spend some time together. My wife, Lorraine, was pregnant, suffering with morning sickness, and would not be comfortable or helpful driving across the country. I cannot remember the exact dates, but work started on January 21, 1981, and we arrived early enough that with Dad's assistance, I was able to rent an apartment and do some other transactions well in advance of work. The cross-country trip was a 4-day drive.

He was not one to just spin the wheels—he always wanted to see and understand things along the way. We stopped at the Herbert Hoover National Historic Site in West Branch, Iowa. I didn't know much about President Hoover, and I was inclined to dismiss him as the guy who caused the Great Depression because of ignorance of economics and insensitivity to the poor. But Dad pointed out his personal recollection— that Hoover instituted standards such as the quart for milk, standard sizes for mattresses and sheets, standards for plumbing, and all sorts of engineering and building requirements.

I grew up in a house that was built in the 1930s, about the time standards were coming into use. My father was a do-it-yourselfer, so I remember him fixing plumbing and wiring in the house. He replaced water heaters, plumbed for a new automatic washer, and built new bedrooms in the basement. Plumbing was a particular problem. Steel pipes were all different dimensions and gauges and all had to be cut and threaded on site. Threads could be different pitches, and sometimes left-handed. There was a seemingly infinite variety of valves and washers. This was the chaotic world that my father grew up in. He understood it and was not intimidated by a project, but he was happy to see new standardized building materials being introduced.

He also knew of the relief effort that Hoover administered for starving Europeans during World War I. Hoover's program lasted from 1914 until 1923—ending just 3 years before Dad was born. One thing on display at the Hoover museum that Dad pointed out was a collection of flour sacks which had been sent to Europe as part of the relief effort. The European beneficiaries had embroidered the empty sacks and returned them to the US as a thank-you. We also paused at the very humble Quaker church on the property and Dad pointed out that the men and women in the congregation were segregated. That is what a conversation and a rest stop was like with him.

We stopped at the Carl Sandburg birthplace at Galesburg near Peoria, Illinois. We listened to a recording of Sandburg reading his poetry. Carl Sandburg was famous for his six-volume biography of Abraham Lincoln. He was also Poet Laureate under President Lyndon Johnson. He wrote the famous poem "Chicago," which reads in part:

Hog Butcher for the World,
    Tool Maker, Stacker of Wheat,
Player with Railroads and the Nation's Freight Handler;
    Stormy, husky, brawling,
City of the Big Shoulders . . .

Dad recited that much to me from memory.

It was very cold that winter. We went through Wheeling, West Virginia, and Dad mentioned Walter Reuther, the labor organizer. We passed over the Ohio, the Monongahela, and the Youghiogheny Rivers. They had pushed huge blocks of ice up onto their banks.

We took a detour to visit Littlestown, Pennsylvania, near Gettysburg. There we visited his Army buddy Guy Conover. Dad had spoken of him occasionally over the years, referring to him simply as Conover. Conover was very warm and happy to invite us in for a chat. He had a war souvenir, a Mauser, the German infantry rifle, which he had refurbished to use as a deer rifle. Mausers had a heavy stock that extended almost to the end of the barrel; Conover had cut his down to a lithe minimum—it looked nothing like the original. They exchanged war stories. Conover had won the Bronze Star when he was taking his turn walking out front of his squad "on point." He drew fire while in the open, but suppressed it by himself with a carbine. Obviously, there must be more to the story. He would have been about 19. Dad was not much for war stories. He had won the Bronze Star, but I never heard him tell how or why. He was among that large group of soldiers who earned the Combat Infantry Badge before September 2, 1945, all of whom were awarded the Bronze Star without written citations. Conover was of a different temperament— happy to talk about the war. Conover did most of the talking during our visit. As we left, Dad turned to Mrs. Conover and said, "You should know that Guy was a good boy during the war." That was Dad's combat commendation for Conover.

Dad told me aside that he liked to sleep with Conover because he was warm; sleeping on the ground in Germany in the winter of 1945 was so cold. Soldiers were each issued a "shelter half" and they would pair up to put their halves together to sleep. Dad had suffered frostbite on his feet during the war and his feet continued to give him pain all his life, particularly in the cold.

Dad became a little nostalgic when we finally arrived at Ft. Meade. He had been stationed there after the war and helped with the effort to discharge the large numbers of soldiers returning home. He remembered the names of many of the roads going through base, such as Mapes, Ernie Pyle, and Llewellyn. Other than that, there were few landmarks that he could remember. In fact, he was a little disoriented. Acres and acres of frame barracks had been torn down, leaving acres and acres of grass. There had been a train stop on base which he had used to travel into Washington or Baltimore—that was gone. Dad told me he had had a girlfriend in Baltimore named Josephine. I believe she was a Polish Catholic, which would be nothing remarkable in Baltimore. I actually spoke to Josephine on the phone. She remembered Dad and recalled, "he was the picture of health with rosy cheeks."

Dad made a curious remark as we were looking at the very large NSA campus with its grid of roads, fences, and floodlights. "This is very impressive; I wonder how long it will all last." I never had the imagination nor inclination to wonder about the impermanence of things.

As Dad got older—or maybe as we got older—he became freer with retrospection, evoked by common daily experiences. While looking at a contrail of a jet airliner he said it reminded him of the closing days of the war, seeing the sky filled with contrails of Allied planes flying east. When asked if this had bothered him he said, "No; it was comforting knowing these planes were flying east, and this irresistible destruction was falling on distant German targets and not the other way around." On another occasion before running the "Beat the New Year" footrace in Sugar House Park on New Year's Eve, he was at the starting line, shivering in his running clothes before midnight on December 31. He commented, "This is how our prisoners felt, stomping their feet, huddling together, trying to keep warm."

He recorded a more blunt assessment in his diary in 1979, some 35 years after the fact:

> It seems almost cowardly now to complain about my discomfort during the war. I am forced rather to remember the collective agony of humanity through it all and also the individual tragedies I witnessed first hand . . . After all, I did come home.
>
> . . . Sometimes we imposed ourselves upon the citizenry and lived in their houses or barns. Sometimes they left to stay with other citizens as we commandeered their homes. We were not good guests. I believe our assuming their homes may even have been a violation of the laws of war. Their homes were looted by us interlopers and in some cases GIs took severe unfair advantage of the women. Also their meager food was looted and their homes damaged, bedding, etc. stolen. Of course there is a great difference among soldiers. Expectedly, some were coarse, mean and cruel; others were genteel, careful, even courteous to the conquered German citizenry. But regrettably the kind ones, either through lack of boldness, or fatigue, timidity, or other reasons were ineffectual in really preventing or avoiding leaving many scars of war. It seems to me that by far the worst part of

war, the really hellish part is the dehumanizing of virtually every-one who experiences it. Even the victors are victims.

I never knew directly of a case of rape. I suspected it in some cases but often it seemed that the women and others acquiesced or submitted to the soldiers more out of intimidation or desper-ation than by force. Except, of course, to purchase favors with a can of GI beans or milk chocolate or canned milk from a des-perately hungry or frightened girl who has hungry parents and children at home seems to me to be a special kind of rape. This kind of thing occurred often, some of the men later bragging about what they got for such a low price. These "men" like all of us were hardly adults. I was 18 years old, turned 19 at this time. This is an impressionable just-out-of-high-school age. I came into this mess from a conservative social life of well-behaved teenagers. I had firm and loving warning from anxious parents, and I know I had the faith and confidence of siblings and friends. I was really an innocent abroad. I came home gratefully and quietly rejoicing and blessing God for the rearing, teaching, and love which sus-tained me, if not heroically, at least humbly through the war. I know I could have behaved better, been more bold, even valiant. If I could do it again I would be better but when I came home I could embrace my parents, look into their eyes and not blush.

ARMY SURPLUS

There were other trappings of the war. We had a stack of olive-drab towels that we used in our bathroom as I was growing up. We also had wool army blankets on our beds. Dad used old ammunition cans as tool-boxes. His combat boots laced above the ankle, and above that there was a cuff that closed with buckles. He cut the cuff and buckles off the top of his boots and wore the bottom, lace-up part for years when working in the yard, or, for example, when we built our ward meetinghouse in 1964. He dyed some old army shirts and wore them to class at the university. He had a fatigue hat that was like the soft, eight-sided Marine cap. He wore that hat when picnicking or doing chores around the house, and he kept it, I believe, until his death. It was quite ragged in the end, and on an occasion or two he had to retrieve it when Mother tried to throw it away. Once when we were hiking in the Uintas she threw it off a cliff, but Dad got a long stick and patiently fished it back. In the winter he wore a mackinaw that may have been part of his uniform. It's hard to tell what he brought home and what he bought at the surplus stores. It seems that there was no shortage of military surplus in the 1950s; it was everywhere.

Mom and Dad were frugal, but they were also poor. That's why we were using olive drab towels. Dad did not seem to mind wearing pieces of his old uniform. At least he never mentioned it.

In the late 1960s, there was a broad peace movement in response to the Vietnam War. The patriotism of World War II seemed to dissolve away. Hippies and peace demonstrators appropriated old uniforms as an ironic, counterculture fashion statement. I wore Dad's mackinaw to high school. Dad took a ho-hum attitude to this Che Guevara chic.

WAR SOUVENIRS

Though Dad had put a bit of distance between himself and the war, he did have some war souvenirs. Others were lost in a fire in the spring of 1946 that also destroyed his parent's garage where the souvenirs were stored.

Things that survived included a Mauser; a Luger loaded with its original bullets; a beautiful Nazi dress bayonet, as long as a small sword, nickel-plated, with a stag-antler hilt; binoculars; a German helmet; a U.S. helmet and helmet liner (which may have been his own); a Nazi armband; and several articles of clothing from his own uniforms. The German helmet was burned in the fire, leaving it rusty and the webbing gone. Dad used it on his workbench to hold loose nails and screws. He said he wanted to make a lampshade out of it for his desk. But that never happened.

There came a point when we children moved out of the house, and Mom and Dad were contemplating selling their house. Dad had a yard sale and sold most of his war souvenirs. I was incredulous and asked him why he had sold them without offering them to me. He said, "They were mine, and I didn't want them any longer."

This is the incongruous thing. Dad never seemed to dwell on the war like some men do. He never joined clubs. He never took us hunting, and even said that he didn't like guns; that he had shot them enough. Nevertheless, he kept the Mauser and the Luger, even after the yard sale. And years earlier, when we were little, about 1958 or so, he bought another gun—a single-shot .22 rifle for target practice. He used to take us to the range and teach us how to shoot. We never shot the Mauser; it was too heavy for children. I don't believe we ever shot the Luger in his presence. Despite his antipathy or disinterest toward guns, the Luger was always loaded with those ancient bullets and stored within easy reach in our storeroom. It makes me shiver to think about it now. Often I would go into the storeroom as a child because that pistol fascinated me. I would take it down, load it, unload it, take it apart to some degree, play with the safety and the trigger mechanism. And Rem would play with it with his little Teutonic friend Ralf Czerny; he would actually put the pistol up to Ralf's head. When I was older I asked Dad why he kept it loaded and he said, "What good is an unloaded gun?" Such a response would be more typical coming from a survivalist, but Dad was usually more nuanced in his reasoning. The Luger was not much good, loaded or unloaded. In my experience, it was very unreliable. It would jam easily, and required a very specific load of powder to fire correctly.

I took his Ike jacket at one point and took all the ribbons and insignia off it. I was too insensitive to notice if it bothered him. It must have. After his death, in the 1990s, I tried to restore the jacket. By then it was already difficult to find authentic replacement insignia and reliable descriptions of how to place them.

I also inherited the Mauser and the Luger. I believed at that time they might have historic value. But my relatives told me they were nothing more than incentives for burglars. They were not so attractive that they could be displayed above the mantle. Anyway, Lorraine told me she did not want any Nazi relics displayed in the house. I offered them to Rem, and then to Nyman; neither wanted them. I told Nyman that if no one wanted them I would sell them, and asked him to reconsider disposing of things that Dad had slogged through the mud of Europe with and kept so long. Nyman said: "Look at it this way—maybe Dad was foolish. Sell them and put the money in your kids' college fund." Now little remains—only a Nazi armband that Leslie uses as a bookmark, and his Ike jacket restored with some authentic pieces and some modern replicas.

WHAT IT MEANS

As a child I was proud of my father because of his participation in that great adventure of World War II, even though I had no concept of what it was all about. I thought his Bronze Star singled him out as something special, not realizing that every combat infantryman in his division had also received one. In fairness, our whole society has been simplistic in our comprehension of war. In a silly, crass way we have all vicariously sought some self-justification in war while staying willfully ignorant of the extraordinary complexities, tragedy, and failure of war. Military service has become a kind of currency, and the word *hero* is used thoughtlessly and too often.

Dad had limited use for the word *hero*; come to think of it, he may have used the word only to describe Beowulf or Odysseus. He saw himself as one guy in a multi-million-man army, mostly conscripts, some of whom were lucky, others brave. He employed little quips to dismiss his own heroism. "I only killed one German; he ran himself to death trying to catch me," and, "I won a medal for being the fastest foxhole digger." In his journals and letters he wrote without pretense about longing for mail from home, about taking cover, about gratitude for the occasional "PX ration" of candy or soap, about showing up for a firefight with the wrong ammunition and lying helplessly on the ground, about carrying water in his helmet in a desperate attempt to put out a fire to save the regiment's ammunition supply, about cold sleepless nights, chattering teeth, vomiting, diarrhea, and frozen feet.

It is not a story of heroism, nor even of adventure; it is a story of grace. That is my take. Dad went to war and came home from war with his humanity intact, and for the most part, without physical injuries. And then, very deliberately, he lived the rest of his life. He said one thing on occasion which we children like to remember. When he was confronted with some misfortune or difficulty he might say: "At least I'm not being shot at and it's not snowing."

XI

George
Mission to French Canada
1946–1948

George returned home from military service in the first part of May 1946. By the first week of July he had had arrived in Toronto to begin his missionary service. So he had less than 2 months of civilian life before setting out on his next adventure.

The LDS church's missionary service was receiving so many applications from discharged servicemen that it was difficult to absorb them all. George was working at Jewel Tea, a door-to-door retailer, trying to save money for a mission when he heard a rumor that the next batch of missionaries would enter the Mission Home in June, and they would be the last to be called that summer. It was a Friday morning when he realized that his paperwork had to be signed and delivered that very day or he would have to wait indefinitely. He had to scramble to get his application in.

He took a bus into town to find his stake president and to get his signature. It was not so easy to make phone calls or appointments in those days. He finally located his stake president at a construction site on the west side of town. That same Friday he turned in the application at the church offices to enter the Mission Home on Monday, 3 days later.

The Mission Home was an old repurposed hotel where newly called missionaries would be instructed on a range of topics such as scripture, church history, how to conduct music, proselytizing techniques, how to dress, how to stay healthy, and missionary demeanor. Indoctrination lasted about 10 days. The Mission Home had meeting rooms, a dining room, dorm rooms, and classrooms. George's group was the largest ever hosted there and it was so crowded that missionaries who lived in Salt Lake City were asked to stay at home and just show up for the classes. George was one of those. He started his indoctrination on Monday, June 24, 1946; in a departure from usual practice, his official "call" was dated a day later.

This was a different experience than the military. There was still hierarchy and camaraderie, but it was more genteel. Neal Maxwell, also a veteran and a missionary to Canada, commented in 1990 that George did not go on a mission to baptize; he went to get over the war. If that is true and not just a rhetorical flourish, his recovery began at the Mission Home. There he was able to meet and speak personally with General Authorities of the church including Levi Edgar Young, Marion G. Romney, Joseph F. Merrill, Thomas E. McKay, Stephen L. Richards, and Don B. Colton. The lectures were edifying. He enjoyed the prayers, testimonies, and particularly the hymns. He describes singing with the missionaries as thrilling. Finally, there was the warm embrace of the new cadre of missionaries, some of whom were friends from Sugar House, friends of friends, or shirttail relatives. Nearly half of them were former soldiers.

His mission farewell—a semiofficial church meeting—was held Tuesday evening, 2 July, and was followed by a reception at the Brooks home. On Wednesday evening he boarded a train; two Pullman cars carried only missionaries. Some got off at Omaha, the others went their separate ways at Chicago. The next morning George and a few others arrived in Toronto. It had been a hectic 13 days with countless essential tasks: acquiring clothing and luggage, getting photos taken, printing programs for the farewell, planning and cooking for the reception. In fact he was not entirely prepared; his parents continued to send him odds and ends such as scriptures and clothing over the next several weeks. One thing he asked for early on was his Honorable Discharge lapel button.

KINGSTON, ONTARIO

Elder Marvin Butler came to Toronto "off the line" (to use a military expression) to meet George and take him to his first assignment. They were assigned to Kingston, a town of 30,000 people and a dozen members, four of whom were active. Missionaries had been pulled out of Kingston during the war years. The two missionaries spent a few days reacquainting themselves with the members and with a list of names left years ago by the previous missionaries. Then they started knocking on doors. Elder Butler knocked on the first few doors then at one point he said, "You take this one." The door opened and then was slammed as soon as George started talking. Elder Butler took the next few doors to give George time to regain his composure. George may have thought he was having a bad day, but as it turns out, that event sums up his proselytizing success; there were very few conversions or baptisms in French Canada over the next 2 years, and none were attributable to George's efforts.

It was not all knocking on doors. There were members to warm up and meetings to organize. A big mission-wide conference for the Mutual Improvement Association, the church youth auxiliary, was held in Toronto in August. All the missionaries were told to support this conference, participating in one-act plays, ball games, picnics, and other activities.

A day or two after this MIA conference, the assembled missionaries took a field trip together on chartered buses to Palmyra, New York, to visit the nearby Mormon pilgrimage sites. There were 55 missionaries including the mission president. This was a very moving experience for George. He effusively recalled the history of the fledgling church in New York. The missionaries climbed to the top of the Hill Cumorah and sang "An Angel from on High" and "We Thank Thee, O God, for a Prophet." They visited the Sacred Grove, where George was called upon to offer a prayer. He visited a street corner in the village that has become famous among Mormons. On this intersection there are four churches—one on each corner. There George recalled Joseph Smith's words and the "division amongst the people, some crying, 'Lo, here!' and others, 'Lo, there!' Some were contending for the Methodist faith, some for the Presbyterian, and some for the Baptist." So there were testimonies, there was fellowship, and a break from the work. On the way back to Toronto they visited Niagara Falls. It was night and the falls were illuminated with colored lights. It was beautiful, "but not to compare with what we had seen that morning in and around the small, insignificant town of Palmyra."

Occasionally in his letters he wrote about the beauty of Canada. Offhandedly he mentioned seeing the northern lights in October 1946.

> Tonight is a very beautiful night here in Kingston. It isn't cold at all and the night is clear and the weather dry. The northern lights are showing now and I do wish you could see them with me. I saw them once in Utah when I was up at Scout Lake and they were red but now they are a beautiful green-blue. I guess as the winter nears they will get to be more and more brilliant.

Street Meetings

The "street meeting" was a staple missionary method to generate interest in the church. The mission president and visiting General Authorities always promoted the technique. Basically, missionaries would stand on a street corner or in a park and hold a church meeting. These meetings were modeled on an agenda similar to a worship service. They would begin with a prayer, and a hymn, then the missionaries would take turns giving speeches or sermons, and finally they would close with another hymn and prayer. Missionaries who were not speaking would sometimes mingle with the crowd and offer literature. The meetings seemed to be effective for finding people to teach. Sometimes they would draw large crowds and would distribute hundreds of pamphlets. Not many people would stay for the entire service, but occasionally someone would linger, and would ask for more information, and a few baptisms resulted.

But street meetings were at least an order of magnitude more difficult, more frightening, more humiliating than having a door slammed in your face. On one occasion a young man approached George during a street meeting and asked for literature. He took a pamphlet and very demonstratively tore it in small pieces and scattered it on the ground. George, always even-tempered in his writing, said it was "distasteful, but his loss." On another occasion a rival evangelical meeting started up across the street and attempted to shout down the Mormon meeting. And of course there were hecklers or people who wanted to contest points of doctrine.

Street meeting, May 1947, Dominion Square, Montreal. George held as many as five street meetings a week; each was as frightening as the first. The woman in the middle is possibly Winifred Wilkinson.

Every now and then the missionaries would be arrested and their literature would be confiscated. They tried their best to coordinate with the police or civilian authority, and they usually had written permission in hand during the meetings. The police always had some opinion on where the meeting should take place so as not to obstruct foot or car traffic; or when the meeting should be held—even specifying days of the week. The missionaries were wary of and deferential to the police, fully aware that the police would not allow the Jehovah's Witnesses the same freedoms they allowed Mormons, and the police had completely shut down public proselytizing in Quebec City.

There was an aspect to religion in Canada that slowly dawned on George. Religion was not so much a matter of conscience as a statement of politics or ethnicity. Missionaries serving in Montreal had one "friend" in the Montreal police force—a Mr. Charles Barnes who was a director of police. Barnes was a high-ranking, very busy civil servant with a spacious office. And he was a Protestant in a police force of mostly Catholic officers. George wrote home that Barnes was a "close friend" of the mission president, Octave Ursenbach, a native of Alberta. The missionaries called on Barnes frequently, and Barnes graciously offered them written permission and even police protection and crowd control. Nevertheless, the missionaries were occasionally harassed by police, and their written permission was sometimes ignored, if only for a few hours. Barnes, serving *ad interim,* resigned in August of 1947, and George wrote home that this put missionary work at some risk.

If street meetings could be frightening, they could also be euphoric. In a typically earnest letter to his father, George wrote on September 16, 1946:

> Last Saturday night I had an experience that I'm sure I'll never forget. Not because of what I accomplished because that was very little, but because of a manifestation of God's help that I will never forget. . . .
>
> We were planning to hold a street meeting here in Ottawa and I was to be one of the speakers. All of us were quite inexperienced; in fact it was either the first or second time for all of us except Elder Smith. It was his third time. He presided.
>
> We opened the meeting singing, "The Spirit of God Like a Fire." I was shaking in my boots. Believe me we were a humble

bunch. . . . There were four elders and four LMs [lady missionaries]. After the song Elder Lionhardt prayed and we sang again. After the second song Elder Smith stepped out and in a most commanding voice called the people on the street to stop and listen, that "we are missionaries of the true church of Jesus Christ" and "Christ has restored His word again and we are here to declare it." Not a lot of people gave him much heed but he kept on talking loudly and seemed very much inspired. He talked about 15 minutes and then introduced me.

I had been praying constantly in my heart for help. I was shaking like a leaf. I stepped out, he stepped back, and I continued to tremble—through my whole talk I trembled. I opened my mouth and began talking. Even though my whole body was quaking and continued to do so, my voice, I was surprised to hear, came forth much more clearly than I had expected. My mind was also clear so that I talked much more clearly and eloquently than I could have in and of myself. Even though I shook during the entire meeting I don't think the listeners knew it. But I did and I know that God helped me, even putting words in my mouth that I didn't realize until after I had said them.

I couldn't have done it alone I know. God helped me and He helped us all. I know He did. Yet He let me shake with fear so that I would recognize His power over me. When our street meeting was over it seemed, though, like we were walking on air.

Satan had his part to play, too, because all afternoon we had been pleading with Elder Smith, our D.P. [District President] to change his mind about it. But his faith was too strong to give in. He insisted saying, "there's going to be a street meeting tonight if I have to do it alone. Don't you have any faith in God's help?" There was nearly rebellion among the missionaries and I am ashamed to say I was rebelling as much as any. . . . Incidentally, we held another street meeting tonight and experienced the same feeling. It's a glorious work.

George held as many as five street meetings, week after week. Sometimes it would be just him and his companion. Each time was as frightening as the first.

OWEN SOUND

George was transferred to Owen Sound in October of 1946 to work with Elder Glenn Sacos (who conducted a missionary choir at George's funeral in 1990). Owen Sound was a port town with a population of less than 20,000, on the southeast shore of Lake Huron. He remained there less than 2 months and none of his letters to his parents during that time survive. George and Glenn inherited a list of contacts to teach, canvassed a few more, and had some promising teaching experiences. But they could not hold church meetings because they did not have a space to hold them. They spent a lot of their time looking for a space, ruling out such places as the YMCA and the public library. The problem was not resolved before George transferred out in January. They also spent some time looking for new lodging, until their landlady agreed to let them stay longer.

DISTRICT PRESIDENT, MONTREAL

George was assigned to be district president of the Montreal District early in January 1947. He served in that capacity for a year, or half of his mission, through December 1947. He served without a companion. (Mormon missionaries are rarely without a companion today.) He lived alone at the church; and traveled to the outposts of his district alone for the first 6 months.

George wanted to be a proselytizing missionary. He wrote home in March:

> Now as D.P. I don't get much of a chance to talk with non-members as I did before but every time I do and every time I get a chance to bear my testimony to them it makes me feel so good. As yet I haven't seen any of the fruits of my labors inasmuch as none of my own personal contacts have been baptized. My reward has come, though, in just knowing that I have been doing a good work.

In the course of his duties as district president he interviewed a dozen or so converts prior to baptism, and he presided at their baptisms. But he did not actually teach anyone who was baptized. His work was largely administrative.

FRENCH LANGUAGE PROGRAM

The fact that the church attempted to proselytize in Montreal using English reveals a fundamental naiveté. It is particularly surprising given that the mission president, Octave Ursenbach, was himself a Canadian. A few missionaries coincidentally spoke French but the mission did not commit to teach French to missionaries until January 1947. Even when the mission finally started teaching in French, it took a while for the program to reach its stride, and printed materials in French were in short supply.

The French language program was amateurish. One thing they did right was to move the elders into a French-speaking boardinghouse. They attempted to study on their own while continuing to proselytize, but progress was slow. In May, George pointed out to the mission president that Elder Woolley only had 4 months left in his mission and probably could not learn French soon enough to be of practical value. Woolley and his companion, L. Stephen Richards, asked to be split up and reassigned to French-speaking companions, an idea that George supported. They also asked to work only with English-speaking members and contacts until they could be transferred, an acknowledgment that they were wasting their time. They were reassigned to French-speaking companions and transferred in late June.

In June, George approached a member who spoke French and Spanish but only a little English. He asked her if she would be willing to teach French to the missionaries. Sister Renee Argualt was a Uruguayan national who had lived in France until she was 14 years old. She agreed to teach 3 days a week. Renee turned out to be very reliable and stuck with the program until after George was transferred. She took upon herself the extra duty to encourage the sister missionaries who were frequently discouraged and who could not get along with each other. One of them, Sister West, finally called it quits and was transferred out in October after struggling for 7 months with the language and a companion she did not like. By November, George and Renee could both report positive progress with the program. George could not speak French himself but he was with a Sister Freebairn when he heard her speak at length with French contacts interested in learning about the church.

George wrote home in June what it was like to reach across the gap of religion while not completely understanding the gap of language and culture:

We elders went across the Ottawa River to the town of Hawkesbury where we had a date to meet with the town council thereof and submit a request to do missionary work therein. We were about ready to leave when the meeting started by the mayor leading his "boys" in a short French prayer and everyone there making the sign of the cross on their chest and forehead. Every one of them were Catholic and the whole meeting was carried on in French until our part came. So you see it kinda took the starch out of us. Nevertheless I stood when the mayor asked in English if there was any more to be put before the council and I stood and talked to them for about 3 minutes. I read to them the first the eleventh and then the twelfth of the Articles of Faith, explaining our views on each one. Telling them that we were willing to abide by whatever they decided and also that we would like to present our message to the people of their city. They wouldn't vote on it while we were there as they had heretofore done with the other proposals that they had expedited while we were waiting, but told us to come back the next morning and we would get their answer. We went back the next morning and found that they could not forbid us the right to tract or distribute literature. The Lord did help us again.

New Companion

George had been serving without a companion for 7 months. He was finally assigned a companion, Elder Don Christensen, in mid-July. Don was a great help, but even with a companion George's opportunity to do the actual teaching was limited. He typically spent 10 to 20 hours each week just to complete mission paperwork. He reported on specific missionaries and their contacts. There were 33 members and 22 missionaries in his district, including Montreal City, the suburbs, and in smaller cities such as Cornwall, Hawkesbury, and Sherbrooke. He often reported 10 hours of travel time in a week for the purpose of visiting missionaries, speaking in local meetings, and interviewing contacts who had applied for baptism. He visited distant missionaries to check on their work, discover their problems and encourage them.

They visited the elders in Cornwall who had another recruiting technique; they had a weekly radio broadcast which turned up at least three interested contacts. The program played recorded church history radio dramas, homilies, music from the Tabernacle Choir broadcasts, and *The Fullness of Times* which was apparently a recorded study course. Once in July he and Don Christensen hitched a ride with a member from Cornwall back to Montreal:

> It was a lovely ride about 80 miles along the St. Laurence [*sic*] River and the canal where occasionally a steamer would pass with its load of coal, pulpwood, grain, or anything. There are miles and miles of canals that the boats must go through as the descent of the water in the St. Laurence is so swift in places and so fast that there must be locks that the boats have to go through. We watched some of them going through locks at Cornwall and it was very interesting. While in Cornwall we also went down to the river and watched the rapids. It was really a sight to behold. For nearly a mile across the river the water is nothing but a tumbling, frothy mass. Swirling over the rocks at a tremendous speed. It was beautiful.

(He always misspelled "St. Lawrence" in his letters, possibly confused by the French "*fleuve Saint-Laurent.*")

WEEKLY REPORTS

Missionaries submitted a letter and a form report to their district president which were forwarded to the mission president each week. Of forms and letters more than 200 pages survive to document George's mission. George's weekly reports show that he put in 80-hour workweeks and sometimes more. The reports tallied separately the hours for study, visits to investigators, tracting (Mormon vernacular for *proselytizing*), church meetings and cottage meetings, street meetings, travel, and downtime such as for illness. They also reported detailed accounts of expenses and printed materials. George tried to live on $50 a month, but often needed more money for clothes, travel, or printed materials. The report forms had a box to comment on health; George always reported "excellent," or "very well." On only one occasion he reported "excellent except I'm tired all the time."

In October 1946 he had three fillings put in his teeth. In June and July 1947 he had 14 more teeth filled and one extracted. He wrote home that he was getting dental care for the first time since joining the military in 1944. He had been suffering from a toothache for about a month prior. The dental work came to $45. There is no mention of these procedures in his weekly reports other than hours checked in boxes over about 6 weeks for a total of 13 hours off "due to illness or other reasons."

Letters to the president, like letters to his parents, were deferential. And when writing to his parents about his mission president, he was reverential. In March of 1947 while serving as president of the Montreal district, he wrote to the mission president:

> Dear President Ursenbach:
>
> Again with pleasure I write to you concerning the Lord's work in this district. As long as I have been working as district president here I have found it trying at times but most strengthening and I do hope that the things I do in this job may be as you would do them yourself, were you here.
>
> I look forward to your letters of counsel and help always. Anytime, President, that I'm not doing things as they should be done I [would] appreciate your help and authority . . . .

That is a mild example of an introduction to his weekly activity report; he wrote similarly week after week. It is not very surprising that he was obsequious in his letters. There are a few rationales to consider: 1. George came from a hierarchical command structure only 2 months prior to his mission. 2. He may have been very insecure in general, and in particular about his fitness to be a missionary or a leader. After all, he had had little successes in school and his parents were not role models in that way. Many missionaries go into the field having never read the scriptures. Just maybe, George was one of those. 3. Hero worship is by no means an aberration in the mission field where obedience is valued above inspiration. 4. Who among us wrote better letters at 20 years old? 5. Finally, even late in life, it was more George's nature to hear opinions than to offer his own.

What follows those introductory paragraphs are complete and detailed accounts of the district's work, mentioning missionaries, contacts, and members by name. To look at the whole, he comes across as earnest, conscientious, comprehensive, and fully compliant with the mission's most detailed reporting requirements.

He always found complimentary things to say about his companions and fellow missionaries, even when highlighting problems. He was always positive about the work, even though it was moving at glacial speed. At least he would report what the work was doing for his personal growth.

A formality he extended to the mission president and to other missionaries, he signed those letters with his full name—George Thomas Brooks, and "Most sincerely your brother" or "God bless you," and often used his title, "Montreal District President."

LETTERS HOME

George's letters home were similar and almost formulaic. They were earnest, sentimental, and to-the-point. They were typically two pages, typed, single-spaced, but in many cases much longer. The first part responded to questions and thanked family members for recent letters or cash; apparently he did not often write individual letters to his siblings. Then he talked about the work, acquainting the family with the names of people he was working with and relevant details about Canada or the weather. Then he talked about expenses and how his clothes were holding up. It is not clear who paid for the mission; apparently his parents contributed. However, George occasionally instructed his parents how to access his military savings. Finally, George invariable thanked his family and expressed his love for them individually and including his infant nephew, Stephen. In particular he addressed his parents and expressed how happy he was to be a missionary. A typical example—in March of 1947 he signed off:

> I am so happy to be out here in the mission field. I love this work more and more every day. I realize that you folks are doing a lot for me and sometimes I wonder if the effort I put forth is repaying you for it. So many times I fall and make mistakes that I just wonder if they put the right guy in the job as DP [district president]. I hope I'm doing alright, and if I [am,] it will be

because of your faith and prayers that I can feel with me all the time. I love you. Tell everybody hello for me and all my friends that I miss them. I love you all and God bless you.

His parents responded quickly but the letters were typically very short, maybe only a single sheet of stationery paper, handwritten, shared among all family members. Sam, his father, was laconic with a tendency toward platitudes. As an example, in January 1948, Samuel wrote on the bottom of a letter written by George's mother, Winnifred:

Dear son—am at the exchange office to get a draft to send you. We are so thrilled to know you are having the experiences you are. Get lots of them. They are an education themselves. Just as good as the cash. May the Lord watch over you always that you may grow and grow. Plenty room at the top. Dad

Bobby Dean, his 19-year-old sister, was the outlier. She reported gossip of George's friends. She sometimes wrote with a playful eye dialect. She was the only one to address concerns specific to George beyond such banalities as bank drafts and worn-out shoes. In May of 1948 she wrote:

Another thing. Is you is or is you aint going to the Y [Brigham Young University]. You know you'll get an allowance [GI Bill] each month besides your books and tuition. If you don't go when you get it free you're cracked! So, will you go? If you're gonna go I'll start looking for an apt. for us. Whydoncha ever answer me when I ask you about school next year. You always beat around the question like it was some kind of a disease. If you're not planning on going to school you'd better say so—but—I hope you go cause only eggheads wouldn't go when they have the chance!

To speculate about George's motives relative to college, he had a girl-friend and possibly wanted to resolve that before committing to rooming with his sister at the Y. Also, he had never been particularly academic and he may have been ambivalent about school.

George wrote a letter to his little brother Sam Jr. on his 13th birthday in November of 1947. In it he preached a tiny bit, but also included this charming description of Montreal:

> Do you remember that street down by Liberty Park? The one with the grass out in the middle of it? Well the street here in the front of the Church is just like that and when it snows here they have a big truck with a snow blowing machine on it that pushes the snow out of the way and picks it up and blows it where they want it. They blow it right on that grassy strip in the middle of the road and the snow gets so high on that strip that you can't even see across the road to see the cars and busses on the other side. . . .
>
> Then too—Montreal is on an island, a big island right in the middle of the St Laurence River and it gets so cold here that the big river, about a mile across, freezes solid. The men go down there in the winter and cut big chunks of ice out of the river and store it in sawdust for summer use. A lot of ice we used in our refrigerator [icebox] last summer came in that way.
>
> The river is deep, too. So deep that big ocean steamers can come right up to Montreal even though Montreal is so far in from the East coast. That is, they can come up in the summer but in the winter the ice won't let them.
>
> You see Montreal is a very interesting city. Though it is on the American continent and is so close to the English-speaking people they still speak French here. In some small villages they don't speak any English. That is because a long time ago, a few centuries, the first people to settle here were French and they still don't speak English.

A few curiosities turn up in these letters which speak to the economy of the times. George justified having a coat altered at the cost of $25 arguing that an equivalent new coat would cost $50. Possibly it was a military overcoat which he was having re-tailored and dyed navy blue. He complained that Canadian winters were cold and this coat was so very warm. Also he asked his parents to look for shirts with detachable collars which he could not find on the local market. He pointed out that he could launder collars for 4¢ but a shirt cost 15¢. His shirt size was 15½ x 34. On one occasion he asked his mother to retrieve his parachute and cut it up and make silk scarves for him to give as Christmas gifts. Evidently, the parachute was one of his war souvenirs, though he was never a parachutist.

WINIFRED WILKINSON

It was probably in January of 1947 when George met Winifred Wilkinson, a sister missionary, for the first time. She had some family ties to Manti and southern Utah and had some friends in common with George's mother. She and George both served in Montreal from January through September 1947, at which time she was transferred to Kingston.

George and "Wynne" corresponded while in the mission field—a practice discouraged or forbidden today. None of those letters survive. George also wrote to Wynne's mother who invited him to visit in Idaho on his way home from his mission. There are gaps in the correspondence between George and his family. In November 1947 George responded to some concerns of his parents, saying:

> I am also thankful for the advice. . . . Believe me, mom and dad, you don't have to let it worry you too much. I was attracted to Sister Wilkinson, and still am. I like her very much. But I still intend to spend quite a bit of time in school and at home before I think of getting married . . . the four years difference in our ages is a big issue. I'm not forgetting that either.

In January of 1948 he wrote home, "If you knew her I think you'd fall in love with her too." Then he reassured his parents yet again, "I'm not going to spend valuable missionary time thinking about it or her." In a February letter he wrote:

> I received a lovely letter from Wynne Saturday. She is still in Kingston and I still think of her and as much of her as I ever did. She asked about you and is rather worried about what you might think of her. I think she sent you a Christmas card at Christmas and is rather disappointed at not hearing from you.

Towards the end of his mission, in May 1948, he told his sister Beverly that he intended to visit the Wilkinson family in Idaho Falls on his way home to Salt Lake. "I still can't make up my mind if we should get married or not. The truth of the matter is, I don't think I know her well enough, yet. She seems to be pretty certain of it. I don't know if I have faith that the Lord will help us with this—if He doesn't I don't see how we'll figure it out."

Family lore has it that George and Winifred were engaged. He may have even bought a washing machine in anticipation of marriage. But details of a visit to Idaho Falls, or whether he gave her a ring, are not known.

NEW MISSION PRESIDENT

George got word in May 1947 that President Ursenbach was to be the new president of the Lethbridge Alberta stake. Ursenbach continued on as mission president through August when he was replaced by Floyd Guymon "F.G." Eyre. George quickly warmed up to the new president, saying he "is just like one of us except when it comes to giving advice and then he is so far above us. He is so spiritually minded. . . . I wish I could be just like him."

TIMMINS, ONTARIO

Conferences were always happy times, time to emerge from isolation, share testimonies, and see old friends. George attended a mission conference in December 1947; there were about 140 missionaries in the mission at that time. George was released from his assignment as district president at that conference. Only two people had been baptized in Montreal while he was there. Others in the district had been baptized, but in the large, very Catholic, and very cosmopolitan city, there were only two.

George was next assigned to Timmins, a town of about 30,000, halfway to the Hudson Bay, the farthest north where missionaries served. The economy of Timmins, and the neighboring hamlet of Porcupine relied on gold mining and forestry. When he arrived in Timmins he heard surprising and happy news that nine people in Montreal had requested to be baptized.

Now free from his administrative duties, his letters home reflected a new relaxation. He sent newspaper clippings and described the sport of curling in some detail. His weekly reports to the president, of course, became shorter, about a half page. In February 1948 he wrote to President Eyre, "The weather is brutally cold and it may, in the future, prevent us from going out [proselytizing]. We will go out all we can."

As his mission wound down he started to plan for his return trip and for his future. He mentioned coming home in almost every letter to his parents in 1948, and even in a few letters to the president.

In March he was stricken with appendicitis. He became violently ill and walked with his companion to St. Mary's Hospital in Timmins. His companion left him in a hospital bed to contemplate a crucifix on the wall as he suffered through the night. The doctors took his appendix out on Good Friday. On Saturday he was cheery; with pain under control he wrote to his parents not to worry. He was released from the hospital the following Friday. He was still recovering in mid-April and describes his convalescence as "maddening inactivity—lots of [time to] study."

Occasionally he would visit the town of Orillia in the Toronto district to sing in part harmony on live radio; he was a baritone with good range and excellent pitch. In May he was instructing and meeting regularly with seven families.

In May he wrote a letter home which rambled a bit about a bucolic picnic he shared with some members.

> After Sunday School we were getting ready to go to the Taylors' home but they came for us and drove us out . . . to a very pretty little lake called Slab Lake where we spread out a big lunch Sister Taylor had prepared, and ate it while the blood-red sun disappeared in the west over the northern Ontario bush. It had stopped raining and except for a chilly wind, was ideal. No insects this early in the season. A boat placed on the lake by the parks commission offered a pleasant time for us; we were the only ones at this lake. There are thousands of lakes through the bush and it seems that every family has their own lake where they go. . . . All it amounted to was . . . eating our dinner outside instead of inside, . . . seeking to justify ourselves [eating a picnic on the Sabbath]. After the lunch was eaten and the sun taken back, we went back to South Porcupine . . . The whole day was lovely, rain and all.

George, c. 1946.

JUNCTURE

He persuaded his family to come out and tour with him. He particularly wanted them to see Palmyra the way he had seen it, and the great city Montreal. They agreed, and planned from January through April to bring the family, maybe even Beverly. But they later demurred, saying they were unable to buy a car. He shrugged off his disappointment, suggesting maybe it was for the best. For a while he considered returning home alone via Baltimore and Ft. Meade so that he could reconnect with his army buddies and tell them his gospel message. Then he thought he might return by way of Calgary, suggesting that it would be cheaper for his family to meet him in Calgary and see the Stampede. But that idea did not excite them, either. He then said he would skip the Stampede to spend some time in Montreal saying good-bye to members of the church there. He planned to travel through Idaho Falls to meet the Wilkinson family, his girlfriend's family. Beverly tried gently to dissuade him from going to Idaho Falls—maybe helpful advice to a young man buffeted by so many changes and decisions.

In a letter to his sister Beverly, May 22, 1948, he asked about his brother-in-law Clarence and his business.

> You know, Beverly, that's what I want to do, get into a small business of my own like that. Brother Dan Taylor here is that way. A few years ago he quit working underground in the mine and started a small variety store. Now he has one of the most prominent businesses in South Porcupine. The sooner I can start in on something like that, the happier I'll be, I figure. . . . Maybe I'm all wrong.

About that time his mother, Winnifred, encouraged him to bring home some British porcelain or china which was either cheaper in Canada, or simply not available in Salt Lake City. He exchanged letters with his mother about Spode, embossed Wedgwood, and Irish Belleek.

The impression is that of someone in transition, not knowing what he wanted or needed, and loved ones ill-equipped to help or notice. George was released on July 5, 1948, and likely reached home about July 9th. He was 22 years old.

XII

Marriage
First Child
1948–1951

George and Lillis had a romance that became part of the idyllic mythology of the family. The in-laws, aunts, uncles, and grandparents would retell the story at family gatherings, or recall archetypal fragments of it. Over the years, George and Lillis were always playful, even a bit silly together, and there was never any doubt about their loyalty and kindness toward each other.

Paths Cross

Lillis became aware of George for the first time when he spoke at stake conference in July or August 1948. Lillis had moved into his ward just before he returned from his mission. She said that she was not overly impressed with him. It must be true that she paid little attention to him because she said it so often throughout her life.

Soon George was assigned to be the gospel doctrine teacher in the Sunday school. George called everyone in class by their first name except Lillis; he called her "Miss Remington." She wrote in her scrapbook, "I paid little attention to him and he seemed to pay little attention to me."

In the fall the church young adult group held a dance at Fairmont Park. Lillis watched him that evening as he danced with each of the other

153

girls; there were many young people in Lincoln Ward. She wrote that he was a good dancer, and she was finally able to acknowledge that she was very put out by him. Other fellows asked her to dance, but not George. It could have been shyness on George's part; it was much less likely an oversight. Alternatively, it could be an example of the disconnect between their individual senses of humor. George was a playful prankster—Lillis not so much. He was trying to get her attention and she was not about to reward his behavior.

Their paths crossed again at a dance in January 1949. This time Lillis was on a date with a fellow named Lawrence Angebauer and George was with someone else. George traded three dances to dance with Lillis, a courtesy that seems quaint now. He tried to trade a fourth time but Laurence refused, pointing out that Lillis was his date.

Lillis hoped that George would invite her to a dance at the Student Union at the University of Utah, but he took another girl from Lincoln Ward, Arda Wetzel (later Arda Wetzel Leatham). Tommy Oaks from Lincoln Ward took Lillis.

Finally, George called and invited her to a formal dance at the LDS Business College. He borrowed Clarence Walker's car. Clarence, his brother-in-law, had a 1935 Plymouth with a roof that leaked freely. It rained that evening and the only thing that protected her formal gown was an old Army raincoat that was in the car. They had a good time at the dance and a pleasant time afterwards talking in the car in her father's driveway. She said, "'I had such a lovely evening. It has been so fun.' He looked at me and smiled and said, 'It has been fun. I think I'm going to marry you.'" She dismissed the suggestion with a laugh and went into her house. That was their first date. They were not engaged yet and they continued to go out with others, but they saw each other every day from that night on until they were married.

ENGAGEMENT, MARCH 1949

They went to the play *Othello* on Saturday evening before Easter at Kingsbury Hall at the U. After midnight, Easter Sunday morning, they drove to 11th Avenue, the highest street overlooking the city. He presented her with an Easter gift, a glass box in the shape of a chicken containing a pair of white gloves on a bed of Easter grass. She had been shopping for gloves and was delighted with the gift. She put them on to check the size and found a ring inside a finger of the left glove. It was slow to dawn on her; she thought for a moment maybe it was her birthstone. When she pulled her hand out, she was wearing a diamond. Thus, they were engaged. But in her heart she was immediately worried about the size of the diamond. It was too big. She wondered if it would be safe to own or wear a stone so big. She worried about George's judgment; after all, he was a broke university student in a dead-end job. As soon as she said yes, he pulled the real ring out of his pocket, one of a more modest size. The diamond on her finger was glass and had only cost 60¢.

Though it was very late, they went across town to announce the news to their parents. The Remingtons cooked a breakfast of ham and eggs at 3 AM. Finally, Lillis went to bed, but looked at her ring until it was time to get up for Lincoln Ward's Easter sunrise service at 6 AM.

It was a whirlwind romance. They had shown emphatic disinterest in each other in the summer, their first date was in March, they were engaged in April, and they were married on a Wednesday morning, June 22, 1949.

Lillis spent part of the engagement in a body cast. She had broken her back at work lifting something. The cast did not seem to prevent her from going to dances or shopping for her trousseau; she remained active. At a dance another couple accidentally bumped her on the dance floor, and they were stunned at how solid she was under her diaphanous gown. Happily, the cast came off a week before the wedding. One of her friends knocked on her chest to be sure.

WEDDING, JUNE 1949

Salt Lake City was a smaller city then, and maybe there was not much news to print. The *Deseret News* printed a column on the engagement and later printed another detailed column on the wedding, both with photographs of the bride. The length and journalistic style of these articles exhibit a charming attention to the details as if the *News* were documenting high society.

> . . . A traditionally styled white satin gown was the one chosen by the bride for her wedding and reception. Her fingertip veil of white bride's illusion was caught to a beautifully pearled crown. Her bridal ensemble was complemented by a bouquet of deep pink rosebuds and a shower of lilies of the valley encircling a

George and Lillis, June 1949.

white orchid corsage. Mrs. Samuel Markely [Edna Colton, a childhood friend from Vernal] was the honor attendant to the comely bride. Miss Cleo Remington, a sister to the former Miss Remington, Miss Necia Cardwell from Canada, Miss LaRue Hadlock, a cousin to the bride, and Miss Barbara Brooks, a sister to the bridegroom, completed the bridal party. They wore formal ensembles of pastel shades, and carried white gladioli caught with matching ribbon streamers.

Samuel Brooks Jr., a younger brother of the bridegroom, served as best man. Ushers were Clarence Walker, Newell Remington, Don Larson and Allen Price. . . .

And so it went. The marriage ceremony was performed in the Salt Lake Temple by Marion G. Romney, who was an Assistant to the Quorum of the Twelve Apostles.

After the wedding they enjoyed a wedding breakfast at the Brooks home; members of both families were invited. That evening the Remingtons hosted a reception in the Lincoln Ward Relief Society room, with about 60 guests. Lillis borrowed her wedding dress from her cousin, Colleen Young Slagle. The wedding cake was a fruitcake that weighed 43 pounds and was made by a competent amateur, Mrs. Spakman of Layton, who did not charge.

HONEYMOON

At the end of the evening, as the reception wound down and as George and Lillis tried to get on the road, some of the guests attempted to abduct the bride. Perhaps these misbehaved friends in formal attire thought that they were sanctioned by a venerated tradition of shivaree. George was not amused. He was defensive of Lillis, not least because of her recent back injury. Reliable details of the incident are lost. It seems George became quite physical with the assailants. It is probable that he bit, kicked, and shoved both men and women. Some versions of the story have it that he broke someone's collarbone or maybe it was an arm (possibly David McClelland), and he put a woman in a trash can (probably Janet Richards). A fragment of the story that he himself told was that he took Lillis to the car, put her in first, then he followed her. A man put his hands on George to drag him out of the car. George turned around, put his foot in the middle of the man's chest, and kicked him out of the car. Certainly he was capable of that kind of physicality. He weighed 190 pounds and was a half-inch shy of 6 feet tall. In a short while he made his point, and they made their escape.

They spent their first night at the Tower Motor Lodge on south State Street; the next day they drove on to southern Utah to visit the national parks and George's relatives in St. George. They borrowed Fuller Remington's new car. The Brooks clan of St. George threw another party in their honor.

University Studies

It was about this time—either just before or soon after their marriage—that George went through some evaluation of his future. His high school grades had been poor. During his mission he had expressed no greater aspiration than to be a store clerk or a small business owner. He had no particular goal to attend the university. He was a university student in the spring of 1949, but possibly only motivated by the GI Bill. He worked at Purity Biscuit as an assembly-line baker, making trays and trays of cookies. About this time he also sold shoes at Sears and Roebuck. There was no role model of a scholar or a professional in his life. Similarly, Lillis had no role model of a scholar or professional in her family with the exception of her brother Newell. At least Lillis had gone to nursing school, and had attended a couple of quarters at BYU.

Family lore has it that in a moment of resignation, George said to Lillis that he was content to be a salesman at Sears and Roebuck. Lillis, as the story goes, responded, "You may be a salesman if you like but you must take advantage of the GI Bill and finish a university degree." It was a line in the sand for her.

Before fall quarter, 1949, George quit his job at Purity Biscuit and enrolled for 20 quarter hours, leaving Lillis to pay the rent and support them both. These were hard times financially. They must also have been hard times emotionally for the both of them. George, the poor student, was putting all his chips on one bet: that he would succeed academically. Lillis was betting all on George.

It is not clear when he took his first class. If, for example, he enrolled immediately upon returning from his mission in 1948 (which seems unlikely), and if he attended summer quarters, he would have the standard 12 quarters to graduate in August 1951. He was a student in the spring of 1949, but it appears that he committed seriously to school later, probably after the wedding, and then carried heavy class loads. He took class seriously, earning the first *A*s of his life.

APARTMENT ON ALDEN STREET

Lillis and George lived in the Remington home for a few months. Lillis's sister Lois had recently given birth to her first child, Stephen, and Mother Remington had moved into Lois's house to help out. Fuller was often on the road selling insurance. So on those pretexts George and Lillis were able to live in the Remington house without much disruption, though Don, Cleo, and Ted were still single and living at home.

Around August they moved into a basement apartment on Alden Street near Stratford Avenue for $55 per month, completely furnished. George studied and Lillis worked at LDS Hospital. They arranged their schedules so that they could ride the bus together. They didn't own a car and would walk a mile to Sugar House to see a movie, or go shopping. For greater distances they would take a bus or even a train.

PREGNANCY

Lillis tried to accommodate George and his studies even after she became pregnant in November. She started to suffer morning sickness in January 1950 but continued working full time. George would take the occasional job to help out. He worked as a mailman over the Christmas holidays. Carrying a mailbag in the cold weather aggravated his combat injuries. A doctor advised him to give it up and prescribed shoe inserts for him but by then the season was over. He also worked at ZCMI but was laid off in March.

Lillis wrote in her diary on January 1, 1950:

This year has had a most pleasant beginning. I work 48 hrs a week at the L.D.S. Hospital and George is carrying heavy class loads at the Unv. of Utah. Our hours are long but we are enjoying our life together. Even though we have very limited money, no car, we do enjoy many friends. Mother and Dad invite us to dinner at least twice each week.

There is a hint here that the Remington parents were helping the newlyweds with a food subsidy twice weekly. George and Lillis were living in poverty reminiscent of O. Henry's *Gift of the Magi,* too distracted to notice. On one occasion some friends dropped by unannounced and Lillis was able to prepare an impromptu dinner party using only canned goods. So it can be said they did not have an expansive pantry.

Yet they did find a little discretionary money to go out a bit and enjoy each other's company. They bought season tickets to the Masterminds and Artists lecture series at the U, and in January they heard Risë Stevens, mezzo-soprano of the New York Metropolitan Opera, sing in the Tabernacle. They also attended plays at the U.

In mid-January, soon after Lillis announced to her family that she was pregnant, they took the Bamberger train to Ogden to pick up a tailored wool suit for Lillis. It cost a month's rent and an expense of travel time without a car. It speaks to their budget priorities. She wrote:

> It cost $58.00, a great extravagance, which we really shouldn't have paid. He wanted so badly to do it and I do like the suit. We had dinner in Ogden and a lot of fun returning home by train that evening, catching the bus to our apt. I enjoy riding the bus when George is with me.

In February, they bought a spin-dry washer for $130. This was a generation of washer prior to automatic washers. It had two tubs. The larger tub had an agitator. Clothes and detergent were put in there, and water was added with a hose from a faucet such as from the kitchen sink. Then the washer was turned on and left to run for a while. The water could be drained through another hose into a floor drain, then new water would be added to rinse. Finally, the clothes would be moved to the smaller tub for a high-speed spin to extract much of the water. It was so exciting to have a new washer. George had a lot of fun going through the apartment looking for things to wash.

Frequently, Lillis would write things in her diary such as this from Thursday, March 2, 1950:

> Geo. was waiting for me when I got off work. He has a bus pass and came to the hospital after school to meet me. It is always

more enjoyable to have him with me. We stopped in town tonight. We went to the coffee shop at Hotel Newhouse for dinner. Their salads are very good and also their soup. It is a lovely place to eat and quite inexpensive. We had a very enjoyable evening before catching the bus for home. I still feel nauseated much of the time but my work keeps my mind off it most of the time. The anticipation of the baby makes it very worthwhile.

They went to the movies almost every week. Sometimes they would go with friends or with Newell. Lillis wrote that on March 8, Newell went with her and George to see a double feature, *Malaya* and *Admiral Byrd's Expedition*. "Newell is good company. We enjoy being with him. He has a very sad home life. [Newell's marriage was failing.] He works very hard and has few escapes or diversions from his work and studies."

In March they bought an *Encyclopedia Americana* from Newell, who had a job selling them door to door. Again, this reflects their values and budget priorities. However, they did comment that Newell, unlike his father, was a timid and pathetic salesman, and that may have been a factor in the decision to buy.

Lillis complained about her nausea, her intolerance for diesel smoke from buses, and sometimes about medical expenses. But more than that she was very happy—looking forward to a baby and happy to be current on expenses. As an example, on Wednesday, March 8, 1950, she wrote:

Today I went to the doctor for my monthly check-up. It is so wonderful to feel our baby move. I am doing well with my pregnancy. I have had nausea and vomiting but it is getting better. The fumes from the cars and buses make me nauseated. It is difficult to avoid the smell because I have to wait at bus stops to catch my bus. Today I paid $15.00 on our doctor bill. We are up to date on our payments.

In April, Lillis and George attended his mission reunion. Lillis insisted on wearing her new maternity dress. Her old clothes still fit, but she really liked the dress, and she particularly wanted everyone to know she was pregnant. Some of her friends would be there.

STADIUM VILLAGE

Lillis finally quit her job in June. She had not felt well since becoming pregnant. George took a job with the Fuller-Toponce trucking company as a driver and dock worker. In this job he dropped a steel plate on his big toe, an additional injury to his foot, which never fully healed. He continued to study at the university, but this new job gave Lillis some needed rest in the last 10 weeks of her pregnancy.

It was about this time, June 24, that they moved into married student housing at Stadium Village, land and barracks recently deeded to the U from Fort Douglas as part of the postwar draw-down. George rented a truck and Lillis's brothers helped him move. George could now go to class without taking a bus. Lillis was no longer working, so transportation was not an issue with her.

FRICTION WITH IN-LAWS

It was common knowledge that Lillis did not get along with her mother-in-law, Winnifred, and had problems with other women in the Brooks family. In one of her longer diary entries she writes in some detail about an early and illustrative incident. Obviously, this is one uncontested version of a story. Other than that, it needs no further comment:

> Sunday Aug 13, 1950
>
> My baby is due today. No labor pains as yet. Geo. and I had planned to take a picnic lunch and spend part of the day in Memory Grove. I'm very uncomfortable and ready to have my baby. I have looked forward to being alone today with George all week.
>
> Mother Brooks called early this morning and declared she had many errands for Geo. to run. (She has a car of her own. She also has her husband, Sam Jr., and Barbara to help her with her errands.) I told her Geo. was to priesthood meeting and we had plans for the day. She was very rude to me as she most often is and demanded I have him call her which I did.
>
> Geo. called his mother and by the time he had finished talking to her he had agreed to spend the day with her at a Branch family [George's paternal grandmother] reunion in Fairmont

Park. Without asking me we drove to her house in Harvey's [Lillis's brother-in-law's] car. Mother Brooks kept George busy the remainder of the day.

Sam Jr., Barbara, Beverly, and Clarence all had their own things to do. Bev and Clarence went home to take a nap. Barbara went with girl friends. I sat on a cement bench for several hours in the park. My back ached, my feet were swelling, it was hot, I didn't know the people, I was large with pregnancy, Geo. was not with me, Mother Brooks always ignores me or is sarcastic in her relationship, Dad Brooks is never mindful of a situation.

Finally in the late afternoon when many had left I suggested to Geo. I should like to go home. Geo. actually asked his mother if he could go. I tried not to show my disappointment in him. He could never take a stand with his mother. He disliked his relationship with her but could never stand up to her. She constantly put demands on him that were unnecessary and unfair and he never seemed to be able to tell her "no." He disliked her for it and always felt guilty because of it.

I stood up and said to Geo. "I'm really quite uncomfortable. Would you please take me home?" His mother responded instead of Geo. and said, "Take her home and you can come back." He took me home and left me and went back to the park and stayed until 9:30 PM that night. I had no way to reach him had I needed to go to the hosp. I was very angry. I felt he had been very inconsiderate of me, and his mother had been very unkind. I was angry they were using my family's car for their use when they had one of their own.

Mother Brooks is not a kind woman. She is a bright and talented woman but shrewd and cruel at times. She was dishonest and even treacherous at times not only with me but with many others as well. She has never been kind or even civil to me since I married George. George's father has always been nice but never seems to take any stand to make things right when he sees his wife being unkind and unfair.

Tonight I disliked them all very much and I am greatly disappointed in George. I feel he is very immature in his relationship with his mother. I have decided I will not continue my

marriage with this kind of a relationship. I went to bed before
George came home.

Monday Aug 14, 1950

George and I had words this morning over his mother. I
pointed out to him how impossible it is for me to please her, how
unkind, dishonest she has been and is, not only to me but how
vicious she is with anyone who crosses her or does not please her.
She is ruthless in her dealings with people. George agreed with
me and said he would visit her without me from now on. Our
conversation left me feeling terrible. I feel George avoids rather
than understands the situation.

New Baby, 1950

They bought a secondhand baby buggy. George would entertain
himself sometimes by wheeling the buggy around the house pretending
he had a baby. By mid-August they had the crib set up, a new chest of
drawers, baby clothes in place, and a bag packed for the hospital. Lillis's
sister Lois and her husband, Harvey Hirschi, had left town on vacation
and had loaned their car to George and Lillis to use when she went into
labor. Lillis tried to put the thoughts of her mother-in-law out of her
mind and enjoy the anticipation of the new baby.

Lillis went into labor at 5 AM on August 18. She arose from bed, and
she passed the time in the early morning hours by scrubbing and waxing
the floors. Then she defrosted the refrigerator. Those who knew Lillis will
find that part of the story amusing but not particularly surprising; she
was industrious and her house was always clean.

Dr. Howard Sharp, a resident, delivered the new baby at 2:15 PM
while her doctor, D. R. Skidmore, was scrubbing in. The baby weighed
8 lbs., 8 oz. He was wide-awake from the beginning. Lillis had worked
in the nursery for many months and felt qualified to comment, "I have
never seen a more beautiful baby than mine. He has dark hair, a handsome face, and beautiful body. I have never felt such joy as when he was
laid in my arms."

Her diary ended abruptly on August 18, 1950, with the birth of
George Remington "Rem" Brooks. (Over the years he was called variously

George R, Georgie, Little George, and *George Jr.* In high school, George R finally put an end to all that silliness and started to answer only to *Remington* or *Rem.* That is the name used in these following chapters, though sometimes anachronistically.) Maybe some diaries are lost; more probably Lillis simply did not keep a diary again until 1961—years after Nyman, her fourth and last child, was born.

Lillis's friends at the hospital placed her baby closest to the show window. Visiting hours were relaxed for George, another professional courtesy; he was allowed to visit at any hour. When the baby was a little older George took him to class and showed him off.

In May 1951, Lillis became ill. Part of her problem was sleep deprivation because 9-month-old baby Rem did not sleep or eat well. Also, she thought she might be pregnant again and should stop nursing. The doctors contested that idea, suggesting that maybe she just *wanted* to be pregnant. By July she was 15 pounds under her normal weight. She was too sick to work and finally she moved into her mother's house. Edith Remington tended Lillis and the baby for about 7 weeks until George graduated in August.

GEORGE REMINISCES ABOUT LILLIS

In January of 1976, after almost 30 years of marriage, George reminisced in his journal on what he admired about Lillis:

> I was impressed with her quick wit, her air of total adequacy in any situation, her posture, her walk, her ambition, her efficiency. . . . She was always frank and open. . . . She always helps me succeed. She is . . . neat and well groomed. . . . She handles money well, a willing but careful spender. She prepares marvelous meals . . . with a flair. Her plates and tables are beautiful. She is a good housekeeper and cleans quickly. . . . She has great faith, prays regularly. . . . She is a conversationalist. She insists upon visiting together and . . . I still find myself hour after rewarding hour talking with her, sometimes until early morning. . . . She makes and holds many friends. Strangers are attracted to her. Old friends of 40 years back still keep in touch with her. Almost daily she talks with her mother. . . . I have never for one moment wished that we had never married. Always I have felt fortunate

to have found her. . . . Our marriage has . . . been an exception-
ally good one.

The end of a journey does not always remember the hazards and
distractions along the way. In retrospect it seemed so inevitable that they
would fare well. But George did not start out as a natural academic. Lillis,
despite living on her own for 6 years, still needed frequent and extraordinary help from her parents, even for food and a bed. George was capable
of action and resolve, but sometimes lived in a quandary. Lillis was ready
to call it quits over her mother-in-law's insults. Neither of them was prepared for the expenses of their new life together.

XIII

Indian School
Washington Terrace
New Babies
1951–1955

GRADUATION

Lillis attended George's graduation on August 30, 1951. It was the first time in weeks that she had gone out in public. She was just starting to get over her illness. She had been suffering from sleep deprivation with her 1-year-old baby, George Remington. Rem was a poor sleeper and a finicky eater. Soon it was indisputable that she was pregnant again and suffering from morning sickness. Her illness was severe enough that she and her baby had been living and recuperating at her mother's house almost 2 months. She also lived briefly in the home of her Brooks in-laws.

The graduation ceremony was held outdoors in front of the Park Building at the University of Utah on a beautiful evening as the sun was setting. George gave Lillis a corsage of yellow roses. After the program it was the Remingtons who threw a party in George's honor, with a cake, "Congratulations George," written on it. Most of the Brooks and Remington families attended, along with some friends, Kendon and Enid Naylor and their parents, and Richard and Bonnie Larsen.

George, graduation, 1951.

INTERMOUNTAIN INDIAN SCHOOL 1951–1952

George completed the last weeks of school while Lillis was sick, sometimes sleeping at the Remington house on weekends. He also applied for jobs. He was offered a teaching job with the Salt Lake City public school system for an annual salary of $2,300. He was also offered a job with the US Department of the Interior as an elementary school teacher at the Intermountain Indian School in Brigham City, UT, for $3,100. He accepted the Civil Service appointment and on July 30 he moved to Brigham City alone to set up an apartment before graduating.

It was a boarding school primarily for Navajo children through high school. Some elementary students would be as old as 15 and many could not speak English. None in George's class had prior schooling. A few members of the staff were Navajo themselves, and bilingual.

The sprawling 200-acre campus had been built as the Bushnell General Military Hospital during the war. It had a capacity for almost 2,000 patient beds plus accommodations for staff and for visiting relatives. It was a new and well-appointed facility that needed only a little work to be converted into a school.

Students arrived mid-August and George helped them find their rooms, find the cafeteria, and even how to use the showers. He lived weekdays in Brigham City and would commute home on weekends, sometimes sharing gasoline expenses with a colleague. By that time he had a car which gave him a little trouble on the 2-hour drives between Salt Lake City and Brigham City. Before school started he studied up on Navajo culture, put together a lesson plan, attended faculty meetings, went through some orientation, and completed the application process. His letters to Lillis reassured her about his job and the apartment that they would rent. But mostly his letters expressed worry and concern for her recovery, her nutrition, and his infant son, Rem. Two outliers, written on the days when students were arriving, give a glimpse into his personality and sensibilities:

> Tuesday evening [August 14, 1951]
>> Dearest Lillis:
>> This morning at about ten o'clock the students started arriving in Greyhound buses. I was working in the dormitory for the older boys (17–18). The first thing we did was to help them with

their showers and inspect them for any body lice or evidence of disease. After showers they went to eat. After they ate we inspected and counted all of their belongings, clothing, etc. A record is kept of it all so that if any of it is missing it can be traced. When I was counting their clothing I thought I had never smelled anything as foul as one of their open suitcases. Most of their clothing needed laundering long since. I suppose that washing clothing is a rare activity on the reservation; not due so much to their uncleanliness as to the scarcity of water. It was also quite a revelation to see how few clothes most of them have. Many of them had only one pair of jeans besides the one they were wearing, no underwear, one to four pairs of sox (usually the one they were wearing, only), three or four shirts, usually in very poor shape. These people must live in dire poverty, they have so little. I only saw one watch; that was an Ingraham, the "dollar" type. One of them had a portable radio, one of them had a box camera, other than those things there was almost nothing except the very rudiments of necessary clothing. Every one of them, however, seemed to own a bottle of some kind of Brilliantine pomade. The group seemed to be all strangers to each other. There was very little talking among themselves, most of them are new to the school this year. As soon as we had checked all of their clothing the matron of the dormitory, a middle-aged Navajo woman, took all of their clothing and threw them into the automatic washer. Believe me, most of the shirts and Levis were pretty stiff. But the boys did get right to ironing their own shirts when they came out of the machine. In the afternoon I took a group of ten of them [to] the canteen. On the way I got lost in the hallways and I would likely be lost yet but one of the old students who had been here last year rescued me and the group or we might be still wandering around the halls yet. That was the first time I heard any of the group laugh. They quite enjoyed that.

There were over five hundred came in today. There will be like groups on Thursday, Saturday, and Monday. Our dormitory is about one quarter full.

I expected a letter from you today but none came. I suppose that the mails just aren't too dependable as far as trying to keep on a schedule is concerned. I'll keep trying to write to you every day. And I love to hear from you every day. But when I go to the mailbox expecting a letter from you and there is none—gosh I feel sorry. I hope that you are continuing to feel better. Is staying at Mother's proving to be a rest for you? What is the latest about my little boy? Mrs. Kee, the dorm attendant where I worked, has a niece staying with her who is just the same age as George [Rem]. She has straight black, dutch-boy style hair and the prettiest bronze skin you have ever seen on a baby. Her big brown eyes are just as alert as a young puppy's. She's really beautiful. I held her for a few moments and she didn't seem to mind it a bit. Lillis, you just got to come up here right away. I can hardly wait to have you with me again. I love you so, and miss you terribly. Do get well.

I managed to do my laundry this evening in an automatic washer and dried it in an automatic drier. Nuthin' to it. I used Tide.

Well, Lillis, it's nearly 10 and I've got to get to bed. The evenings are the worst for me. That's the time I miss you the most. I hope that at this time of night you are sound, sound asleep.

I can hardly wait until tomorrow morning when I just know I'll get a letter from you. How about it?

Sleep tight, honey, I love you tremendously.

All yours,

George

On the following day he wrote:

Wednesday morning [August 15, 1951]

Dearest Lillis:

Since I wrote you yesterday morning until now there has been almost nothing happen which I can write about. I've been almost bored stiff. Yesterday afternoon and this morning I've been arranging the names and ages of the boys in this dormitory and typing a roster, several rosters, for Mrs. Kee. There are 88 boys here in this building of the ages 14, 15, and 16. We are four above capacity. They put extra bunks in two of the rooms to take care of them.

Yesterday afternoon Mrs. Kee and I went shopping in town together. I took her in my car. We went to Penney's to buy her little boy a couple of pairs of jeans and some shirts. When she had bought them she gave her boy a dime and told him to hurry and go spend it. He rushed out into the dime store next door. She and I waited out on the sidewalk for him for quite some time. He didn't come—and he didn't come. So we went in to see what was keeping him. We found him in a state of pathological indecision at the toy counter. We tried to hurry up his choice by suggesting things, but all to no avail. Finally he decided he wanted marbles but he couldn't see anything at that store he wanted in marbles so he dashed out and up the street to the next dime store. Mrs. Kee and I sauntered after him and when we got to him we found him in the same situation as before; he had changed his mind en route. So we started suggesting again. Finally (it had to happen sometime) he made up his mind and bought a tablet and a pencil. We went out to the car and started home. No sooner had we gotten started than he decided that he should have gotten something that he, as he put it, "could use more." So that's that.

Yesterday when I got back from lunch and walked into the hall I saw standing in one corner of the hall, leaning over a wastebasket, one of the littlest, youngest of our boys (probably about 12, supposed to be 14). He was crying as though his little heart would break. He was trying to dry the tears with a soaked paper towel from the washroom. I went to him and touched him on the shoulder and asked him what the matter was. He acted as though I weren't even there and just went on crying into the wastebasket and his pulpy towel. I patted him for a moment and then Mrs. Kee came and talked to him in Navajo. She said a lot of sweet Navajo words to him but he just couldn't stop. She left him for a few minutes, she told me that he was just lonesome and homesick. (I know just how he feels.) Later she went back to him and took him in to some of the bigger boys and told them to take care of him and keep him happy but he sat down and just kept crying. I had given him one of my clean handkerchiefs. He must have cried for a half hour. Finally he stopped. I was just wondering all the time how the little 7, 8, and 9-year-olds over in the other dormitory get along. I'll bet that the dormitory attendants really have a lot of comforting to do.

You, Lillis, better hurry up and get well so that when the apartment is ready you can come up here or you're going to have a 25-year-old boy crying into a soaked paper towel because he is lonesome. Understand?

Give my little boy a big kiss; I wish I could give my wife one myself. Gee I love you. I can't stand it much longer without you. I'll try and write again tomorrow.

Bless you,

George

Lillis joined him in Brigham City around September 1. She was pleased with the spacious apartment which came furnished with appliances and hardwood furniture. They had two bedrooms, a dining room, a large eat-in kitchen, and a screened-in porch with an extra bed. Their entrance hall was large enough that they used it for a library and study room. It cost them $45 per month. They lived on the second level of a four-unit apartment. Their neighbors in the building were the Begay and Shortie families, Navajo staff members; and Glen and Ida Oldroyd. Among the four families there were 11 children living in the building.

There were many cherry trees on campus and Lillis would harvest and bottle the cherries. But the most appealing part of the experience was the social life. The school was so isolated there in Northern Utah that the staff bonded quickly with each other. Most of the staff were young couples like themselves with young children. They held dances, house parties, faculty parties, picnics in the nearby canyons, swimming in a swimming hole at an old cement plant, and gabfests of all kinds. They socialized with the students, inviting them to their apartment to cook fry bread. And there were faculty versus student basketball games. They were also active in the Brigham City Sixth Ward. George sang in the choir, taught the elders quorum, taught in the MIA, and was in the Young Men presidency. They had had many friends there.

Rem was 1 year old at the beginning of the school year. He was an agile child who had learned to walk at 9 months. He was happy and social. He was good at climbing. At 18 months he climbed a ladder to a second-story window on one of the apartment buildings. Lillis was distracted with guests at a party. It could be that she was ashamed of ignoring her baby while attending to guests. The details of her embarrassment are not the sort of thing that she would write down. As the story goes, Lillis called the fire department to get him down. When they recovered Rem, safe and sound, Lillis was hiding in the apartment, either too shaken or too embarrassed to take delivery of her little boy. Ordinarily she was assertive and capable. This was one occasion that revealed a weak spot.

SECOND CHILD

Lillis continued to suffer morning sickness until Dean was born. She finally stopped nursing Rem, fearful that she was starving the new baby. She was angry that the doctor had disputed her symptoms of pregnancy, and she was ashamed that she had allowed herself to lose weight, putting the new baby at risk. As she lay in the delivery room, now under a new doctor's care, and watched the staff put the chloroform mask on her face, she thought, *I can't believe this backwoods hospital is still using chloroform.* The drug had fallen into disfavor in most US hospitals a decade earlier.

Dean was born in the Cooley Memorial Hospital on February 27, 1952; he was 18 months younger than his brother. Lillis was relieved to see he was a healthy baby with a good weight. And yet she continued secretly to observe the differences between Dean and Rem. She wondered whether she had mismanaged her pregnancy. Rem was coordinated, a good pianist, and a high school athlete; Dean was not. It was a private, nagging worry unsupported by evidence that finally, in her old age, she disclosed to her daughter, Leslie.

The other 11 children in the apartment block, mostly the Begay and the Shortie kids, loved to visit the new baby. They would visit every day, make a fuss over him, and ask to hold him.

WASHINGTON TERRACE 1952–1955

The next summer George rode the Greyhound bus south to New Mexico to gather the next class of students from their dispersed desert homesteads and escort them to Brigham City. He brought home some beautiful souvenirs—some kachina dolls and a Navajo rug made with undyed wool in the natural colors of black, brown, gray, beige, and white.

With that task completed he signed a contract in the fall with Weber School District for $3,300 to teach sixth grade. Over his career it appears that he was always trying to maximize his salary. But in this instance there might have been an additional motive: the mission of the Indian school might have rubbed him the wrong way. In later years George commented that the Intermountain Indian School was well intentioned, but the Indians didn't like sending their children so far away for months at a time, and they took issue with the cultural arrogance. George recalled that ballroom dance was one example of a subject the Navajos did not value or understand. Many boys would refuse to dance with their sisters or even distant female relatives (whom they called *sister*). In other classes sometimes the students would put their heads on their desks and simply withdraw. It was very passive and it was difficult to tell if the students were protesting or simply disinterested.

In the fall of 1952 George and Lillis bought a house at Washington Terrace, the same wartime boomtown where Lillis's parents had lived. They borrowed money for the down payment from Lillis's father. It was a white frame house like so many others in the neighborhood. George put up a 5-foot chain link fence to keep the little boys out of traffic. Rem climbed over it and Dean dug a hole under it.

The elementary school was large with 1,000 students. Wheatley Taylor was the principal. One of George's colleagues at the Indian school, Owen Burrell, also signed on that year at Washington Terrace.

The students and staff liked George. Just before he was to start the next school year, the Weber superintendent, Parley Bates, cold-called George and asked him to be the principal at Arsenal Villa. That was on a Sunday, August 30, 1953. Of course he accepted.

Arsenal Villa was in Roy, UT, not far from Washington Terrace. It was the smallest school in the Weber district with 230 students, eight teachers, a janitor, and a school lunch program. George would also teach.

Part Time Work

Money was still tight. They lived from paycheck to paycheck. But Lillis recalled that they were blessed and always had enough. They would both take occasional odd jobs. George ran a youth club at Washington Terrace called the Teen Canteen which provided recreation and dancing. He also worked summers at American Can Company in Ogden on a mind-numbing assembly line making tin cans. On two occasions American Can Co. gave George checks for $20 for his suggestions to make the assembly line more efficient. As a faith-promoting story Lillis recounted how they were blessed to have that job.

In the summer of 1953 Fuller Remington was working in Spokane and he needed his car. George and Lillis drove Fuller's new Kaiser to Spokane and returned to Utah with his older Frazer. The Frazer had mechanical trouble all the way home. The garages in the towns along the way did not have parts to fix it. They reached Boise at midnight.

George had to be in Ogden the following morning to keep his summer job at American Can Co. He was too exhausted to drive and went into the back seat to take a nap. As George slept, Lillis thought how badly they needed that job. They owed money on their down payment on their house. Lillis was pregnant with Leslie and she had not yet acquired a driver's license, but she felt she was entitled to call in a blessing. After all, while living frugally they had always kept faith with their tithing and LDS building fund assessments, even in wards where they knew they would never benefit from the new buildings.

As George slept, Lillis slid into the driver's seat, and prayed that the car would start and keep going. It did start and she drove it through the night to Ogden. All the traffic lights in Ogden were green and she did not stop until she reached home. When the car stopped at their house, it would not start again, and had to be towed to a garage. She regarded that experience as a miracle.

George worked a swing shift and would return home about 1 AM. Several of his teaching colleagues also worked at American Can Co.

Lillis worked a few shifts at St. Benedict's Hospital running the iron lung machines; not all nurses knew how to run the big machines. She also worked a couple of shifts at Dee Hospital in Ogden in 1953—enough time to learn some gossip on some staff members.

THIRD CHILD

Leslie was born at Dee Hospital on November 24, 1953. Dr. Curtis delivered her and George was with Lillis from beginning to end. While sedated and uninhibited, Lillis freely recounted all the hospital gossip she had learned, even identifying and accusing a doctor who was present. Leslie was the seventh grandchild and the only granddaughter on her

Brooks side. George, ever the tease, went to Salt Lake City and told his family that he had another boy.

Lillis spent a few days in the hospital recovering, and George spent a week in bed at his mother's house with a back injury he had sustained while helping to build the new ward meetinghouse at Washington Terrace. For the next 3 weeks the Remingtons cared for Lillis, her new baby Leslie, Rem (3 years old), and Dean (21 months).

When they returned to their house in Ogden they discovered that Mother and Dad Remington, and Lillis's cousin Walter Dow had repainted the inside of their house, washed the rugs, mopped and waxed the floors, cleaned the windows, hung new curtains, installed a carpet, and done some ironing. This generosity of the Remingtons with their children was not uncommon.

POLIO

In the spring Lillis became involved with the polio vaccine trial and helped administer it at schools. Today there is little memory of the scourge that was polio. The iron lung was emblematic of the horror of the disease. It was an early respirator design, an airtight chamber that completely enclosed a patient except for the head. It could force the patient to respire by cycling the pressure differential inside the chamber, all the while whistling and puffing through the gasket around the patient's neck.

The disease was so frightening that when double-blind trials were announced in 1954, Lillis agreed to administer the vaccine in order to secure one for Rem. Today it is difficult to imagine mothers in large numbers volunteering their children for a vaccine control group. Lillis wrote, "I was lucky enough to be called." (Most doses were given to school-age children.)

> Soon after he [Rem] had the dose we heard over the news several children had died from the trial doses. The next day my pediatrician called and told me not to worry. My child's dose had come from Park Davis Lab. Cutter Labs in Calif. had made an error and had given live viruses in their shots instead of the dead viruses.

She told variants of this story for years. In another story she told of watching a 5-year-old child, among the first to be vaccinated, atrophy and waste away.

On July 27, 1954, Rem was taken to Salt Lake to have his tonsils removed. That was another occasion when Mother Remington stepped in to tend. She cared for Rem at her home during his recovery for about a week. She also sewed him a new outfit to wear.

VALUE ADDED

Lillis felt that she and George, had grown and learned during their 3 years at the Terrace because of the variety of responsibilities they took on in quick succession. They took on debt for a house and for a car. They had three children. He had taken a job as principal. At church he was elders quorum president, Sunday school superintendent, and gospel doctrine teacher. She was counselor in the Relief Society, the Primary, and in the Young Women organization. They had paid into ward building funds since the beginning of their marriage. In Washington Terrace, George was in charge of fund raising. This was a task that forced George to be assertive outside of his comfort zone. He also observed which schemes succeeded at raising funds. So many, such as the proverbial bake sale, were an expense of time and effort with no financial benefit. These were days when the church assessed local congregations to pay for the construction of new buildings with money and sweat equity. The church also gave local leaders broad latitude over how to raise funds. In the end, George felt that the local leaders were not discreet enough with the members' personal finances and commitments. He quit his fundraising job to take himself out of that loop.

The little family was growing. It seems there were always diapers on the clothesline flapping in the breeze. George and Lillis were playful with their children. They would take them to the park or to the mountains. They would collect guppies in Mason jars and keep them as long as reasonable in the house. In the winter George would pull the kids around the neighborhood on a sled or on a snow shovel. The neighborhood itself was sandy and dreary with few lawns or trees. The radio was always playing in the morning at breakfast. Davy Crockett was the pop hero of the day. The little boys had coonskin caps. George played ukulele and taught the boys to sing "The Ballad of Davy Crockett." Rem and Dean

Brooks family portrait, c. 1954. George wore a flattop haircut until the 1970s. Lillis wore glasses all her waking hours.

had plastic toy ukuleles of their own. One day one of the boys hit his brother with a toy ukulele and broke it. The brother retaliated in kind and broke his own ukulele. Then Lillis swatted them both with George's ukulele and broke it; she had a propensity to swat the kids with whatever was closest at hand. Nevertheless, George continued to play his ukulele and to teach little songs to his children. From then on his ukulele would rattle and buzz when he played it because it had a crack down the back. A year or two later Lillis did a full penance and bought a new ukulele for George for Christmas.

Salt Lake City

Their last summer at Washington Terrace in 1955 was hectic. George was back at the University of Utah working on a master's degree. Lillis worked full time at LDS Hospital to help pay expenses. They got up each morning at 5 AM to feed the children and to drive them to their Remington grandparents to be tended. At 3:30 PM they would all drive back to Ogden and George would drive to American Can Co. to work the swing shift. Lillis would take care of the countless domestic chores alone. They were trying to purchase a house in Sugar House, but the transaction proved to be complicated, and dragged on through the summer.

They had some money invested in a quasi-US government corporation which managed Washington Terrace. When they tried to withdraw it, they discovered that the corporation's treasurer had embezzled the money and dispersed it in accounts belonging to his relatives, then he died before he could be brought to trial. The money was not recovered. George and Lillis had intended to use that money for a down payment on the new house. It was $1,000 but seemed like a million to them. Quickly, and without being asked, Lillis's Aunt Lucilla loaned them $1,000 and Fuller Remington loaned her another $600.

It was a great relief to move into the new house at 936 Wilson Avenue. Rem was not yet 5 when they moved, Dean was 3, and Leslie was 1. The house was 1,200 square feet with one bath. It cost $15,000—more than they had intended to pay. There was no carpet, so the house echoed a bit when the children would run around. And at night as the children lay in their beds they could hear their father typing his master's thesis, tap, tap, tap, late into the night. Financial problems continued. Immediately after they moved in they had to treat the house for termites; they also replaced the hot water heater and the roof. And the man who bought their house in Washington Terrace defaulted on the loan. But by the end of 1956 they paid their debts to Dad Remington and to Aunt Lucilla who had closed ranks around them in their time of need. Lillis continued to work full time in Salt Lake City and George worked part time as he worked on his master's degree.

The decision to move to Salt Lake City was an obvious one. It would put George nearer the University of Utah as he finished up his MA. It would put Lillis nearer her work at LDS Hospital. It would put them nearer to the Brooks and Remington families. The new job at Garfield Elementary at 1838 South 15th East was just about walking distance from the new house, and it would pay a little more—$3,480. Another part of the decision was to establish the children in a neighborhood and school district before they started school. Salt Lake School District seemed like the better bet than Weber District for career and for education. Just days after his fifth birthday, little Rem began kindergarten, walking the half mile to Forest School, completely unaware that his education was a part of the motivation to move to Sugar House.

XIV

The New 1952 Plymouth

George and Lillis bought a new car in 1952 while living at Washington Terrace, and paid it off in 2 years. They were modest and frugal and did not buy many new cars. Indeed, they did not buy another car for 10 more years, and possibly only two other *new* cars in their lives.

The pale green 1952 Plymouth that they bought now seems unthinkably primitive. Of course no cars had lap belts until the 1960s; the children would just rattle around in the back. They had a child's car seat for baby Leslie which was very insubstantial, a half inch of foam and vinyl over Masonite that unfolded and simply hung over the seat with hooks like umbrella handles so that she could sit high enough to see out the windows—no protection, no restraints, no padding, no support. The Plymouth had a windshield made of two flat panes of glass with a chrome seam down the middle. It did not have power steering and thus the steering wheel was big so as to improve the mechanical advantage of human muscle. When the car was stopped it was very difficult to turn the wheels. It had drum brakes front and rear—again, no power assist. It had six cylinders in a straight line, three forward gears with a manual shifter on the steering column; the dashboard was steel; the numbers on the speedometer were in the Art Deco style; the car had bench seats both front and back to seat six people comfortably. The car seemed to be cavernous, like a cathedral. A child could sleep on the shelf in the back window, and they often did at drive-in movie theaters. A child could also sleep on the floor if the floor were built up a bit with blankets to cover the hump in the middle where the driveshaft ran—all cars were rear-wheel drive.

SINGING

The car did not have a radio. Some cars did but radios were an optional expense. Everything was AM—no one broadcasted or received FM. Car radios of that vintage had vacuum tubes, so a radio would take a while to warm up before it would actually play. That is significant because it hints at so many other small cultural shifts. If a family could not listen to the radio in the car they would sing together on long trips. Sometimes Lillis would make requests—"George, sing a hymn." One of her favorite hymns was "A Poor Wayfaring Man of Grief" which had many verses. George knew them all. He seemed to have an endless repertoire. He knew a lot of silly songs, some lost in the folk tradition. One example verse of an amusing, maudlin ballad went like this:

> 'Twas Saturday night in the corner saloon
> The miners came in with their gold.
> And Father blows in all his wages for gin.
> While Nellie blows home in the cold.
> The doors swing in, the doors swing out
> While some pass in and others pass out.

This lengthy ballad tells of a drunken father and a destitute family and the heroic but futile efforts of daughter Nellie to bring home her father and his money.

Singing tradition was not unique to the Brooks family. Other families also sang, though the repertoires may have varied. That being said, George did have a good voice and good pitch by any measure. He attributed that to his Welsh heritage. He was a baritone with a good range.

Back to the topic of the car: Of course, no cars had air conditioning. On long trips, particularly in the desert west, motorists often carried a water bag. This was a bag that would seep water through all sides so that it was always a little damp, and the surface evaporation would keep the drinking water cool. The bag hung on the bumper of the car with a rope so that it was in the wind as the car moved. When motorists would stopped for a drink of cool water in the middle of nowhere, it was always a little counterintuitive to drink out of the bag, now encrusted with dead bugs and highway debris.

The Brookses were unwittingly part of the ascending automobile culture. They would take the car to drive-in root beer stands. Fast food was served through the window and consumed in the parking lot. They traveled to Yellowstone, sometimes washing and picnicking by the roadside. They visited relatives in California or St. George. They vacationed in Denver.

The interstate highway system did not come to Salt Lake City until the 1960s. The old highways each had a special mystique—not just Route 66. US 40 for example, went across country. It was Colfax Avenue in Denver, crossed the treacherous Rabbit Ears Pass, went through Lillis's hometown of Vernal, it was 21st South in Salt Lake City, it crossed the Salt Flats, went over the Donner Pass, and on to San Francisco. US Route 89 followed the Wasatch Front and passed through most of the Mormon settlements in Utah. It was State Street in Salt Lake City and Main Street or Center Street in many of the Utah hamlets.

In 1962, George bought a new Studebaker Lark and they became a two-car family—a common term to describe the increasing wealth of the middle class. The Lark had a transistor radio, a quick V8, George paid extra for the optional lap belts, and there were very rudimentary cup holders on the door of the glove compartment (which George called "the gin bin"). With the Lark, Lillis refused to drive the Plymouth any longer, saying it was too difficult for her; though really, the two cars had very similar controls. They both had three manual forward gears with the shifter on the steering column. The Plymouth was still around when Rem was learning to drive in 1966; that was the car he was trusted with.

In its final days the Plymouth left the family stranded on several occasions with trivial problems. Cars of that generation seemed to be easy to fix, but they needed frequent and routine maintenance. They needed ignition components replaced or adjusted, such as distributor caps and rotors, wires, points, and ignition timing—components not even found in modern cars. They needed to be greased and have their bearings packed. Even upholstery had to be replaced or repaired. In September of 1967 the Plymouth was still drivable. George drove it to the scrapyard and sold it for $9. At that time the clutch was worn and the floor was partially rusted through so that the road was visible as it passed underfoot. Yet it was beautiful to look at, a dawdling outdated homage to the modernism of the early century.

XV

The House on Wilson Avenue
1955–1959

Rem was a great help getting the family acquainted with their new neighbors. His birthday was coming up and his parents had promised to take him to a movie—*Fantasia*. He went out in the neighborhood and invited all the kids to go to the movie with him. Soon the neighborhood parents were over at the Brooks house asking if this were true. Either because George was a good sport, or maybe because Lillis always found it difficult to back down, they put on a good face and took everyone to the movie. Seat belts were not an issue in those days and all the kids—eight or so—crowded into the car.

HOUSE AND NEIGHBORS

Lillis felt that the day would come when they would outgrow the house and would move again, probably when the kids were entering high school. But as Robert Frost pointed out, way leads on to way. They ended up staying put for 30 years.

Though the house was small (about 1,100 square feet plus an unfinished basement), it had a beauty and quality that Lillis appreciated. It had a canvas ceiling in the formal rooms and hardwood floors. It had a gothic arch between the living room and dining room, and repeated in the doorway to the study, and in the built-in bookcases flanking the

fireplace. It had deep crown molding in those three rooms. It had beautiful hardware, door knobs, chandeliers, and bath fixtures. The fireplace had
an onyx facade. There was a covered patio in the back yard, freestanding,
supported with Tuscan pillars, and enclosed with lattice work. It matched
the lattice fences and gates and their repeating arches and columns. The
builder-owner, Mr. Arnold Clawson, and his new bride were the first
occupants of the house. The many refined details can most certainly be
attributed to his emotional involvement in the construction of the house.

For the kids, the most important amenity was the irrigation ditch
passing right in front of the house. Water rights dating to pioneer times
are still a peculiarity of Utah law; someone downstream in central Salt
Lake City owned some water rights and their water would flow every
Monday from early morning until noon during growing season. The kids
would alert each other on Mondays with a shout: "The ditch is running."
They would come out with boats and buckets and sometimes garbage can
lids to dam the water and flood the street.

The neighbors were an eccentric collection. Across the street lived the
Czerny family of German refugees; the father had served in the German
army in World War II. He played the violin, sometimes practicing outdoors on summer evenings. The Andersons lived next door to them. Ted
Anderson was a music teacher, a trumpet player, and a member of the
Mormon Tabernacle Choir. He also could be heard practicing. The man
next door was a butcher who would butcher stacks of deer in his garage
during hunting season, and the smell of warm, newly-killed deer filled
the air over several days in October and November. The church assigned
him to be a home teacher to the Brooks family. He was likely an alcoholic
and was either permanently impaired or drunk when he would make his
monthly visits. His wife, Grace, was Lillis's visiting teaching partner for
years. The Roothoff family lived directly across the street. The father, Dirk,
raced pigeons and raised them in his back yard. He exercised them in the
evenings, letting them fly in circles around the neighborhood; he would
whistle to call them home. A couple of neighbors owned or rented water
rights and they had big gardens. There were several schoolteachers in the
neighborhood, a school custodian, a house painter, a couple of accountants, a railroad superintendent, a grocer, a banker, an engineer, a steel
worker, and a chemist. Most were Mormons and attended the same ward.

There were many children and, as the years passed, they spent a lot of time together at church, at school, and playing in each other's yards and houses. Neighborhood children had access to each other's basements, garages, and even parents' bedrooms. On summer days children would stand on a neighbor's porch and shout to call out their friends to play.

Lillis and George furnished their house not too quickly, but as quickly and as nicely as their budget would allow. Lillis special-ordered the local construction of a sofa for the living room. She ordered the fabric from Italy but it was lost when the *Andrea Doria* sank in July of 1956, and had to be reordered. That gives a sense of her attention to such details. Her tastes leaned toward formal styles.

George received his Masters of Arts degree in education administration in August 1956. Commencement was held on the lawn in front of the Park Building and the children attended. The long hours of typing late into the night had paid off.

LEON RIGGS

There are no diaries or letters from 1957, but that was probably the year that Leon Riggs came to live at the Brooks home. Judging by the few undated snapshots of him, he was about 8 years old, Rem was not yet 7, Dean about 5, and Leslie about 3. Leon came with the Indian Placement program, a Mormon-sponsored program to expose Navajo children to English, city life, and schools.

The Brooks home was small, but a place was found in a drawer in the hall for his clothes. There were only two upstairs rooms which could be used for bedrooms. All the children slept in one. Prior to Leon, the Brooks children would bathe together. When Leon came Leslie started to bathe alone and Leon would bathe with Rem and Dean.

He went to school with Rem, and they became chums, but he was indifferent if not a little mean to Dean. It is not clear why he left the Brooks home—maybe because Lillis was pregnant, maybe because he did not get along with Dean. In any case, he went to live with another family and Lillis worried that he was not well cared for there. At the end of his term he went home and the family never saw him again.

FRICTION WITH IN-LAWS

One of the advantages of living in Sugar House was that George and Lillis lived within walking distance of their parents. But Lillis—and to a lesser extent, George—continued to suffer little insults from Winnifred and Samuel Brooks.

George and Lillis made a habit of visiting the Brooks parents on Sundays between church meetings. (Sunday school was in the morning; sacrament meeting was in the evening.) On one such occasion they arrived to find a photographer and the extended family present in their Sunday clothes. Beverly's children were in their church clothes, but Lillis's children had already changed into play clothes. It was hard to tell which members of the family were in on the conspiracy. So Lillis had the choice either to pose with the family, or refuse to pose. That photograph survives as the only portrait of the extended family. On first glance the picture may not raise an eyebrow, but it is the kind of thing that would annoy any mother.

Samuel and Winnifred gave George the family piano as a college graduation gift in 1951, then asked for it back in 1957. Without protest George said, "Come and get it." Family members came to the house, picked up the piano, and delivered it to Beverly's house.

One Sunday George and Lillis skipped sacrament meeting and went to visit the Brooks parents early, only to discover they were having a dinner party with George's sisters and brother and their families. They all attempted to pretend that they were not actually eating together.

Once Winnifred asked George to prune her apple tree. Then Samuel came home from work and scolded George for cutting a branch off the tree.

When Lillis's niece Lyn Remington died, Winnifred called her on the phone and accused her of preventing Beverly from attending the funeral. Beverly later called Lillis to apologize for her mother's "misunderstanding."

At this late date, with so few primary sources surviving, it is completely mystifying to read Lillis's and George's diaries and wonder about Winnifred's and Samuel's motives. Lillis's diary entries are short and dispassionate, side by side with comments on the weather and her daily list of chores. Everyone acknowledged that friction existed. The Remington parents and the Brooks parents attended the same ward and so Lillis's younger brothers and sister would have a clear memory of Samuel and Winnifred. But the Remingtons were never inclined to speak ill of the

Brookses. When pressed for a comment late in life, Lillis's sister Cleo responded succinctly, "Samuel was friendly enough. I never thought much of Winnifred; she was arrogant, and insulting." Lillis was never inclined to overlook insults.

NEW BABY, 1957

The fourth child, Nyman, was born at LDS Hospital, November 2, 1957. He was delivered by M. S. Sanders. Nyman weighed 9 pounds 4 ounces and was 23 inches long. Even as an adult he continued to be the tallest among the Brookses. He was named after Emil Nyman, the principal at Garfield Elementary School where George worked. Emil Nyman lived only two blocks away and visited often, bringing little gifts for his namesake. George worked at Garfield as a sixth-grade teacher of arithmetic and physical education for three school years between the fall of 1955 and the spring of 1958. Soon after, Mr. Nyman retired and became a lecturer at Westminster College. In retrospect, Mr. Nyman was a good choice to lend his name to the new baby. He was polite, intelligent, generous, and gentle. Baby Nyman was similar in these ways. He was also sensitive to loud noises and did not like to play with noisy toys; pots and pans startled him. He was coordinated and walked early. He was social and not afraid to meet people. And he was handsome.

Lillis quit her job at LDS Hospital in 1957 to care for her new baby. The money she had earned prior to quitting had put the family ahead. They had repaid the debts to her father and aunt which they had incurred with the emergency repairs to the house. They had started to furnish the house, including buying a new piano, carpet, and a new kitchen range. And George had paid for his schooling.

PROMOTION TO PRINCIPAL, 1958

After 3 years teaching at Garfield, and after earning a degree in education administration, George started looking around for advancement. He had also been teaching summer school, which indicates that money may have been an issue. He applied for and accepted an offer to teach in San Jose, California, for the fall of 1958. That job offered $1,500 more annually. By the spring of 1958 the house was up for sale and his intentions were common knowledge.

In April 1958, George received a note from the superintendent of schools, M. Lynn Bennion, congratulating him on his performance evaluation. In June he received another note from Superintendent Bennion noting that George had failed to sign a contract for the fall of 1958; Bennion invited George to talk personally about an administrative position with the Salt Lake system. George was offered the position of principal at Jackson Elementary at 750 West 2nd North, for $5,862 annually. This threw George and Lillis into a quandary. George had also received mail from some of the parents of students at Garfield, expressing regret that he was leaving the Salt Lake district. He finally accepted the principal job in Salt Lake, took the house off the market, and withdrew from the position in San Jose.

The family took a summer vacation to the Bay Area in August. George and Lillis may have been curious to see what they were missing. Lillis's brother Earl was a teacher living in San Leandro, California. He and his wife, Marge, turned out to be wonderful tour guides. They visited all around the Bay Area, the great universities, parks, missions, museums, and historical sites. They drove home through Yosemite over Tioga Pass and through Virginia City. They were happy to get home and pleased in the end with their decision to remain in Salt Lake. Nyman, not quite a year old, stayed with his Grandmother Remington and missed that trip.

PUTTING DOWN ROOTS

Lillis and George were always involved in the church and community. They became more active in Sugar House. Like so many Mormons they took on a variety of church tasks, teaching assignments, and even leadership positions. Here is an attempt to characterize their church activity and other social involvement:

There were three church meetings on Sundays: Priesthood meeting for men and boys of 12 years and older, lasted about 90 minutes, followed by a short break to allow men to go home and accompany their families to Sunday school. Sunday school lasted 90 minutes. There was a midday break, and in the afternoon, sacrament meeting would last another 90 minutes. There could also be choir practice and a variety of leadership meetings on Sundays. Priesthood meeting and Sunday school each required a staff of teachers. Sacrament meeting had two or three assigned speakers chosen from the congregation. One day in mid-week the women's auxiliary—Relief Society—would meet, as would Primary for children under 12 years old, and the Mutual Improvement Association (also known as Mutual or MIA) for the youth or Boy Scouts. These meetings were staffed with teachers from the congregation.

Lillis always served as a visiting teacher, a Relief Society assignment to visit a few women and instruct them in their homes. Additionally, she always had a position teaching children in Sunday school, primary, or MIA. When her boys were in Boy Scouts she held positions in that organization. Sometimes she served in the presidency of these organizations.

Lillis was active in community organizations. From the beginning, she was a member of the Aurora Club—a social and charitable club—and sometimes held leadership or committee positions. That club met monthly with occasional socials. She was a member of the Salt Lake Council of Women which promoted issues of community welfare; and on the Utah Legislative Council—a lobbying group for women's issues. She served a term as vice president of the Literary Art Guild which hosted lectures. She was active in the LDS Hospital Nurses Alumni Association. She was very active in the PTA and served as PTA Legislative Chairman while her children were at Forest Elementary.

It is not necessary to chronicle every detail of her social, church, or civic engagement. It is enough to say she felt a social obligation and contributed the time and effort she could, often while working 2 days a week at LDS Hospital. Participation in organizations maybe was not so unusual in her generation.

George was similarly engaged with the professional organizations of Phi Delta Kappa and Delta Phi, and the public schools Administrators Group. He led special committees to redesign report cards and for educational TV programming. Of course there were also church callings.

They enrolled in a lecture series associated with Brigham Young University and they participated in two study groups; each met monthly. One group was composed of friends they made while living at Stadium Village. The other group was made up of eight married couples with roots in Lincoln Ward. This second group met for 30 years and usually followed a study outline suggested by the Ford Foundation or the Great Books. These close, lifelong friends were Howard and Arda Leatham, Norman and Nelda Miller, Sterling and Colleen Workman, Albert and

Joanne Hibberd, Jesse and Audrey Davis, Don and Rayola Larson, and Rex and Jacqueline Moulton.

FAMILY ROUTINE

Lillis and George enrolled the children in music lessons in the summer after their third grade year. Rem started trumpet, piano lessons, and tap dance. The tap dance did not take, but was handy for ridiculing him later in life. When Dean was 9 he started on clarinet and piano. Leslie started on flute, piano, and ballet. And finally, Nyman took viola lessons. Orchestra classes were part of the school curriculum; Rem, Dean, and Leslie continued practicing music with the school system into high school. Rem and Leslie also continued private piano lessons into high school and were quite competent in the end. And Rem played French horn in the All-City orchestra when he was 14. Lillis frequently noted in her diary that she drove kids to their weekly music lessons or to performances.

When Rem and Dean were about 9 and 8 they also took swimming lessons at the YWCA. Lillis taught them to ride the bus and let them commute on their own. She would not worry so much about their physical safety riding the bus alone, but would fret about them losing their bus fare. She would tie their nickels in a handkerchief, reasoning that money in a handkerchief would be harder to lose.

She was also afraid that her children's lives might appear to be too advantaged, and she instructed them that they should never so much as mention that they were enrolled in music or swimming lessons; but they could respond truthfully if questioned. Somewhere between modesty and superstition she was wary of too much success.

The kids got a dog in 1959—Spooky—the first in a series of unfortunate pets. Spooky quickly died of distemper while still a puppy, even though he had received his shots. It was so sad to watch a puppy get sick and die.

George taught arithmetic at summer school even after he was a principal. His duties as principal encroached into summer vacation; he had to do inventories and prepare classrooms for the next school year. The Brooks children were often pressed into service, moving furniture and heavy stacks of books. But even principals had some time off in the summers, and George and Lillis would take the family on short summer vacation trips.

George cooked breakfast on Saturdays as a matter of routine. Some of his breakfasts were experimental. For example, he would bake spam or fruit or corn or other ingredients into waffles. Sometimes he would color them with food coloring. He would make syrup with 2 parts sugar, 1 part water, and a capful of maple extract. George was always off on Saturdays, and also had free time on weekdays during the summer.

In the summers the children would be enrolled in short classes such as tennis or ukulele. Lillis cultivated the practice of reading to her children, particularly in the summers of these first years on Wilson Avenue. Sometimes she would read to the children as a group, sometimes individually. She started with the Bible, but would also read magazine articles and novels. The family attended the monthly children's plays at Pioneer Memorial Theatre from the time it opened in 1962 through 1966; by then Rem was in high school and the children were outgrowing it. They attended the children's concerts of the Utah Symphony beginning in 1959, which were performed in the Tabernacle. The conductor, Maurice Abravanel, would give short interpretive lectures between the musical selections. George served as a volunteer usher and would always save seats for his children in the balcony just above the orchestra. Sometimes they would visit the Utah Museum of Fine Arts or *Hudnut* as Lillis called it, after the donor, Winifred Hudnut. It was on the campus of the University of Utah. These were things that Lillis and George enjoyed and they also believed were important exposures for their children.

But it wasn't all high culture. They took the kids to Fort Douglas to play on an old airplane which was preserved as a monument. They frequented a grove of trees on the University of Utah campus behind the old library or George Thomas building on 14th East. They played in Lindsay Gardens on the Avenues or in the Peace Garden in Jordan Park. They hiked Ensign Peak or did target practice at the police shooting range at the foot of the peak. They played on the grounds of the capitol. There were many picnics and short hikes in the canyons. They played at Fairmont Park, fed the ducks, or caught polliwogs in the stream. There was a cold-water spring in the park (now buried under Interstate 80) where the children would float boats. Dean had a wind-up submarine which would navigate in circles, and dive and surface. George would set its rudder and control surfaces and let it go which would fill Dean with anxiety. George would also take the kids swimming at the pool in the park. The boys would change clothes in a huge open room with benches along the four walls. They would put their clothes in a mesh bag and give it to a coat check attendant. The lavatory was not much more than a steel trough along the wall which served as a urinal for several men and boys at the same moment. It all seemed so undignified and exposed. But it was OK while George was there. He wore the funniest swim trunks—baggy, red, with pictures of yellow fishes. And he carried his things in a duffel bag which he had fashioned out of the leg of some worn-out trousers.

In 1959 the family traveled to Lava Hot Springs, Idaho. Nyman was 20 months old; this was his first trip. He was a good traveler and enjoyed playing in the pool and in the park. The trip only lasted a day or two; after all, the children were young.

On this particular occasion Lillis had to return quickly to Salt Lake City to throw an engagement party for Helen Sanford who was marrying Lillis's brother Newell. There were 20 guests including Newell's aunts and cousins. The party required a delicate touch; Newell's divorced wife, Winnifred Kennard, was a lifelong friend of the Remington family, and mother of Newell's three sons. Helen thanked Lillis in a note dated July 22:

Dear Lillis,

Your party of last Saturday was without doubt one of the nicest I have ever attended. The color scheme, the flowers, the tables—all were beautiful. The food was so good. But the nicest part of it all was the kindness of you to do it.

I sincerely appreciate the way you and the rest of your family have treated me. I know now you have accepted me because of Newell. I hope soon it will be for myself also.

Thank you again for the opportunity of meeting your aunts (and cousins). And also the butter dish. It shall be used!!!

Love,

Helen

This note is illustrative of Lillis's special aptitude for entertaining. She collected china, crystal, silver, and linen. She would spend hours making favors and table centerpieces appropriate for the season or for the occasion. She was careful to present food attractively and on correct serving pieces. These things, along with dining etiquette, were important to her even as they were ignored by her children.

That summer Earl brought his family to Salt Lake City from California. The Remington cousins and in-laws hiked to Timpanogos Cave and picnicked together. And it seemed that there was a pajama party every night at one house or another with kids sleeping on the floor in sleeping bags. Even without Earl, Salt Lake City cousins had frequent sleepovers.

The children were young, but there was a sense that the parents also were still very young.

XVI

Reading to Children

George and Lillis easily had 1,000 books in the house as their children were growing up in the 1950s and 1960s. Additionally at various times they had subscriptions to *National Geographic, Harpers, American Heritage, Smithsonian, Time, Look, Life*; children's magazines such as *Highlights for Children, National Scholastic, Weekly Reader, Boys Life*; professional magazines, church publications, and the daily newspaper. Most of their books were stamped with a rubber stamp "From the library of George Thomas and Lillis Remington Brooks." Most books also had a little gold monogram on the spine—a ligatured *G* and *L*. They were impatient with people who borrowed and neglected to return their books. It was quite an investment and it was more than what most people had. The library included references such as atlases, dictionaries, an *Encyclopedia Americana* and a children's encyclopedia. They had histories such as the *Personal Memoirs* of Ulysses S. Grant, the *Outline of History* by H. G. Wells, *The Echo of Greece* by Edith Hamilton, *Inside Russia Today* by John Gunther, *The Discovery and Conquest of Mexico* by Bernal Diaz. They collected literature, sometimes complete works, such as O. Henry, Bennett Cerf, Tennyson, Shelley, and of course Shakespeare. Once Lillis gave George a paperback book for his birthday—*The Age of Reason* by Thomas Paine. Once Harvey Hirschi asked George when he found time to read—a fair question given the many demands on his time. George said, "I read while waiting for my turn to use the bathroom."

George, and more often, Lillis, read to the children. They read from earliest childhood until the children were grown and perfectly capable of reading to themselves. As Rem got a little older, sometimes Lillis would ask him to take a turn reading a paragraph or chapter to the others. Particularly in summer there was a set time to sit with her and listen to her read. As often as not she would read from the scriptures, or from a children's adaptation of scripture stories. But they also read novels. George read Robert Louis Stevenson's *Kidnapped* to Dean alone. Lillis read Charlotte Brontë's *Jane Eyre* to Leslie when she was 12 years old. George was more likely to read something *ad hoc* that he had recently found interesting. There was an occasion, for example, when he read to the children from Edward Gibbon's *The Decline and Fall of the Roman Empire*, which he was reading for his study group: "The recruits and young soldiers were constantly trained both in the morning and in the evening . . . and the effusion of blood was the only circumstance which distinguished a field of battle from a field of exercise." Of course the quality of writing and the drama of these passages would stick in a child's memory. He did not have the entire *Decline and Fall*; he had only the portion which was included in his *Great Books*. In addition he had several boxed sets of paperbacks from the same *Great Books* series which he followed in his study group.

On another occasion he read a poem, "The Steam Shovel," by Eunice Tietjens:

> But he, the monster, swings his load around—
> Weightless it seems as air.
> His mammoth jaw
> Drops widely open with a rasping sound,
> And all the red earth vomits from his maw.

Almost every Christmas George found time to gather the children and read *The Story of the Other Wise Man*, by Henry van Dyke—a tradition that continued even after his children were married. It is a sentimental story with florid language. ("'. . . I am waiting to give this jewel to the prudent captain who will leave me in peace.' He showed the ruby glistening in the hollow of his hand like a great drop of blood.") George had several tattered editions of this small book; one was marked up to help him abbreviate the readings so that his audience would not lose interest.

Literacy extended to writing. Many people of that generation wrote letters; after all, long-distance phone calls were expensive. So when Rem went away for a mere week to YMCA summer camp, his kit included a little portfolio with stamps, envelopes, stationery, and a pen. He was expected to write home every day, even though he would almost certainly return home before his last letters would arrive. To his credit he did write and told the family of the camp culture, kitchen duty, and the funny songs that they sang. That was 1961; he was barely 11 years old.

XVII

The Family Grows Up
1960–1963

LILLIS'S DIARIES

Scrapbooks, a few letters, and recollections provide the storyline for the 1950s. Lillis's diaries began January 1, 1961. To be sure, the pages of Lillis's diaries were each written within the narrow scope of a single day—to be remembered for a while and then to recede toward some vanishing point. But when taken together as one would read a novel, a very different perspective emerges. The days and their tasks form like waves of greater purpose to flow over friends and community and children and grandchildren. The adults were aware of life's components, the laundry, shopping, dinner parties, music lessons, civic meetings, doctor appointments. But to paraphrase Wordsworth, the children, self-absorbed in their newborn bliss, behold not whence it flows.

In April of 1960 the family took a trip to southern Utah. They toured Zion and Bryce National Parks, the Glen Canyon Dam which was under construction, and Hoover Dam. (George called it "Boulder Dam," quipping that Hoover was not worth a dam.)

1960 was an election year. George and Lillis were caught up in the optimism and charisma of the John Kennedy candidacy. George served as a delegate for the state convention to support Kennedy and he took the children to the conventions and rallies. He also enlisted the children to hand out handbills door to door. Lillis served as a poll judge.

Emil Nyman ran for the state House of Representatives, as did Clarence "Clarey" Neslen, who was the husband of George's secretary, Leone; the kids helped campaign for them as well. Both were Democrats; both won in the primaries and lost in the general election.

A Terrible Nightmare, 1961

In 1961 Lillis was still worried about her sister Cleo and her father and their recent surgeries. About March 1, Lyn Remington, Lillis's niece, was diagnosed with leukemia. Lyn died a week later; she was 1 year old. Rem and Dean were pallbearers. Michelle "Mickey" Hammond also died of leukemia in August. She was the 3-year-old daughter of Lillis's cousin Carmel. Mickey's funeral was held while Newell was in the hospital with cancer.

Newell had been studying at Yale on fellowship when he became ill. His illness came on quickly and progressed quickly. Lillis first noted his illness in May, then wrote in her diary about his decline a few times each week. Newell had good days and bad. He received X-ray therapy and sometimes reported pain in his pelvis, spine, lung, or shoulder. George noted in the diary in July that Newell was dying. H. D. Lowery, Don Remington's father-in-law, offered to pay for Newell's flight home, then later he offered to pay for a private plane. The Remington family collected and sent $645 to Newell and Helen. They returned to Salt Lake City on a commercial jet airliner on August 5.

George's father, Samuel, was hospitalized for a month at the Veterans Hospital at this same time—from July 4 through August 8—with a heart attack; and George's mother, Winnifred, was bedridden with gout.

Lillis continued to chronicle Newell's stays at the Veterans Hospital, his pain and atrophy, episodes of sedation, a treatment of nitro-mustard gas, and his visitors. Relatives and friends from St. George and Vernal came to visit him.

Newell lost so much weight that once while receiving visitors he let his hand hang over the side of his bed and his ring slipped off his finger onto the floor.

Newell resumed his teaching job at South High when school opened August 30, but he taught only 2 days. He died October 22, 1961 at the age of 39.

Lillis called it a terrible nightmare. It was no worse than the typical agony of mortality. But it was Lillis's personal agony. Newell had been her

Newell about 31 years old. He died at age 39.

closest friend, accomplice, and confidant from birth. They had played and grown up together at the Rector mining camp like Jem and Scout. They had attended classes together and shared friends all through school. To paraphrase Emerson, she loved him as herself, as a self of purer clay; his parting dimmed the day, stealing grace from all alive. She had come home crying from the hospital visits. She had listened to him speculate about death. She had relived the collapse of his first marriage. She lamented the lost promise of his intellect and of his gentility. And then she moved on, a wife and mother—and now, the older sister.

All the while her staccato diary was interleaved with the smaller issues of 1961. The US broke diplomatic relations with Cuba. East Berlin was walled in. Lillis bottled 280 quarts of fruit and tomatoes that fall. She bought a puppy for Dean while Newell was ill, but gave it away 6 weeks later because she did not have the patience to train it or care for it. The family visited Vernal, and watched cement being poured to build Flaming Gorge Dam. The children were persuaded to collect money for UNICEF on Halloween instead of candy. George and the boys thinned sugar beets at the stake farm. Dean was not doing well in school; Lillis called meetings with his teachers, the principal, and social workers. She finally had him tested. Though test results vindicated his intellect, the teachers continued to neglect and mistreat him.

At the end of the year Lillis summed things up:

> We take time to pause and consider our many, many blessings: our good health, our wonderful family and our choice friends, our interesting and stimulating work, our fine neighbors, our great country and outstanding leaders, our testimony of the truthfulness of the gospel and our faith in the future.

THE NEW BISHOP, 1962

George was called to be bishop in January 1962. He was 35 years old. That was when the family installed a private telephone line; they had been using a party line. The immense demands of the new calling were a surprise for George and the family.

Within 2 weeks, on February 6, a neighbor across the street, Helene Czerny, died leaving young children. George spoke at the funeral.

Thereafter, Lillis often prepared meals or special treats for the Czerny children and watched them out of the corner of her eye. It turned out that there were some 70 widows living in Richards II Ward, some of whom were indigent or shut in. A lot of people depended on George not just for kindness and spiritual support, but for general welfare and navigating everyday life, grief, and child care. Over the years, a ward member would die about every month, and sometimes as many as four in a month. It was not just old women, but breadwinners, returned missionaries, and infant children of young parents also died on his watch.

The telephone would ring constantly in the evenings, and sometimes would wake him after he had gone to bed.

Sometimes when people are put in new and difficult roles they succeed merely by showing up and following rote formula. George developed some habitual disciplines and fenced off blocks of time to help him through the recurring tasks of his new calling. He often carried a little portfolio or clipboard, and while sitting in a waiting room or waiting for the curtain to go up at a play, he would write letters to missionaries or jot down thoughts for the next funeral. Time was in short supply and never wasted.

Sometimes a challenging role requires a departure from rote formula, or even a bit of enlightenment. This was the case with his next assignment: to build a new ward meetinghouse. In their married life, George and Lillis had been involved to one degree or another with five ward building projects, and had found them all distasteful. There were two Richards wards meeting in the same building. George was the younger and the junior of the two bishops. Nevertheless, he was assigned to be the lead in contract management and fundraising.

In those days a congregation was to raise half the cost of a new building, so Richards I and Richards II Wards would each have to raise 25% in money or labor. Also, buildings would not be dedicated until the debt was fully paid on the building. ("Dedication" could be viewed as a rite of acceptance of the building by the church, though the title and liability for debt would never be in doubt.) The building that was built in Washington Terrace, as an example, carried debt and was not dedicated even 5 years after it was completed.

George and Lillis had been fatigued by their experiences with previous building funds which had relied on cookie sales and collecting old newspapers. George took a different approach to fundraising. He asked people for small but unflagging periodic donations. He periodically interviewed each household in the neighborhood, if they would hear him—both Mormons and non-Mormons. He explained the benefits and costs of the building in some detail. When acceptable he would also discuss with these individuals their relative capacity to donate either money or labor. Richards II Ward held only one "fundraiser." That was a joint Richards I and Richards II kick-off banquet, which raised very little money. These funding interviews are mentioned frequently in Lillis's diaries as George continued to hold them several years in a row.

Surprisingly, many non-Mormon neighbors contributed money and labor. More surprisingly, the ward met its assessment by the time the building was completed. As suggested before, the neighborhood was not wealthy. There were many widows, and many of the wage earners were blue-collar with young families.

The building plan was announced on Sunday, June 3, 1961, 4 months after he was assigned to be bishop. Fundraising began immediately though the actual demolition and rebuilding did not begin until 1966.

SAMUEL BROOKS DIES, 1962

Lillis was still in mourning over Newell when she was confronted with new distress and fear. Her mother, Edith, got sick in March 1962 with adhesions, probably a result of her 1942 bowel obstruction. She also suffered a pelvic abscess. She was in the hospital from March 17 to April 20 during which time she also had a cholecystectomy. When she was released, Lillis visited her at home every day to administer penicillin shots. Lillis wrote in her diary on April 27, 1962, that she quarreled with her father because he wanted Lillis to sign a document to release Edith's savings account to him, which Lillis refused to do. This indicates that Edith was too sick to sign for herself or that Fuller thought her death was imminent. But Edith survived.

Late in the year George's father suffered another heart attack. Samuel was hospitalized for 8 days at the Veterans Hospital. He was of a good weight and active, so his death on October 23, 1962, surprised the family. It was a year and a day after Newell's death. Samuel was 76 years old. George wrote the obituary. He had visited his father a couple of times,

The carefully groomed family, c. 1962. Front: George, Leslie, Lillis. Back: G. Remington, Dean, Nyman. All eyes look impassively and slightly to the right of the camera. Only George smiles. Lillis has removed her glasses. Dean is suffering a bout with cold sores.

but regretted that he had not taken flowers. Nothing is quite so final as the death of a parent.

Still, there were a lot of flowers, if not in his hospital room, at least at the funeral. Samuel was not wealthy or influential but he managed to collect a lot of friends and acquaintances. That was reflected in a well-attended funeral. One floral arrangement in the shape of a block letter *D* came from Dixie College; Samuel had been the first student to enroll there. Lillis helped Winnifred write thank-you notes for the many flowers after the funeral. The task wore her down a bit and she complained of pain in her arm and back for the next few days and she started wearing a supportive corset. She occasionally complained throughout her life of pain in her back and arm, and her diary is full of other things that could have aggravated a chronic weakness—canning fruit, incessant housework, lifting patients at the hospital. A few days later she noted in her diary that Eleanor Roosevelt had died.

FAMILY VACATIONS, 1962

The family took three short vacations in 1962, to Disneyland, Denver, and to a mountain cabin. Given the other things that were going on that year it is remarkable that they were able to get away at all.

They spent a couple of nights in a cabin above Midway, Utah, with Don and Marilyn and family. The cabin belonged to one of Marilyn Remington's relatives. They spent leisurely days hiking, picnicking, and swimming at the nearby Homestead resort. It is funny how such little things can loom large in memory. This is one vacation that Lillis looked back on and frequently mentioned. It reinforced an enduring and special relationship between Lillis and her brother Don who was 7 years younger. They went again to that cabin in 1964, and took many other trips together throughout their lives.

NYMAN STARTS SCHOOL, 1963

Lillis fell into a happy pattern in the 1963–1964 school. Nyman's birthday was in November and so he was almost 6 years old when he began kindergarten that fall. He attended a half day in the mornings, then he would walk the half mile home at noon, and the two of them would have lunch together, then read together, then take a nap. It was a great pleasure for Lillis to spend time this way with her youngest child. Often he would then follow her around as she completed her errands and appointments. On one such day she bought him a toy gun and asked him if that type of gun was what he had had in mind. Typical of his gentle and precocious conversation, he said, "No, this isn't what I had in mind, but it will satisfy me." Lillis usually worked at the hospital on Fridays and on those days Nyman would walk to Grandmother Remington's house, which was only about two blocks from the school.

The kitchen at the Brooks home had a small dining nook; it was really too small for a family of six to eat together. George ordered a specially-made table to fit in that nook and seat four comfortably. To eat together in those close quarters Nyman was relegated to sitting by himself at a cutting board which could be pulled out like a drawer from the counter. The last child to the table would sit at the corner of the table. And that's how they all fit in the little dining area. Everyone was facing each other, except Nyman who sat behind and a little above George on a kitchen stepstool. When Nyman wanted to contribute to the conversation at the table, he would reach out and turn George's head to face him.

George would cut the boys' hair. In January of 1964 he cut Nyman's hair very short, probably because short was the easiest thing to do. Nyman, 6 years old, cried and cried because he was "bald." George finally bought him a creampuff to calm him down. But on the following Sunday Nyman was too embarrassed to go to church and asked if he could have a wig. This reaction should not have surprised George. The other boys had complained about their haircuts for years.

XVIII

Temper

George and Lillis had tempers which they sometimes expressed with swearing or with corporal punishment. Their swearing could be amusing. Their curse vocabulary was limited essentially to "damn" and "hell," or "damn it to hell." Sometimes George would use the euphemisms "infernal" or "tarnation." Very rarely they might use another term such as "horse's ass" but only if it really were the most appropriate expression for the situation, or if quoting someone. Lillis, for example, was happy to retell the story about her sister-in-law's father, H. D. Lowery, an attorney who had been jailed for contempt when he called a judge a "son of a bitch." All of the Remington clan would swear quite casually if only with "damn" and "hell." But they did not tolerate such language from children.

Maybe it is a bit more shocking to know that George and Lillis would spank their children; *beat* would be too strong a word. The context of the times may not justify their behavior, but it is worth mentioning. There was a lot of spanking—and beatings—going on in the neighborhood. Corporal punishment was still common in school. The shop teacher at Irving Junior High, Mr. Cutler, would occasionally hit students with a long dowel rod, not in a fit of anger but as a measured penalty where the student was asked to stand in front of the class and take it. The band teacher, Mr. Karl Engar (Lillis knew him from Vernal where he had also taught) was a wonderful and enlightened man. But he would sometimes hit students with a cello board which would whistle as he swung it. In 6th grade, Mr. Dale Waldbillig used a breadboard as a paddle, which he called "the board of education." Miss Charlotte Gallyer (who was about 65 and had also instructed George when he was in 3rd or 4th grade at Forest Elementary) had a veritable penal code and a range of corporal punishments, beginning with a slap with a ruler on the back of the hands for small infractions.

To make the context complete, George's mother, Winnifred, also spanked him. In February 1976 he reminisced in his journal:

> I know I gave her more far more anxiety than the others. Even though I knew I was bad, I also knew that she would be consistent with her chastisement . . . She would paddle with hand, willow, coat hanger—usually quite cooly. I must not give the impression that I was beaten or battered. And then, I always knew that the hug, the kiss, and the lap were there when feelings had subsided. I felt loved and accepted, never quite as much as Bobby or especially Beverly, but never rejected. But my ineffective conscience generally allowed me to do what I thought was exciting thereby re-launching the whole cycle.

The dark corollary is that there were some kids in the neighborhood who were beaten so badly by their parents that you could hear them screaming if you were near their house while it was going on. Once David, next door, could be heard screaming from his basement bedroom as his addled alcoholic father Kenneth yelled and beat him. Rumor has it that Evan, around the corner, had to leave the house to avoid listening to his brother's screams as their father Cooper beat him. So there was not a lot of shame nor overt social restraint associated with spanking kids.

George and Lillis would hit their children with an open hand on the face, butt, or wherever was in reach. They would also hit with rulers, yardsticks, hairbrushes, or wooden spoons. With Lillis there was a bit of spontaneity or improvisation when it came to the precise implement. And after the fact it sometimes became a point of pride or humor to brag, "She hit me with a spatula that had still had cake batter on it!"

George's practice usually had more method. He had a designated ruler which he kept above the heating duct in the basement. The children slept in the basement. When he sent them to bed at night they would sometimes talk or stay awake and play in their bedrooms. This was sure to annoy George. He would call down and tell them to knock it off. The next escalation, he would yell, "Don't make me come down there." Then he could be heard coming down the stairs, one of which would squeak. Then the children would hear the ruler being dragged across the heating duct. There was probably no turning back at that point.

If George were really angry he would also pull hair, and sometimes hair would come loose in his hand. If a child would cry and take too long to compose himself George might threaten to spank him again. Lillis's ironic and dismissive threat was, "Oh, shut up or I will give you something to cry about."

They never blackened eyes or broke bones, but sometimes they would leave a bruise. Once Lillis left a welt on Rem's back that looked just like her hand. He was probably about 9 years old. This happened at the inconvenient moment when she was trying to get him ready to visit the pediatrician. Dr. Kenneth Fishler had the habit of looking at every inch of a child's naked body and questioning him about every little mark. Poor Lillis was so rattled in anticipation of the doctor's visit. She applied ice packs, apologized again and again to Rem, and tried to come up with a plausible story. In the end, Rem made it through the exam without detection.

George rarely hit Leslie but there were a few occasions, such as the one Leslie wrote about possibly in 1965—she would have been 11 years old. To Lillis's credit, she saved this little gem of ephemera, maybe because it gave her pause for introspection. The letter reads:

> Dear Dad,
> You are wrong! *This* time you are really wrong!

> Dear Mom,
> You can't be wrong because you never come right out and say yes or no. Try it some time. And besides: "every great advance in natural knowledge has included the absolute rejection of authority."
> Sign –
> [Then she signs with an angry self-portrait in ballpoint pen.]

Leslie's engaging note hints at the roles of authority and passivity that the parents may have taken in their marriage and in child-rearing.

Leslie also remembers when she was about 12 or 13 washing the dishes one night, sassing Lillis. Her dad took a wooden spoon and hit her about five or six times on the back of her lower legs. She was bruised with each whack, leaving the marks of a spoon. She refused to cover them until they healed, transitioning from purple to yellow over the next days, although she did not actually tell anyone what had happened. But the marks were obvious enough that George noticed them the next day. With surprise and reflexive denial in the face of evidence he said, "I didn't hit you that hard." But of course, he had.

George rarely hit Nyman, possibly because Nyman was more polite and compliant. But once George hit him with a little wooden batten from a window blind. Like Leslie's experience, welts were still visible the day after. But unlike Leslie's experience, when Nyman showed the marks to his dad the next day, George quickly apologized and never struck Nyman again. Nyman believes this was evidence of growth in parental wisdom. Or maybe exhaustion.

What bothered the children more than getting hit was that Lillis could neither admit to nor retreat from an error. George was loyal and supportive of Lillis quite literally to a fault, demanding respect on her behalf. To his credit he finally turned away from spanking. But he never seemed to understand the damage he caused by vacating fairness and honesty to facilitate Lillis's pride.

XIX

Lowell Bennion's Ranch, 1963
(Dean's Recollection)

There are some moments that we remember with more clarity, or maybe only with more sentiment. Our summer at Lowell Bennion's boy's ranch near Victor, Idaho, was one of those. It was the summer of 1963; Nyman was 5, Leslie 9, I was 11, and Rem was turning 13. As young as he was, even Nyman has memories of that charmed summer. He recalls the smell of nettles, hay, horses, and the dusty smell of the tack shed. He recalls discovering a porcupine at dusk and thinking it was some sort of strange bird. There was a badger that lived near our house which would scurry across the field like a low-flying magic carpet. Nyman also found a roost of bats. And he recalls the silence and the incredible darkness of the nights.

First, a note about Lowell Bennion. My path crossed his about 4 or 5 times in my life—the first time was the summer of 1963; these are my personal impressions. He was a prominent man from a prominent family of educators. Indeed, a building was named after his father, Milton Bennion, on the University of Utah campus. Lowell was founder and director of the LDS Institute of Religion at the U, and he had published many books, including Mormon Sunday school manuals. He had studied in Europe. When he would speak at a fireside (an informal Mormon study group) he would often quote German philosophers, particularly Kant. He founded and ran a food bank in Salt Lake City, often making home deliveries with his pickup truck. And he founded the boy's ranch in Idaho. So Dr. Bennion was an intellectual, an educator, a philanthropist, an author, and a doer. It is no surprise that my parents admired him. Dad met Dr. Bennion in the University of Utah education department. Though Dr. Bennion was 20 years older than Dad, I'm sure Dad would be pleased to regard him as a friend. Dr. Bennion seemed to prefer to hire educators for the summer work at his ranch.

The Bennion boy's ranch was in view of the Tetons, in a place that was so remote that we had to carry in what civilization we could in our suitcases. We lived in a house that had electric lights and its own running cold water supplied from a tank. Everything else was very primitive. The house had a cast-iron wood-burning kitchen range that contained a small water heater in it. The house had no central heat, and even though it was summer, the nights were cold. Sometimes I would light the first fire in the morning to take the chill off the house. We could not see or hear the rest of the ranch from our house. This is how Mom described it in one of only two surviving letters:

> . . . Our house at the ranch is high on the mountain away from the bunkhouse and main lodge. . . . Our house is a two-storied frame. Two bedrooms upstairs, small living room, nice kitchen and entrance hall, and bath room on main floor. From my front window I can look across the green valleys below and see three high peaks of the Tetons. Behind us rises a huge green wooded mountain, to the side of us a hay field, and to the other side a wood, small canyon with a lovely stream where I cool my milk and watermelon, butter and cheese. Wild flowers everywhere of every color. Leslie keeps flowers on the kitchen table at all times. . . .
>
> Yesterday I walked up the hill to our house and there was an adorable baby skunk on the path, a large water snake on my step and a beautiful baby fawn right in front of the house. . . . There are small animals of all kinds that can be seen from our living room window. . . .
>
> We are having a wonderful time. The days are warm and the nights are cold.
>
> Hope you are all well. Tell Lois, Don, and Ted hello. Haven't any of their addresses. Wouldn't write anyway. If you needed

us you could call Victor, Idaho, and send a runner to Lowell Bennion's Ranch. We have no telephone, TV, radio, or paper at the ranch. It's wonderful.

Subtle as it is, this letter is an example of Mom idealizing a situation, as if she were a bit embarrassed to tell her mother just how primitive her living conditions were. Certainly the experience was magical and there was no need to put a good face on it. But to say the house had a "nice kitchen and an entrance hall" is not quite consistent with the austere, cold cabin that I remember. Our cabin, and indeed the whole ranch, was very rustic—no heat, poor lighting, unfinished floors, little hot water. Maybe there was "an adorable baby skunk." As for the porcupine that Nyman found, it turns out there was a bounty on them; one of the boys killed it and gave Nyman 50¢ as a finders fee. Outside there was the wilderness, the forest, the uncertainty of what lived there, the quiet, the darkness. Once in camp we were told a bull moose had been observed in the area. The news came like a rumor in a refugee camp, impossible to assess but easy to worry about. And the ranch was remote; I stepped on a nail and had to be driven miles and miles to get a tetanus shot.

Down the hill from our house there was a main building which served as a dining hall, kitchen, office, a large open dorm room upstairs, and personal quarters for Dr. Bennion. His bedroom was a very spartan closet; his wife stayed in Salt Lake. There was another building appropriately called the bunkhouse, which had another open dorm room and some showers. There was a third building which was a tack room and maybe some stables. There may have been other buildings. There was no pavement on the property.

Organized discussions promoting objective thought and examining contrasting opinions were part of the camp's agenda. Our parents participated in or directed some of those discussions in the evenings. Dad was also tasked with performing and directing physical labor. Mom may have provided some first-line healthcare but mostly she helped in the kitchen. She would wash the dishes by hand and dry them with a dishtowel. Dr. Bennion would chide her for not allowing the dishes to air-dry, insisting that dishtowels spread germs. Of course, as a nurse, Mom was already aware of germs, and she would chide him for drinking raw milk, his inexplicable preference. It was a dialog that went on all summer.

The labor agenda for the boys and for the adults was the same—to build the ranch infrastructure. Labor might include painting barns, bucking hay, logging, or building fences. We had several projects that summer. Dad built a big locker to secure garbage cans. It was said to be bear-proof, though I doubt it was. It was made of rough-hewn untreated lumber, some of which still had bark on it. This garbage locker was patched up with wire screen and it was a huge improvement for the ranch because it immediately abated the flies which were a real nuisance. Dad assisted or was assisted by a local man named Dale Markham who was a Mormon bishop. He brought up power woodworking tools and set them up outside. He cut and planed the timber into lumber. Markham's wife, Carol, came to the ranch occasionally, and once brought a peach cobbler. The other adults quietly made fun of her because she was such a bad cook, but Markham seemed to like the cobbler. It says something about effort—and about expectations.

Dad also built a support to hold a dinner bell. The bell itself was actually the steel tire off an antique tractor, something that had been abandoned on the property. It had a beautiful tone. We also spent a lot of time foraging in the woods for timber to build a jack fence. Even as an 11-year-old, I carried a lot of heavy logs, by myself or with the help of other boys.

Dad was occasionally sent on errands into town, sometimes to Driggs (also a backwater) and sometimes to Idaho Falls. Dad was out of his element on these errands. Once he was sent to buy some weaner pigs. He had no idea what a weaner pig was, and in fact thought he was told to buy *leaner* pigs, or possibly *wiener* pigs. On another occasion he was sent to buy some milk cans. He tried to get clarification on how to shop for milk cans and Dr. Bennion simply told him to buy quality cans and not think so much about the price. Evidently he bought the best milk cans available, demonstrating that sometimes price should be a consideration. Bennion looked at them and commented in his understated way, "These are probably the best milk cans I will ever own."

These forays into civilization were sometimes combined with short shopping trips, ice cream, or sightseeing. Lillis and George took Nyman to Idaho Falls to see the falls and the temple. Lillis was shocked at the number of drunks on the streets of Idaho Falls, and the number of liquor stores, but pleased with the temple visitor's center. They also took Nyman on a day trip to Yellowstone to see the bears; they saw many bears in those days before the "do not feed" rule. They also saw Old Faithful, the mud pots, and returned to the ranch in time for supper.

Another component of the ranch program was recreation. This could be horseback riding, hiking, swimming, or a variety of games and play. For example, the boys and adults built what they called a whirligig, a big toy with a seat hanging on a rope that other boys could spin or flip around with muscle power. Camp social life was meeting in the evenings and playing parlor games, telling stories, or singing. There were some songs, such as "The Deacon Went Down," which required us to make up verses in a call-and-response style. One boy would sing words for a new verse, and the rest of us would echo back. For example, one boy owned a car at home—it was a 1956 Ford. For whatever reason this car had become a standing joke around camp. When it was his turn to make up a verse it went like this:

> Boy: O you can't get to heaven
> Group: O you can't get to heaven
> Boy: in a '56 Ford
> Group: in a '56 Ford
> Boy: 'cause a '56 Ford
> Group: 'cause a '56 Ford
> Boy: will displease the Lord.
> Group: will displease the Lord

Of course, this is not the funniest gag in history, but it seems remarkable that these boys, including us little Brooks kids, could make up verses like this on the fly all evening long. And so it was with the parlor games. One game involved two teams sitting on opposite sides of the dining table. One team would put their hands under the table and pass a quarter among themselves. At some point they would put their fists above the table and allow the other team to inspect them and to guess who had the quarter, and in which hand. Then the team would simultaneously slap their hands on the table. Sometimes by luck or by skill the other team could hear the quarter hit the table and could tell which hand it was in. It sounds silly.

There was other entertainment. Once Dr. Bennion invited one of the locals up to show off his trick horse. The tricks in this horse's repertoire included sitting like a dog, sticking its tongue out, stealing the owner's hat, rolling over, etc. Then there was the melodrama in Jackson Hole. In one scene Leslie recalls the handsome hero finding the damsel in distress drowning. The hero said, "I'll save you!" then proceeded to take off his gloves very elegantly, one finger at a time.

Other hired hands were LaMont Merritt and his wife, Shirley, of Star Valley, both also schoolteachers. They owned a string of horses and hired them out to the ranch for work or recreation. Even as young as we were, Rem and I were taught to saddle a horse and to put the bit in its mouth. LaMont also shoed his horses and treated them medically. Once the Merritts invited Dad, possibly Mom, me, and Rem on a 20-mile horseback ride through the forest—what an adventure for us children. The Merritts were careful how they assigned horses. Shirley took the least disciplined horse for herself, and was thrown off but not hurt. She commented that she fell on her butt and injured her pride. She was quite embarrassed because the horses were hers, and she was an experienced rider; I think she actually competed in barrel races. At one point a bear and its cubs crossed our trail right in front of us. They were each a different color—one almost beige, one rusty and the mom was dark.

Another man, hired in Salt Lake, also an educator, was Fred Buchanan. He was Scottish and spoke with an accent. Some of the boys called him somewhat unimaginatively "Scotty." Fred played the bagpipes. Sometimes in the evenings he would walk a distance from camp, wearing his kilt, and play his pipes. Obviously, Fred had also packed as much civilization in his suitcase as he could carry. As I write I don't know if I am doing justice to the magic of that summer. Fred was single. He was probably in his late 20s. Leslie, at 9 years old, had a crush on him. He tried to teach her a little Scottish culture and this song sticks in her memory:

Come along, come along, let us foot it out together
Come along, come along, be it fair or stormy weather
With the hills of home before us and the purple of the heather
Let us sing in happy chorus, come along, come along.

Fred went on to get a PhD and became an important thinker and author on topics of education in Utah. In 1996, he published *Culture Clash and Accommodation—Public Schooling in Salt Lake City, 1890–1994*. In it he mentions Lowell Bennion and other Bennions. He also mentions my father on page 242: "The board then appointed George Brooks, the amiable and much respected Personnel Director, as Interim Superintendent. Brooks made it clear that he was not a candidate for the position and that he was only willing to serve until a permanent replacement was found."

Some lifelong friendships were established at the ranch. Dad and Mom continued to associate with Fred, for example. LaMont and Shirley had dinner at our house in 1966 and their son Mark had Thanksgiving with us in 1978. Rem was in touch with Daniel Snarr, one of the boys at the ranch, even decades later after he became mayor of Murray.

At the end of the summer Leslie and I were sent home on the train. I cannot remember why we did not return with my parents. The train was a whole new adventure. We rode through the night, sometimes dozing, to be awakened when cars would be side-tracked or coupled. Many on the train's staff were African-Americans, and just a bit exotic in the Mountain West. They wore crisp white jackets. They were duly attentive but impersonal with us children traveling alone. Grandfather Remington met us in Salt Lake on the platform. The station's great hall echoed and smelled of tobacco, the smell of travelers, and gentiles. What a gift my parents gave us that summer.

XX

Civics and Sentiments
1964–1968

CHURCH ACTIVITY

Take the month of March 1964 as an example; there were only 5 days in that month that Lillis's diary did not record a church meeting or activity. To review each church activity, particularly during the years George served as bishop, would be at once astonishing and monotonous. But more to the point, one's church activity gives no insight into one's life if everyone in the community is also active in the church. It is important to correct for that distortion when sifting out what made George and Lillis remarkable. Out of the thousands of pages in Lillis's diaries, here are a few example days to acknowledge the church's enormous presence that will otherwise be minimized in this story:

Sunday, March 1, 1964

All of us to church. Dean ordained a deacon. Very excited. Passed the sacrament for the first time today. Geo. busy with meetings and interviews and visiting most of the day.

Monday, March 2, 1964

. . . Carolyn and I furnished the refreshments for an in-service meeting (apple pie). I baked the pies while I baked a meatloaf and potatoes for dinner. Geo. to the Adult Aaronic

School. He picked me up after. He had a late interview. Didn't get home till late.

Tuesday, March 3, 1964

. . . Prepared Primary lesson. Nyman, Leslie, and I to Primary. . . . Geo. late getting home from a meeting. . . . Geo. R and Dean to Mutual. Geo had an interview. I finished making arrangements for the program for the Relief Society birthday party.

Wednesday, March 4, 1964

. . . George went to Bishop's meeting later in the evening. . . .

Friday, March 5, 1964

. . . Dean to a ward show with his boy friends. The rest of us watched the Church play-off in basketball on TV.

Sunday, March 8, 1964

All of us to church. Geo. fasted most of the day until late in the evening. . . . Marie Gurrick went to church with me. George was late getting home, had interviews.

Monday, March 9, 1964

. . . George R., Dean, Geo. and I to court of honor. George R received his Star Scout. Dean should have had his Second Class. George to Adult Aaronic School after.

Tuesday, March 10, 1964

. . . I washed, prepared Primary lesson. Read to Nyman. Leslie, Nyman and I to Primary. Dean and Geo. R. to M.I.A. George to a meeting. . . .

Wednesday, March 11, 1964

. . . I went to Relief Society Anniversary party in the afternoon. Geo. also attended. I drove to pick up singers from Roosevelt Jr. High. Nelda Miller, Carley Demman, and Naoma Coleman all drove to pick up the singers. I gave them 3 pies as their treat for an excellent program. . . .

Friday, March 13, 1964

. . . George went to a scout meeting at Hawthorne Ward in the evening.

Saturday, March 14, 1964

. . . George and I to the Young Marrieds' Party in the evening at Max Campbell's. . . .

It would seem that there would be no time for anything else. But 1964 was the year that George built a bedroom in the basement for Rem. The family started swimming in the evenings at South High, usually twice each week. George and Lillis began making frequent visits to George's mother, Winnifred, who was struggling with the loneliness of being a widow; personal interactions with her continued to be touchy. She had tried to take a young woman into her home as a boarder, but that had not worked out well. George took 9 hours of algebra, geometry and mathematics at the University of Utah. The family hiked Bald Mountain—"Old Baldy"—in the Uintas. It was an annual event they started years earlier. At almost 12,000 feet and with a small glacier obstructing the trail, the 4-mile round-trip hike was just the right challenge for the young children. Lillis served on jury duty from late September into mid-November. She also remained active on the Legislative Council and in her other clubs. And they were involved in other matters.

CURB AND GUTTERING, 1964

George petitioned the city in 1964 to install curb and guttering in the neighborhood. When houses were built in the early part of the century, the dirt excavated from basements and foundations was often simply dumped in the street. Many streets in Sugar House were therefore highly cambered, and many did not have curbs. George took his children with him to the City Commission meetings in March and in April to argue for leveling the streets and installing curbs. The meetings, as it turned out, were heated, neighbor against neighbor. Two neighbors who lived in the same block on Wilson Avenue as the Brookses—Glenna Cannon Black, and a Mrs. Dean—were very angry and abusive of George, and of Wilford Kimball, the stake president, who both spoke in favor. Mayor J. Bracken Lee and his commission sat impassively as they listened to the opinions. A decision to install curbs would require each property owner to pay an assessment based on frontage. So George had put himself in a position of advocating for this assessment on all of his neighbors at the same time he was asking his neighbors for money to build the new ward meetinghouse. But he was unapologetic. At some point the city agreed and the streets were torn up in July.

ALLEN PRICE

One of George's mission companions came by to visit about the time the new street was constructed. Lillis's diary notes on Thursday, August 13, 1964, "George to school at the U of U. Allen Price came and visited with me all morning." It may be subtle, but *all morning* signals that Lillis was annoyed with the unannounced interruption. The next day when she came home from work she wrote, "Geo. took final exams at U of U. I worked at L.D.S. Hosp. Allen Price was at home visiting with Geo. When I came home. He told us that Ellen Jane [Allen's wife] had left the church and he is thinking about it."

On Saturday George and Lillis were entertaining some old friends from Washington Terrace, Keith and Elaine Midgley. Keith had just completed graduate studies in Indiana and was on his way to join the faculty at a college in Washington state. Lillis wrote, "Had a nice visit with them. Allen and Ellen Jane arrived before they left. A rather heated argument arose between the two over religion."

The following Friday Lillis and George threw a big luau party in their backyard for some ward members. They set up the ping-pong table to seat 13 guests. They had a great time. After the party, at about 10:30 PM as Lillis and George were cleaning up, Allen and his sons dropped by and they talked. Allen was in crisis. His marriage was falling apart and he was losing his religion. He was showing up unannounced at all hours.

Lillis had suffered for months with pain in her shoulder, arm, and chest. Perhaps she over-exerted with the luau, or work at the hospital. Perhaps it was playing tennis with Rem. That summer Rem would awaken her early in the morning to play, and sometimes they would play 10 games. Finally her doctor put a cast on her arm from her shoulder to her wrist to force her to rest it. Then he cut the cast so that she could remove it or wear it bound together by rubber bands. Over the next couple of weeks, while she was in pain, her mother came over to do the ironing.

Allen came by on a few more occasions. George was always busy but not too busy for a friend. Allen helped George excavate for a concrete pad in the backyard, and helped construct forms, and cut and fit reinforcement wire. This was hard labor. Allen was a solid man and worked hard. He came another day early in September to pour and finish the concrete; they poured 5 yards (or about 500 square feet of surface). Afterwards they had a barbecue with Allen, his sons who had also helped, and with a neighbor, Roland Gee. They all stood around admiring the finish. On one level, this story illustrates how men bond through physical exertion. However, the important point of the story is that Allen showed up to lean on George in a time of crisis.

We all have friends. On occasion maybe we have said to them, or they have said to us, "If you need anything, let me know." Regardless of good intentions, there are times when we are alone—when we realize that we have nobody truly capable of comprehending our despair. In such a crisis Allen turned to George.

Years later, after George's funeral, Allen came again to visit Lillis when she was a 67-year-old quadriplegic. He asked her for some of George's clothes. She gave him a sports jacket and some ties. He wore them all the time and told Lillis how good he felt when he was wearing something of George's.

UNCLE OTTO

Someone gave a desert tortoise to the Brooks children as a pet, possibly in the summer of 1962, in the days before it was understood how threatened the species was. They named him Uncle Otto. He would graze on the lawn all summer. Then in the winter he would hibernate in a cardboard box in a cool place in the basement. At the same time Leslie had a cat who would occasionally sit on Uncle Otto and take a ride; Uncle Otto was oblivious or indifferent to the cat.

What Uncle Otto lacked in intelligence he made up for with persistence and patience. He could see under the gate and he presumed he could crawl under it, apparently unaware that his domed shell was much higher than his eyes. And so he would push and push against the gate without making progress. But occasionally factors would align in his favor and he would escape, startling the neighbors. The Brookses painted their address on his shell and someone would pick him up and return him. But paint would not stick for long. They also drilled a hole in the edge of his shell, put a key ring through the hole, and attempted to tie him up that way. But given time, he could tug against his leash and get away.

One day he disappeared, never to return. Lillis, in her heart, took responsibility for ignoring the peril he lived with in the backyard. In the summer of 1964 the streets in the neighborhood were being reconstructed. Uncle Otto looked just like another rock. It is presumed that he got out of the yard and was taken away by an earthmover. Lillis never really confessed to the family, but wrote in one of her undated manuscripts:

> It was on one of these days I was surprised to find him behind our back fence on the parking area on my return home. There was road construction taking place. I unloaded my car with the thought the children would soon be returning from school and return him to the yard. Before they arrived, a scoop shovel came by and scooped him up and carried him away. It was a great disappointment for all of us and a serious error in judgment on my part. The shovel was not there when I arrived home. We had enjoyed him for several years.

ELECTION YEAR, 1964

George was elected to serve as a Democratic state delegate again in April 1964. His brother, Samuel Jr., was elected to serve as a Republican delegate. Politically, 1964 was an acrimonious year both locally and nationally.

Utah school teachers were paid at rates below national averages. Governor Clyde appointed a study group to recommend the way forward. In the spring of 1964 the governor's advisors recommended allocating $6 million to education in emergency funding, and recommended the governor call a special session of congress to come up with a permanent fix. Clyde quickly dismissed both of the recommendations—and also his task force.

The UEA (Utah Education Association) which represented the vast majority of Utah teachers *and* administrators voted on Saturday, May 16, to "recess" for 2 days—the first strike of public school teachers in the United States. Lillis wrote in her diary:

> U.E.A. held meeting and decided all teachers of the state would take a two-day recess in protest of Gov. Clyde's action against the teachers. We listened to T.V. reports most of the evening. The teacher situation is grim. Strong feelings between the educators and the governor.

Then on Sunday, May 17, George had his typical busy church schedule. Lillis wrote, "Principals called into special meeting concerning the school situation until 10:30 PM. The school board instructed the principals 'to be in their classrooms or they'd be without a job.'"

On Monday and on Tuesday George reported to work, and the children went to school. But school was closed and the children came home early, except Dean. Dean was attending Jackson Elementary across town and relied on George for a ride home. Only two or three Jackson teachers scabbed and they suffered loud verbal abuse on Wednesday when the other teachers came to work. Teachers voted on Tuesday not to sign contracts for the fall. So that was part of the election-year drama.

Lillis also wrote about the Republican National convention, which she characterized as "sickening." This was a convention of internal struggle—moderates against conservatives. Barry Goldwater and the conservatives carried the day. Lillis and George were Democrats, but Lillis recorded that she feared a collapse of the Republican party.

On July 13 Lillis wrote: " . . . watched the Republican convention in San Francisco. It was frightening to see how Goldwater railroaded everything thru the convention. A great am't of bitterness at the convention."

On July 14 she wrote: "We listened to the Republican convention in the evening. It's sickening to see Goldwater controlling everything at the convention. Rockefeller and Romney booed at the convention when they tried to be heard."

On July 15 she wrote: "We discussed the convention and how sick we were over Goldwater and his machine running everything."

On Thursday, July 16 she wrote: "Barry Goldwater was nominated to run for pres. on the Republican ticket. What an idiot! Hope it doesn't divide the Republican party in half."

On a more personal level, Lillis wrote on October 14, "Geo and Sam [Jr.] had words over Reed Benson speaking at fireside. It was decided he [Benson would] not speak. Sam very unhappy." A fireside is an ancillary church meeting, often in a private home, where prominent church members or people with some expertise are invited to speak or lead a discussion. George and his younger brother Samuel Jr. were living in the same ward; George was bishop, and responsible for implementing the church's nominal prohibition of partisan politicking in church meetings. Reed Benson was a prominent member of the hyper-conservative John

Birch Society, which zealously promoted itself among the religious as an ethical imperative. He was also the son of Ezra Benson, a member of the Quorum of the Twelve Apostles. Many people in Utah were easily confused by such cross-purposes. This kind of disagreement was part of the background noise in the 1964 election year.

George's term as delegate lasted until the next presidential election, 1968, and other political issues continued to get attention in Lillis's diaries in the succeeding years. For example in 1965 she wrote that she had "touchy" conversations with her Relief Society visiting teachers on civil rights. Lillis would have been on the progressive side of that exchange. The next day, March 25, 1965, she wrote an uncharacteristic page-long harangue, illustrating how sensitive the times were.

> A white woman killed in Selma Alabama by a member of the Ku Klux Klan for being a civil rights worker. Pres. Johnson is taking firm stand against the Klan. Many L.D.S. people still blame the colored people. They feel the coloreds should be satisfied with nothing and be satisfied with the slums subservient to the whites. It's heart breaking to see how terribly they have been treated and the potential that is going to waste by not allowing them the same privileges as the whites.

The kids passed out handbills all summer in 1964. Lillis was a poll judge in November. The whole family was invested in the political process. Lyndon Johnson—Democrat and John Kennedy's surviving vice-president—won the election in a landslide.

XXI

Bowling Green State University and the Summer Trip Back East, 1965

George continued to take classes after hours at the University of Utah in 1965. Sometime in May he won a scholarship to study math education at Bowling Green State University in Ohio. The courses were held in July and August.

The scholarship to BGSU included a stipend for George's transit, rent, and groceries. George and Lillis had been saving and planning for 2 years, hoping someday to take a lengthy heartland tour with their children. They had saved $500. The stipend and savings came together in 1965, and planning for a long road trip began in earnest. The drive from Salt Lake City to Bowling Green was more than 1,600 miles. The trip they planned would more than double that mileage, taking them into Canada as far as Quebec, down through Maine, to Washington, DC, and back to Ohio before classes started—an ambitious, precision-planned 2-week tour. The Interstate System was brand-new in 1965. It was unusual for a family to travel across the continent on vacation—something very special.

George and Lillis pored over maps and books prior to the trip. Their itinerary was packed tight, and planned to finer details than most people would bother with. They measured routes and calculated mileage to be at each point of interest while the sun was up and the museums open. They consulted Fuller Remington, who as a traveling salesman had a good sense of travel times.

Grandfather Remington was 74 but still working part-time. He always had a nice car; he loaned his new Dodge Monaco to the Brooks family for the trip. The Monaco was a large, beautiful sedan with push-button automatic transmission and a huge trunk. It was larger, more comfortable, and more reliable than George's Studebaker Lark. With characteristic generosity Edith Remington also offered to tend their cocker spaniel, Trixie. The day before departure, friends and ward members came to the house to say goodbye. They brought boxes of cookies—some homemade and some store-bought. Beth Tolley, wife of George's second counselor in the bishopric, brought a boxed lunch of fried chicken for the road. Others brought brownies, pickles, rolls, and other picnic items for the trip. It was an unexpected expression of warmth and friendship.

The family had breakfast on June 29 at 3:30 AM at the Remingtons', then set out in the dark, empty streets. They drove 800 miles the first day, to Grand Island, Nebraska. Mindful of time and money, they usually picnicked in parks along the way, or ate while the car was rolling. Lillis prepared sandwiches in the car. George did most of the driving, but Lillis would drive a few hours midday when George was most likely to be sleepy. George was a better driver, and was also better and quicker at interpreting the maps, and remembering the route. They carried an AAA TripTik. This was a made-to-order spiral-bound map with each page showing 20 to 70 miles of the route. The kids were taught to help with map reading. They arrived in Bowling Green on the evening of the second day, already a day ahead of schedule. To drive 1,600 miles in 2 days takes some stamina. Lillis quickly changed their plans to spend the extra day in Boston. They spent less than a day in Bowling Green, concluding some transactions at the university and finding an apartment to rent. Then they hit the road to start touring.

LETTERS

Lillis wrote a letter to her parents almost every day while riding in the car. Then later, while living at Bowling Green, she wrote to them twice or sometimes three times each week. Her letters at times were like a travelogue, giving a sense of her awe at the great bridges and waterways and the sheer expanse of the continent.

She was conscious of money and reported the prices of many things, including gas, groceries, lodging, and admissions. Motels went for $10 to $18, for example. They spent 90¢ to cross a toll bridge from Detroit into Canada. Highway tolls in New England and New York once totaled $4.90 in a single day. Groceries in Bowling Green were cheaper than in Salt Lake City because there was no sales tax on food; otherwise, the prices were about the same.

She was ever aware of the family's good luck or "blessings" during the trip. They were fortunate to find a spacious apartment at the last minute, within walking distance to campus and with two broken parking meters in front. She noted rainstorms that did not begin until after touring was done for the day. She remarked on how quickly and easily they found parking, even when traffic and parking were congested. She noted traffic accidents that apparently occurred mere moments ahead of them. Strangers would volunteer to give them directions in crowded cities. Clerks would allow them to enter venues before opening times or after closing times. And on one occasion they were fortunate to cut to the head of a very long line inadvertently by entering through the wrong door.

Whenever the family would visit a wealthy home or neighborhood—such as the fabulously opulent Casa Loma in Toronto, or Franklin Roosevelt's home at Hyde Park, or even the home of George's friend Rhoda Bierstedt in Darien, Connecticut, Lillis would comment, "Lois must see this house." The two sisters seemed to enjoy daydreaming about houses and furnishings.

At the end of each travel day they would look for motels. There were more "mom and pop" motels and fewer corporate chains in those days, so the person at the desk was often the owner and had discretion to bargain. George's bargaining position was that he did not need a bed for every person; some children would sleep in sleeping bags on the floor and they should not pay. George would look on the map for the old US highways that predated the interstates, knowing that there would be older, cheaper motels along those routes. George was happy to walk away if he didn't get the price or quality he wanted. He usually asked to see the room before the deal was done. Lillis would insist on tidying up a bit before checking out, even making the beds, reasoning, "They know we are from Utah and they will assume we are Mormons. We must leave a good impression."

CANADA

The visit to Canada was in part a nostalgic return to George's mission field. But it was also an education for the children—their first lesson in foreignness. The Canadians spoke differently, used different money and the imperial gallon, and they cherished a different history. George took the family to the Plains of Abraham above the St. Lawrence River where both General Wolfe and General Montcalm died in battle. George said that the French residents continued to deface or blow up the statue of General Wolfe on the anniversaries of the battle—an important insight into Canadian sensibilities that George explained to his children.

They also visited some large Catholic churches which had a spirit of old-world mysticism. St. Joseph's Oratory in Montreal was decorated with an arch made of crutches that had been discarded by healed parishioners. The church preserved the pickled heart of Brother André, a local canonized priest credited with healings and miracles. There were pilgrims outside ascending the many steps on their knees. Sainte-Anne-de-Beaupré in Quebec preserved the body of a nun in a glass crypt. Frescos and art were everywhere. There were angels and constellations in the architecture. Outside on the church grounds one could stroll past life-sized Stations of the Cross. In a letter to her Remington parents dated July 4, 1965, Lillis recalled the day this way:

> . . . We spent a fascinating day in Quebec and Ste. Anne de Beaupré. The children played on the Plains of Abraham and we climbed to the citadel and the beautiful Château Frontenac (where Churchill and Roosevelt met during the war). We walked up and down the steep narrow streets. Watched the artists on the streets and visited the 14 Stations of the Cross on Ste. Anne de Beaupré. We drove thru the beautiful parks and watched the steamers and freighters coming up and down the river.
>
> The entry to Quebec across the huge bridge (high enough for ships to go under) was so beautiful and impressive. Lovely homes, universities, monasteries, convents line the way. All the signs, advertisements and everyone reading and speaking French. Most frustrating. Most all guides and policemen and most people on the street speak both English and French. They understood us but we couldn't always understand them. . . .

> We visited St. Anne's Cathedral this morning and the 14
> Stations of the Cross. We climbed the mt. The cathedral was
> magnificently beautiful but it was like the county fair. Everyone
> wandering about taking pictures, paying to see her bones, buying
> souvenirs in one corner, lighting candles, kneeling and praying.
> When we came out Leslie said, "That was barbaric. I feel like sing-
> ing one verse of 'We Thank Thee, O God, for a Prophet.'" In one
> cathedral they had a pickled heart of Father André and another
> they had St. Anne in a glass tomb so we could see her. Leslie said,
> "There is nothing spiritual about it. It makes me ill! I long for my
> own happy beliefs and my own church." We visited these today
> because it was Sunday. I had to smile at her reaction. . . .

The quoted conversation with Leslie seems glib for an 11-year-old.
It is most certainly a complete fabrication. It is an example of how Lillis
could be unreliable as a witness, sometimes allocating her opinions to her
children. She could also mold the memory of an event to fit her idealized aspiration. If anything, the children were awestruck by the cathedrals.
Leslie was taken with the art and ritual, and wondered if it would be
appropriate for her to cross herself during her private prayers. Nyman
remembered the great dome on St. Joseph's Oratory, but did not recall a
carnival atmosphere with people snapping pictures (though it is likely that
George took pictures). Dean remembered the candles and the pilgrims
on their knees, but did not regard it as barbaric. On the contrary, he was
forced to consider his own devotion and the dignity of his own religion.

They left Quebec by ferry then drove into Maine along the Kennebec
River. They stayed in a rustic motel cabin near Hinckley where the river
was so wide and calm that they thought it was a lake. When the mist
lifted in the morning it was clearly a river, full of logs floating downstream to the mill—a practice that is now illegal. All of Maine was beautiful, but the setting of the motel was so beautiful that George and Lillis
decided to get a late start and let the children play on the grassy bank
until checkout time. They caught an eel and chased a muskrat.

The Itinerary

It would be tedious to list all the museums and battlefields (though
they are catalogued in detail in Lillis's letters and diaries). A typical day

might include visits to five or even ten venues of cultural interest. Lillis and George projected their insights onto each: the *USS Constitution* lionized by Oliver Wendell Holmes in "Old Ironsides"; Walden Pond, where Henry David Thoreau lived and meditated; New Bedford, which inspired *Moby Dick*; Yale University, which evoked memories of Newell; Plymouth Rock, where they found the name of Lillis's ancestor Samuel Fuller; they visited the Arlington grave of President Kennedy and watched at a discrete distance a funeral for an officer killed in Vietnam; they sat in the Senate gallery and heard Bobby Kennedy announce the death of Adlai Stevenson and give an impassioned tribute to him, then they exited the chamber to find the flags around town lowered to half-staff.

While in the New York area they stayed 3 nights in Darien, Connecticut, in the home of Gustave and Hazel Bierstedt, parents of Rhoda, one of the teachers on George's staff at Jackson Elementary. Rhoda was there waiting for the family with dinner on the patio. Gustave and Hazel were out of town. Rhoda cooked breakfast and supper for them each day. Gustave was a well-to-do executive for the telephone company and they had spent some money furnishing their large and elegant house with colonial American antiques. It was like sleeping in a museum. Virtually everything in the house from chairs to tableware was antique. George and Lillis slept in a poster bed that was so high that George said they could not see each other across the bed when they said their prayers.

On Friday, July 16, they returned to Bowling Green, but took a windshield tour of Pittsburgh on the way, around the Golden Triangle, and gawked at the steel mills and the smokestacks dumping soot into the air. They took a cable car to a 1,000-foot promontory for a panoramic view.

The aggressive tour was exhausting, particularly in the muggy heat of New York and Washington. The children sometimes complained of headaches as they cycled into and out of air-conditioned buildings. It was also expensive. Lillis mused about the costs this way in a letter to her parents:

> Actually it hasn't been very much when you think how many of
> us have been eating, sleeping and paying . . . We cashed in all
> of our bonds ($500) and it has not cost us more than that. . . .
> Everyone else we've talked to who have taken similar trips have

spent more and done less. . . . The stipend from the school will cover our rent, utilities, . . . and practically all of our food if we're careful . . . What more could you ask? . . . Five hundred dollars couldn't have been better spent. I don't regret one penny of it. . . . We have been truly blessed. The trip has been so right from the beginning.

BOWLING GREEN, OHIO

The apartment in Bowling Green was on the main floor of a turn-of-the-century house at 220 E Court Street, right across the street from the Wood County Courthouse. Lillis went shopping for groceries and to buy sheets, towels, and other furnishings. She also helped the landlady, Mr. Arlene Kirkland, clean the filthy apartment. Commenting on the previous tenants, Lillis said, "I cannot believe that a family and a dog can make such a mess in two short years." Rental units were hard to find in Bowling Green. Several of George's classmates lived in smaller units far from town, and one lived in a 16-foot camper trailer with his wife and three children. So the family felt lucky that their house was spacious, furnished, and had a private place for George to study. It did not have a washer, so Lillis did a lot of laundry by hand in the sink, or walked to a laundromat. The house did not have a telephone and so the family tried to schedule occasional phone calls during the week when it was presumed or planned that people would be home to answer. Lillis planned phone calls in her letters to her mother, then would walk into town to find a pay phone. Long-distance phone calls were expensive and billed by the minute, so it was important to have a pocket full of change and an agenda of the important topics.

The family settled in as if for the long term. They made friends with the Wilsons who lived just around the corner on Summit Street. The Wilsons were truck farmers and successful to a degree not possible for farmers in Utah. There was an oil well on their farm which could produce $500 of oil each month. But they capped it so that the land would be easier to till in straight lines. They had a restored antique tractor in their yard which they would start up and play with. Rem was friendly with a nephew of the Wilsons who worked on the farm. Leslie made friends with Linda Wilson, who was a year younger, and continued to be pen pals with her years after. Linda invited Leslie to summer Bible school and other activities. The Wilsons took Nyman to Toledo to shop for farm equipment, and on a different day on their farm, let him ride on the tractors. The kids acquired library cards. They often went swimming at the university pool. Rem played tennis whenever possible with Lillis or Dean. Leslie and Dean took a bus ride to visit Seneca Caverns with the city summer recreation program. Sometimes the kids would cross the street and sit in on sessions of court—usually divorce court.

Social Life

The most important social interactions were with George's classmates and their families. There were about 45 students in the cadre—men and women, old and young, different races—even a few nuns. All were school administrators or teachers. Some of the socializing was scheduled into the program. The cadre ate lunch together every day, which they called the "Exchange of Ideas."

Very often the classmates got together by choice. Enduring friendships developed with Dick and Jane Sardella of Syracuse, New York, and Larry and Marge Ecklund and family of Fresno, California. The wives would get together during the day and let their children play together or even sleep over. They had dinner parties at each others' apartments. They all went to the county fair together and watched the tractor pull contest and the pie eating contest—a cultural education for all of them. The adults sat together and ate barbecue and laughed and talked while they let the kids roam free. They also got together in a park for a "corn roast" which someone had told them was an essential element of Ohio tradition. It rained so hard that day that they could not keep the fire lit. Dick Sardella, always upbeat and amusing, was wearing shorts and a plastic raincoat. He made a theatrical declaration, "We give up, Mother Nature," and started to eat the raw corn. He insisted that the heaver the rain, the better the raw corn tasted. Sometimes George and Dick would study together.

The family was ever conscious of their religion and its eccentricities. Lillis acknowledged in a letter to her mother on August 17 that the Ecklunds were a "wonderful family, very spiritual, Presbyterian." That comment masked a little religious rivalry that existed between Marge Ecklund and Lillis. When Lillis hung laundry out to dry on a clothesline in the backyard, she took special care to hang the temple garments in such a way that it was difficult to tell what they were, with their edges overlapping—and always behind another clothesline hung with more ordinary laundry. Rem's friends teased him gently about polygamy, asking him how many wives his father had. Rem responded, "One was all he could manage."

There were very few Mormons in Bowling Green, maybe only a dozen including the six Brookses. There were Dennis and Page Reese and their baby, Danny; Dennis was studying mathematics at BGSU. There was Vernon and Sharon Saunders and Sharon's young sister Pam. Vernon worked for the church and was on temporary assignment in Wood County to microfilm birth, marriage, and death records in the great handwritten folios in the basement of the courthouse. They actually lived away from Bowling Green, in a trailer house in the nearby hamlet of Luckey. There may have been another young single woman attending college. All were temporary residents. All attended church at the fledgling and diversified Toledo Ward 30 miles away. They would have supper together and watch the fireflies in the evening. But there was no socializing with other members of the ward. On July 18, the first Sunday that they attended church, George was asked to speak in a sacrament meeting. He resisted, reasoning that he only had about six Sundays in Ohio, and his school program had claim on some of those. He felt that his first obligation was to his contract, his cadre, and to the scholarship. The Toledo Ward could have used the support; almost all were converts; of 700 members, only about 15 were seasoned enough that they had been through a temple. Lillis did agree to highlight key passages in 30 copies of the Book of Mormon for the missionaries to hand out. It took her 20 minutes per book, and caused her shoulder and arm to ache.

The family continued to tour on weekends. They took a Saturday trip with the Reese family to the Henry Ford Museum, Greenfield Village, Detroit, and Dearborn, Michigan. They took a guided tour through the Ford assembly line. They visited the Toledo Zoo one Sunday between church sessions. The next weekend they visited the Mormon pilgrimage sites at Kirtland, Ohio, and Palmyra, New York. They also went to Buffalo, and to Niagara Falls, Canada. They saw the Hill Cumorah Pageant and attended a church service on Sunday on the grass at the foot of the hill. Two weeks later they visited Chicago and the great museums there. They dropped Rem off at Chicago's Union Pacific train station so he could return to Utah early to attend a Scouting program. George and Lillis ran into acquaintances in the train station, Eleanor and Lynn Hales. They had coincidentally met friends at other venues on the trip—in New York City, in Washington, and at the Pageant. George commented, "If you stand in Union Pacific Station long enough you will see everyone you know."

The friendship with Dick and Jane Sardella endured for several years. The Sardellas sent gifts when Rem and when Dean graduated from high school in 1968 and 1970. They telephoned on holidays. They also visited Salt Lake City in 1967, and stayed for a week. George and Lillis took them all over northern Utah. They went to a melodrama in Park City. They went to the 24th of July Parade in Salt Lake City and picnicked in the park with the extended Remington family. They hiked Bald Mountain in the Uintas and took a ski gondola ride in Park City. They visited Kennecott Copper Mine and swam in the Great Salt Lake. They went to Temple Square and Welfare Square and toured the city. They went to plays and movies and viewed slides of Bowling Green. They went to church at Richards II Ward and at the Cathedral of the Madeleine. On the last day, Jane cooked an Italian meal in Lillis's kitchen. There was some hope that maybe the Brookses could share the gospel with the Sardellas, but that didn't materialize. On the last day Lillis wrote in her diary, "We bid farewell to the Sardellas. Already we feel a void."

The landlady, Arlene Kirkland, came through Salt Lake in June 1966 on her way to Portland with her children and her mother, Elizabeth Sparrow. The boys, Bill and Don, stayed 2 nights at the Brooks home while the women stayed at a motel. Lillis took them on the grand tour of the city including an organ recital, the Beehive House, the capitol, the copper mine. The boys went swimming. The Ecklunds also visited the Brookses, in August of 1966. Dennis and Page Reese, who had gone to church and toured with the Brookses while in Bowling Green, visited the family in Salt Lake in July 1967. All received the same hospitality.

THE DOG

As the school term approached its end, Lillis's letters to her parents sometimes showed an abashed gratitude for the use of her father's car, for the dog's care, and for hosting Rem's early return. She would make exaggerated pronouncements to express her thanks and embarrassment, such as this on August 2:

> Isn't a dog a nuisance? I feel terrible about you being burdened with it. We would have gotten rid of it if Dean didn't feel so strong about her. He weeps when he talks about her. He has been so concerned about her. Do whatever Ted thinks is best. We will gladly be willing to pay for a kennel if he thinks the dog will be happiest there. We've considered a dozen different things to do with her but nothing seems to be right. . . . I could give her away and not bat an eye. He [Dean] has no idea what you've been thru with that dog. . . . I don't know how you stand it. I would be very understanding if you poisoned her.

Such hyperbole was an occasional feature of Remington conversation. In this case it could be viewed as a substitute for Lillis's inability to thank her parents adequately. Lillis made similar fanciful suggestions to her mother, such as having Rem eat meals with his other grandmother, Winnifred Brooks, while sleeping at the Remingtons. The dog in question was a well-trained cocker spaniel. It is true Dean was homesick for his dog. Edith wrote to reassure him (and possibly to reassure Lillis) in Trixie's persona, such as this undated letter written in late July:

Dear Dean

Will scratch you a note. This is Trixie writing with Grandmother's help. I miss you but not much, as I love my grandmother so much. Because she is good to me. Lets me sleep with her (day or nite). Doesn't even scold when I put mud tracks all over the old sheet she keeps on the bed all the time for me. She has to change it 3 times a week. She has a good washer, and doesn't mind. I pretend like I don't like dog food, so she will mix hot dogs or hamburger with it. She probably is spoiling me, but I'm having real fun. She leaves the door open, so I can run in and out at will. I run all over the neighborhood. Three other dogs I play with in the early morning. The rest of the day they are locked up. Today she gave me a steak bone (even had meat on it). I turned my nose up, she said, "Well, if you won't eat it, at least go bury it." I picked it right up and took it in the bushes and buried it. Don't you think I'm a smart dog?

I still have one bad habit—waking her too early. I go up by her face. If her eyes are closed I lie down and try to be good. If she looks at me I get all excited and bark and coax to go outdoors and play. This morning I kept biting her toes, no matter where she put them. I would find them and gently nip them. It really got her up. I especially like to be by the side of her and lay my head across her neck. She brushes me every day. Hope you will, too, when you come home. Makes me feel good. I hope to get at least one bath before you come home.

By the way, when are you coming home? I won't forget you and still love you. When they rub my stomach they say I look like I'm laughing. I'm losing weight. I'm on a diet. Just eat every other day. I think they are trying to starve me to eat that old dog food. They say they can't afford to feed me what they eat at the table. Once in a while they get real generous or feel sorry because I'm so hungry and give me a bit of buttered toast, or a bite of cheese, or some little treat. My biggest danger is getting hit by a car, as I haven't any sense as far as they are concerned.

Get a lot of rest. You won't get any when you get home.
Love,
Trixie
PS
I like to play hard with my cousin Phoofie, but we are both jealous of the grandparents. But I show him who is boss. (I'm kind to him. He gets mad at me and barks and nips.) Maybe because I'm the biggest and I won't let him near them.

RETURN HOME

George studied hard and got straight *A*s. His study schedule at home was regular, his desk was tidy, his notes and materials were neat, his handwriting was legible, and his pencils sharp. Lillis said his grades were good because he had learned time management as bishop. His grades were better than even those of his cadre who had attended a previous session which George had not attended.

As the term ended, George was worried about some issues in Richards II Ward and anxious to attend to them personally. Lillis busied herself cleaning the house and washing clothes. They took one last trip to a park on the Maumee River and collected shells. They said goodbye to their neighbors, classmates, and new friends. Again, some friends gave gifts of food, and Lillis packed a lunch for the road. Mrs. Arlene Kirkland, the landlady, invited them to a dinner party on their way out of town. That evening they drove to Illinois. On the morning of August 21 they toured the Mormon historical sites of Nauvoo, IL, and Carthage Jail in Missouri, and arrived late at their motel in North Platte, Nebraska. They drove the remaining 700 miles the next day to arrive in Salt Lake City.

Leslie's friends, Rosie and Patti, had decorated the house with welcome signs and banners, and they had baked a cake; Lillis's sister Lois and her mother, Edith, had filled the fridge with food.

They returned home with a bulging sheaf of pamphlets, maps, postcards, and slides. The children brought home college sweatshirts from Bowling Green. Leslie brought home some prints from the National Gallery in Washington; George made frames for them and they hung in her bedroom for years after. George also bought a couple of small souvenirs—a little brass cannon from Gettysburg, another from the *USS Constitution,* also a little bronze Liberty Bell from Philadelphia.

George took many, many pictures over the years, of weddings, babies, cousins, family gatherings. He took pictures on the trip as if he might be called upon at some point to present a lecture or travelogue. He had a German camera with a built-in light meter, adjustable F-stops, shutter speeds, aperture, and film speeds. It was a camera for a serious hobbyist. He preferred slides, which offered wonderful granularity. Pictures were expensive—a single exposure could cost 75¢ with the cost of film, developing, and flash bulb. So it was prudent to compose each frame carefully. Today images seemingly fall from the cloud like rain. But then, pictures were fewer and could hold a family's attention for a whole evening as they were projected on a screen, one by one. George showed his slides to his mother and to his in-laws that year—beautiful slides of faraway places, thoughtfully framed and presented.

XXII

The Last Tennis Game
1967–1969

RICHARDS II WARD COMPLETED, 1967

The old Richards Ward building on Downington Avenue near 9th East (the address was actually on Garfield Avenue) was finally torn down in July 1966 and the new building was completed in May 1967. The new building was dedicated November 19, indicating that both wards had paid their assessments in full. George and his family contributed labor in their free moments. Lillis's diary indicates, for example, that Rem and Dean worked at the site on November 24, 1966—Thanksgiving Day— and on December 26, and on many other days. George worked on his free days in the summer and on weekends during the school year.

George assigned interior color selection and decorating to Genevieve Andersen and Marvel McClellan—two elderly women in the congregation. Genevieve was the wife of Henry Andersen, the former bishop and current stake president. Marvel was the wife of one of George's counselors in the bishopric, George McClellan. They picked a carrot orange for the upholstery and paint—very modern and a bit surprising.

There was a celebration on Friday, May 19, which was billed as a belated birthday party for George. It was potluck, and "gifts" were the final donations to the building fund. George's mother and Lillis's parents attended. The crowd asked George to sing a solo, which he did. They took in $1,650 that evening (the Richards II ward total assessment was probably about $65,000).

He was released from the bishopric in January 1968—less than 2 months after the building dedication. He was called to be an alternate stake high councilman, a move which must have seemed like a reward for a job well done. The new calling was easy and less time-consuming. A stake (like a diocese) is the unit which manages several local wards or congregations. The stake president serves with a council of 12 men, in addition to a few alternate councilmen. Essentially all George had to do was attend a weekly meeting with the high council and speak now and then in the worship services at the different wards. There would be no more personal crises or after-hour phone calls, no meetings scheduled back-to-back with church auxiliaries, no welfare to administer, no budgets, no funerals to perform. In October 1968 he was asked to fill a high council vacancy, and in July 1969 he was asked to serve as second counselor to the stake president, Henry Andersen. This could be characterized as a quick rise through the ranks, though church members would find it distasteful to associate church assignments with status. If nothing else, the assignments indicate a level of competence and trust.

Career and Studies 1965–1969

George worked as principal of Jackson Elementary for 8 years and then was reassigned as principal at Forest Elementary in 1966. These were busy years. Lillis wrote in her diary in February 1967:

George very busy on the new ward chapel. Many worries and much work. Geo. is serving on several committees for the schools. Geo. is president of the Salt Lake Schools Principals Association. He is in charge of the ushering for the [Utah Symphony Orchestra series of] youth symphonies, the representative principal for the So. Elementary P.T.A., on the committee for finance for the S.L.C. Schools, the committee for clerks and secretaries, [on the committee] for volunteer aides, representative to the Council of Social Workers, etc, etc. He never has any time of his own.

In addition, he taught a quarter of math in an adult literacy program in 1966. In 1967 and 1968 he was chair of the Head Start committee.

He took occasional short trips to universities in Utah to recruit and interview for teaching positions in Salt Lake City. And he made a long-term commitment to study after-hours 1 or 2 days a week for years. The Salt Lake Public Schools offered a step increase to employees who had 45 credit hours beyond their master's degree. The step increase was worth $300 per year in his case. It barely made financial sense at the cost of about $41 for a 3-hour class plus books. He took classes in administration, education, math, and also German.

FOREST ELEMENTARY, 1966–1969

Forest Elementary, his new assignment, was on 21st South and 9th East, about a half mile from home. It was the school George had attended as a child. Leslie was about to start sixth grade and didn't want to go to school where her dad was principal so she transferred to Hawthorne on the corner of 17th South and 7th East. Nyman started third grade at Forest that year. Rem was at South High and Dean was at Irving Junior High. So each child attended a different school.

George had a niece at Forest—Marianne Walker, Beverly's youngest child. And there were many children from Richards II Ward at Forest. It was not uncommon for children to call George "Bishop" at school, or "Mr. Brooks" at church. Occasionally even George would make a similar slip, saying over the pulpit, for example, "There will be a meeting in the principal's office."

His tenure at Forest is not well documented. A few details survive in memory, which may or may not shed light on his personality. He moved his desk against the wall so that when people or children entered his office they would be on the same side of the desk as he was on. He had a clock on each wall so people would not notice when he glanced at the time. He had a large window installed in his office wall so that people in the outer office or even in the hall could see him at his desk, and he was thus never out of sight, or alone with a child. He routinely visited classrooms while teachers were teaching. He had a framed quote by Thomas Jefferson on the wall which read:

> I know no safe depository of the ultimate powers of the society
> but the people themselves; and if we think them not enlightened
> enough to exercise their control with a wholesome discretion,

the remedy is not to take it from them, but to inform their discretion by education.

And he had doors installed on the toilet stalls in the lavatories; strangely, no one had taken that initiative in the previous half century since the school was built.

George achieved the 45 credit hours in 1969, as he looked forward toward a PhD. (The summer of 1965 at Bowling Green State University in Ohio was likely part of that grand plan.) He had applied for a Mott Foundation scholarship for a doctor of education at the University of Michigan in December 1968, and received word that he was not accepted on March 10, 1969. That same day, Superintendent Art Wiscombe offered George a promotion to Director of Classified Personnel (personnel other than certified teachers). George was happy to take that advancement while sorry to leave Forest and sorry to be so far removed from students.

He continued to take classes through the summer, and he took exams to enroll in a doctorate program at the U. He had worked at Forest only 3 years.

Lillis and Work

At the end of her stay in Hawaii, Lillis commented that she did not want to work as a nurse after she was married, that it was not a normal life. But in the first months of marriage Lillis supported George as the sole breadwinner while he attended college. And she continued to work at least 1 or 2 days a week until after her children were grown and had left home. Sometimes she said she did not like work, but alternatively she said she liked the professional association with her coworkers, the intellectual challenge, and she wanted to maintain her license. She was asked to give an in-service lesson in April 1968 on blood transfusion, indicating that she did keep current with the nursing practice.

It is not clear how much the family budget relied on her earnings, while it is apparent that her preference to stay home gave George the freedom to advance his career and to serve in church leadership. It seems she had little interest in her own career progression and was content to be a bedside nurse. Periodically she would quit, as she did in May 1967, and again in November 1969, only to return to work a few months later.

As for work in the broader sense, her life was almost defined by activity. She was not known to sit down and relax. She was always busy cleaning something, mending something, preparing something for church, or driving her children to their appointments. When they installed the new kitchen cabinets in 1966, it was Lillis who sanded, stained, and varnished them. When they built new cabinets in the dining room in 1969, it was Lillis who tore out the old knotty pine and finished the new oak surfaces. If she had a pastime it was entertaining guests at dinner parties, which was just more work. She occasionally played tennis with Rem, she did a little gardening, she also enjoyed time with George, walking around the neighborhood, going to the theater, or sitting together for a quiet chat. She didn't seem to have other hobbies or time to herself.

In the fall she would can bushels of fruits and vegetables. (This was not uncommon in households in those days.) Once her cousin Leah visited unexpectedly on a Friday and brought her some cucumbers. By Sunday she was brining them and on Monday she canned them as mustard pickles. Here is her recipe:

Sweet Mustard Pickles

Mustard Sauce Preparation
1½ cups flour
2½ cups sugar
6 Tablespoons mustard, dry
4 teaspoons turmeric
1 quart white vinegar
1 pint water
Stir and mix then cook until smooth. Set aside until end.

Pickled Vegetables Preparation
1 quart cauliflower (cut or break small)
2 large ribs (sticks) celery, cut in small pieces.

Cook cauliflower and celery for 5 minutes.
1 quart cubed cucumbers
1 quart pearl onions
1 quart green tomatoes, cut small

6 large green peppers, cut small

1 large red pepper cut small, or pimento

Put above ingredients in large pan, cover with cold water and ½ cup salt; let stand for 30 minutes, then drain.

Mix Mustard Sauce and Vegetables together. Bottle. Process.

Frequently she complained of pain in her arm or back. It is not always clear which labor brought it on. It could have been lifting a patient. It seems possible that her work finishing the doors in the dining room led to pain. It could have been her incessant housework and cleaning. Another factor, as she wrote on November 14, "I went to the Intermountain Clinic and had an upper GI series and gallbladder X-rays. The doctor told me my pain is caused by a misplaced nerve to my kidney because of the curvature in my spine."

INVOLVEMENT WITH FRIENDS AND FAMILY

Lillis was also busy with her friends. As an example, the name Christine Wilks shows up in her diary about 20 times in the late 1960s. Chris was a smart, cheerful young woman, a couple of years older than Rem. She lived next door for a short while, but her family was a bit unsettled. Lillis kept in touch with Chris as she moved to Idaho and Colorado. Whenever Chris was in town Lillis would invite her to eat or sleep over. She helped Chris apply for college and for a scholarship, helped her file income tax—she once ironed her boyfriend's shirts, and drove him to an appointment.

Another friend, Marion Carver, suffered many years with the pain and disability of multiple sclerosis. Sometimes Lillis would administer medication and massage her to calm her muscles. Lillis visited her monthly and sometimes weekly in the 1960s and 1970s, to write Marion's letters and do other small tasks.

Lillis had a childhood friend from Vernal who spent some time in the state psychiatric hospital in Provo in 1961, possibly for anxiety. Betty would call Lillis frequently and weep, and then hang up and immediately call again. Lillis was fully aware that she could not help beyond patiently listening while tethered by her phone cord, as Betty interrupted her routine. These phone calls continued for many years, and Betty's phone number was scrawled in the cover of one of Lillis's journals.

Lillis studied with an immigrant friend in the ward in 1969 who was enrolled in a nursing program while struggling with English as her second language.

Lillis tried to insinuate herself into her niece's life but was rebuffed. This girl showed up in Lillis's diary about 15 times from 1965 and into the 1970s. In the late 1960s the young woman was spending time with an older lesbian. Lillis wrote stridently about the "sickness" of homosexuality and the impossible naïveté of the girl's mother. In Lillis's defense, it was impossible to understand homosexuality in the climate of the 1960s when even the medical community defined it as an illness. Understanding was made more difficult because Lillis listened only to her brother while ignoring her sister-in-law.

This incomplete list reflects a sense of duty which Lillis could not turn away from. She did a lot of good and provided support for people who could not get it elsewhere. Lillis visited her aged mother-in-law, Winnifred Brooks, at least weekly, usually accompanied by George. Winnifred continued to inflict her moods on Lillis, and Lillis continued to grumble about it. It says something about obligation and reward.

Winnifred wrecked her car in July 1966 and stopped driving frequently after that incident; she was 74. Once in a while Lillis would take Winn for rides or run errands for her. Winnifred continued to have disagreements with the renters in her basement. She relied on George and Lillis to smooth things over. They visited her on one occasion in August of 1968 to find "she was very upset emotionally and went all to pieces when we got there. She cried and wanted to die." Lillis and George had plans to go to a wedding reception that evening so they took Winnifred along for the long drive to Farmington, Utah. They attended the reception while Winnifred waited in the car. On the drive home, Winnifred "became more calm and seemed much better." In 1969 George's uncle Nat Parry (Winnifred's younger brother) got a divorce. He was elderly and, typical of Nat, it was a bit of a scandal. When George and Lillis visited Nat he told Lillis of gossip that Winnifred had spread about her. Later in February 1969 Winnifred had some moles removed from her face and it fell to Lillis to change her bandages. On another visit in 1970 they found Winnifred had taken too much pain medicine and was disoriented. Lillis inventoried her pills and stayed with her until she recovered. Winnifred's rudeness was background noise in Lillis's life. But Lillis was there for her as she became more fragile, more hard of hearing, and more dependent.

Of course, Lillis's own parents were also growing older and needed assistance. She would often visit both homes in succession on Sundays. Thus amusing contrasts sometimes appear in Lillis's diary, such as this one on April 27, 1969: "Geo and I dropped by to see Mother Brooks. She was sarcastic and miserable so we only stayed a few minutes. We drove over to see Mom and Dad Remington. She gave us some chocolates and cookies."

Fuller Remington had a stroke in August 1966. For a while he walked with a walker and would spill food on his shirt; but over time he recovered. He retired from sales at 75 years old. From then on Lillis records that she drove Fuller to Welfare Square where he had found part-time employment. He fell down steps in July 1967 and injured his arm; he was hospitalized several days for a hernia repaired in June 1968; fell again in October 1968 and injured his arm, hip, and head. He had cancer removed from his face in July 1969. Lillis often provided first-line health care, not only for her parents but also for others in the extended family.

SENTIMENTALITY

George and Lillis were demonstrative and affectionate toward each other; some people might say they were silly. Lillis saved many gushy or playful notes that George wrote to accompany birthday or anniversary gifts, or maybe a rosebud on no special occasion. These notes have fallen out of their decaying scrapbooks, and are difficult to link with a date or event. One reads: "Because we're broke, As you may know, And have no dough Which to blow, This note will have to do, By Joe! To tell you that I love you so." Another reads, "How was I so lucky!! Love, George." He gave very personal gifts such as nightgowns, slips, perfume, or jewelry. Once he gave her a sterling silver bud vase, saying, "When I bring you a rose I don't want it in a glass vase."

He amused her. Like an alter ego, he could do things, say things, and behave in ways that she could not. They went to a dinner party with their study group in November 1969 at Don and Rayola Larson's house. It was billed as a Roman theme—after all, they were studying the Great Books. George went dressed in a toga, wearing a laurel wreath in his hair, and carrying a violin—a reference to Nero. One or two others also came in costume, but not Lillis.

Her expressions to him were more modest, or cautious, or private. However, she clearly pined for George in her diary, even when he left only for a night or two. George went to a principals conference in Portland, Oregon, in March 1966. Lillis received a letter from him the next day, and the day after that, and then he returned on the third day. Each day Lillis wrote in her diary, "I Miss George." When he returned he brought little gifts for the children, and a cameo brooch carved from a brown and white seashell for Lillis. In August 1967 George went to a 2-day administrators conference in the nearby town of Park City. Again he called daily and Lillis wrote, "I feel lonesome." Similarly in August 1968 she wrote, "Geo is still in Sun Valley [Idaho]. He called me on the phone this morning. Made me lonesome for him just hearing his voice. I've tried to keep busy in the yard and house while he is gone." When he came home she wrote, "Today is the wonderful day George will be home from Sun Valley." Lillis and George attended a 2-day stake seminar at BYU in September 1969, staying overnight in a dormitory. Lillis wrote, "We had a lovely drive down, a delicious dinner, and un-inspirational talk by Brother Bradshaw. Geo and I put our twin beds together and shared the covers from both beds. It's quite cold." So this pattern of affection, often remarked upon by those who knew them, was also documented in her terse diary entries.

FREE-RANGE CHILDREN

If someone were to ask the Brooks children, "Did your dad ever take you fishing?" or "Did he ever play catch with you?" they might answer, "No; those were not his interests." True enough, but a complete answer might include, "And my parents were too busy." Church and profession encroached on family life. It would be unfair to say that they neglected their children. They took a road-trip vacation almost every year, including 10 days to northern California in 1966, and 2 weeks to the Pacific Northwest, including Canada, in 1968. As mentioned before, they attended most of the children's play series at the Pioneer Memorial Theater, and the Utah Symphony youth concert series. There are mentions of the children going to watch Jacques d'Amboise at Kingsbury

Hall or the Bolshoi Ballet at the Capitol Theater. But the children were also given remarkable freedom.

When Rem was 13 years old he and his buddy Wally Haycock rode their bikes 10 miles along the busy 9th East from Sugar House to Sandy to visit Rem's cousin, Stephen. When it was clear that his parents didn't care, he did it again and took Dean who was 12. Rem and Dean often took the bus downtown to go swimming at the Deseret Gym. Sometimes Ralf Czerny or Jed Pease would come, demonstrating that nobody's parents worried too much. These kids would swim, but also sit in the steam room with a bunch of fat naked old men. The kids frequently slept over at their friends' houses in the summer. They would walk into Sugar House and be gone for hours at a time watching the free movies at Southeast Theater or swimming at the park.

Rem and Leslie used to skip school to go skiing with the tacit approval of their parents. In April 1968 Leslie came home from skiing with a sunburn so bad that she developed blisters across her chin. Lillis called the emergency room to get a pain prescription for Rem's sunburn; his pain took 5 days to subside. Leslie skipped school again to ski in March 1969 and again came home with a bad sunburn.

Rem took a job as a dishwasher at the Kwong Jou restaurant in the fall of 1966 during the school year. Lillis was unhappy with his hours which sometimes lasted until 3 AM. She also worried about him eating a lot of fried pork on his shift. She expressed her concerns to him— an example of her parental involvement—but allowed him to continue working until May when he took a different job at Snelgrove's.

Dean was unhappy and unsuccessful in school. George and Lillis transferred him from Forest to Jackson in 6th grade so that George could keep an eye on him. They called upon his grandmother to tutor and help him with homework. Years later they also transferred him out of South High into East High. So they were aware of a problem, and involved to a degree, but largely negligent and completely ineffective. They often fell back on the strategy of punishing or yelling at him when report cards came out, as she noted March 20, 1968, "Both Geo and I gave [Dean] the dickens for his low grades in school." Dean's grades were so poor it was not clear that he would graduate from high school until the last moment.

After a string of bad teachers they also transferred Nyman from Forest to Emerson Elementary in November 1969.

ELECTION YEAR, 1968

George continued to serve as a delegate to the state and county Democratic conventions in 1968, a dramatic year for politics. George and Lillis almost reflexively supported Democratic positions. They had supported the war in Vietnam but in March Lillis wrote:

"We're becoming more and more confused over the Vietnam War. We question the rightness of the USA being so involved. Thousands of sheep are dying at Skull Valley [Utah] from an unknown cause, possibly chemical or bacteriological warfare experiments by the gov. Over 5,500 have died already.

The US government denied involvement in the sheep incident for 3 decades, but immediate popular skepticism was a factor in declining support for the war.

They took their kids to hear Robert Kennedy speak at the Terrace Ballroom on March 27, arriving 90 minutes early. Lillis and George went to hear Republican Senator Charles Percy speak at BYU March 29. Lillis could have supported his candidacy, or Republican presidential candidate Nelson Rockefeller, but she called Nixon "an egotistical boob." George took his kids with him to the county Democratic convention on June 29, and to the state convention on July 26 and 27.

Just before the election there was a final opportunity for George and Lillis to share history-in-the-making with their children. Lillis wrote on October 12:

It is a beautiful fall day. Geo, Dean, Nyman, Leslie, and I drove around the Temple grounds to see the crowds and demonstrators [protesting] Geo Wallace. He is speaking in the Tabernacle today. We feel bad that Ezra Taft Benson would support a man such as Wallace.

The former governor of Alabama was famous for saying, "Segregation now, segregation tomorrow, segregation forever." It was an inexplicable scandal that he could secure the Tabernacle as a venue for his third-party presidential campaign, not to mention the endorsement of an apostle.

THE LAST TENNIS GAME

Rem played tennis on the South High team and lettered in 1968. He often played with his buddy Bliss Roberts, a ranked player on Highland High's state championship team. For years Rem had also played against his mother. Lillis always won. She won sets if not games. In August 1969 while the family was vacationing at a cabin at Brighton in Big Cottonwood Canyon near Salt Lake City, Rem (19 years old) came down from Utah State University and played one last game of tennis with his mother. He beat her for the first time, 6-2. They never played each other again, probably because as their paths parted they never had another opportunity. Rem had just received his mission call a day or two earlier. It was later that year that Lillis went in for her upper GI X-ray series to diagnose pain. She was 45 years old.

XXIII

Pathways Diverge
1970s

Family pathways began to branch and separate in the 1970. The children graduated from high school and went to college. The boys served LDS church missions. Some took full-time employment, married, or moved out of state. George took on greater responsibilities at work and at church. Winnifred Brooks died in 1977. Edith Remington was diagnosed with melanoma in 1978. Bit by bit, the older generations ceded to the younger. As Lillis sometimes observed, "How surely the end doth come."

George's Career

George served as Director of Personnel from July 1969 until 1973. At that point his title changed to Administrator of Personnel, a nuance that came with a promotion—essentially he became a deputy superintendent of the district. He held that position until his retirement in 1985. George continued to take a class or two almost every quarter at the University of Utah or Westminster College, focusing on education and administration topics. He received an EdS degree in 1973; his aunt Juanita Brooks, author and historian, received an honorary PhD from the U at the same graduation ceremony.

Beginning in March of 1970 George started to travel annually to nearby colleges and universities to recruit schoolteachers. These were usually day trips, but sometimes he would take a few days to visit colleges in Arizona, Colorado, New Mexico, or Wyoming. Even though these trips were short, Lillis would pine for him and mope in her diary. Sometimes she would invite Leslie to sleep in her bed while George was away, and then she would complain that Leslie was skinny and not too cuddly. George took a week-long trip in 1972 to Colorado and New Mexico. He called home every day. Lillis would write things in her diary like, "Geo called tonight from Albuquerque. We miss him terribly. Will be glad when he comes home. Time drags while he is away." Then on February 16 she wrote, "Geo rang the doorbell at 2 AM and we visited until 4 AM. It is wonderful having him home safely. He grew a mustache while away." The mustache was one of his little gags; he shaved it off before he returned to work.

George was also involved with annual salary negotiations which began in February or March. These required a steady temperament, and late hours. At the end there was a scramble to type up the new agreements and contracts and to present them to the board. George's first year for contract negotiations was 1970. He completed the task in August. By comparison the neighboring school district, Granite, stumbled, and teachers picketed into September. It is a subtle measure of his success in the Salt Lake District. Late in his career he commented, "I think I have survived in this position without getting fired longer than anybody else."

George became disillusioned and distrustful with some of his fellow administrators early on, and also with the members of the board. The business administrator, Gary Harmer, for example, hired someone, which he had neither authority nor budget to do. George had to fire the new guy immediately. George wrote and spoke very little about these incidents but Lillis mentioned them frequently. Lillis called his supervisor, Stan Morgan, "inconsistent" and a "difficult distraction." Finally the board reorganized the administration and Richard White became George's boss. White was also a problem. White was nominally in charge of salary and contract negotiations in 1972, but was never present, which paralyzed the process. Lillis called him dishonest and malicious, and asserted that employees at the board office were afraid of him.

Superintendent Art Wiscombe and the board were no help. The board told the administrators in April of 1972 that anyone not attending a retreat with the board would be fired. In the same week the board told George that his job was at risk for budget cuts. It was as if threats were their only tool to motivate employees. In March of 1973 Lillis asserted that poor administration had damaged morale among teachers. Superintendent Wiscombe did little things to keep the staff on edge. Finally, Wiscombe was forced to resign in February of 1973. Then on June 21, Wiscombe asked George for a cash advance on his severance, which George refused. Wiscombe became angry, but by then his anger was inconsequential.

The board asked George on Monday, July 30, to fire 28 teachers for a staff reduction. Then after a long board meeting on the following day they were all rehired.

Board meetings were held on Tuesdays and often ran past midnight, week after week. Besides being painfully long, George felt that the board meetings were chaotic. It seemed that any citizen could show up and raise hell. And the board members themselves were not much better. There were always a few intelligent, well-intentioned board members, but also a few goofballs. One such board member was Jon Bauman. Once he grandstanded in a board meeting by questioning each line item in a budget. He was stumped when he came to the expense for timpani. It soon became apparent that Bauman did not know what timpani were. On another occasion, a woman on the school board showed up on the doorstep of a homosexual school employee to proposition him.

Nyman attended a meeting with George which lasted till 1:30 AM. Nyman was astounded that such people—immature, uninformed, emotional—could get elected. Ms. Susan Keene was particularly ignorant of the issues, argumentative, and rude to other board members that night.

One of the board members, John Crawford, put pressure on George to hire a friend; George did not comply. (George's brother-in-law also put pressure on George on two occasions to hire relatives, which of course would have been illegal. Saying *no* the first time was never enough.)

In 1976 some employees sued the board for age discrimination. One of the plaintiffs was Joe Hillstead, who had served as principal of Irving Junior High when the Brooks children attended there—a hint of how personal the trial would be. This trial created the necessity for friends and coworkers to testify whether Hillstead was competent or whether it was best for him to retire. George was not named in the suit, but had to testify or give deposition for hours at a time on two occasions. The trial lasted a year and in January of 1977 George wrote:

> The age-discrimination trial is all but over. Only the summing-up remains (next Friday). I was obliged to serve as a witness and in giving a deposition. This was all very trying for me. I'm glad it is about over. I feel that no matter which side wins, many people lost in terms of anxiety, worry, hurtful testimony, embarrassment, etc. In deliberating how I have worried over this thing since the fall of 1974 I hope that I have acquired some ability to stop worrying by being more confident, more at peace, more trusting in my Father in Heaven to see me through such ordeals. I hope that this new year will mark some improvement in my ability to . . . have more faith, more assurance. I'm sure this thing is an important lesson for me. . . . I really have very little reason to be a worrier. No great bad things have ever befallen me. I have been abundantly blessed all my life. Things have always turned out well for me. My experience should teach me not to worry.

Clearly the job challenged George's peace of mind and trust in his colleagues. Personalities did not improve as they rose through the ranks. But there was at least one silver lining. One of his official duties was to attend a personnel directors' convention every October. He would take 2 weeks off and drive with Lillis and tour museums, battlefields, or national parks along the way. The first convention, in 1971, was held in New Orleans; the next in Atlanta; then Minneapolis; Montreal; Jacksonville; Washington, D.C.; Milwaukee; and finally George persuaded the committee to hold it in Salt Lake City in 1980.

The October travelogues are a delight to read, even when they are just rolling down the highway. On their first day on the road to Atlanta, Lillis wrote:

> Wednesday, October 11, 1972. We were up early. Geo, Nyman and I left Salt Lake City at 5 AM and had a delightful drive to Salina, Kansas. We have driven nearly 1,000 miles today but it has been very pleasant. We have seen many flocks of birds

flying south. The fields are full of sorghum, grain, and alfalfa, large herds of cattle were everywhere . . .

Thursday, October 12, 1972. Up at 8 AM. It's raining very hard. The countryside is green and lovely. We drove to Abilene, Kansas, and saw the Eisenhower museum and memorial . . . I wrote to Leslie and Mother in the car, and Mother Brooks. We visited the Truman Library and Museum at Independence, MO . . . We also drove by his home . . . It is still raining very hard. We drove to the LDS Information Center at Independence and went on a tour of it . . .

George and Lillis were curious about every back road, and took delight in every town. Going home from Jacksonville, FL, in 1975 they charted a path through Bernalillo and Cuba, NM; Durango, CO; over the Molas Pass, Silverton, Red Mountain Pass, and Ouray. These are roads well off the freeway and over magnificent mountain passes in Colorado. Since they traveled over some routes several times, they were able to visit the less-frequented points of interest, such as the Eugene Field House (home of Dred Scott's attorney, Roswell Field) in St. Louis; or the Betty Crocker Kitchen in Minneapolis; or the monument to Vulcan, god of fire, in the steel town of Birmingham. Sometimes Lillis would kill time on the road by reading aloud to George as he drove. Sometimes he would sing to her. When Nyman went along they would stop and allow him to run for a mile or two along the road to keep in shape for track. Then he would practice his chanter or do homework. Lillis often started her daily writing with, "It's wonderful traveling with George," or, "He is exciting company, a good and interesting traveler, and fun to be with." These frequent affectionate comments in Lillis's diaries are a primary motivation for telling this story; there is never a comment to the contrary in their loving and respectful relationship.

GEORGE IN THE STAKE PRESIDENCY 1969–1979

George was called to serve as a counselor to the stake president in July 1969—the same week he took his new job as personnel director at the school board. Both assignments demanded a lot of time in after-hours meetings. In both cases George complained that the meetings were largely a waste of time because of poor organization and poor discipline. His new authority did not extend to controlling meeting agendas. He always spoke kindly and respectfully of his fellows on the stake high council and in the presidency. But there was a dynamic of everyone needing to be heard. Additionally, the president, Henry Andersen, was a bit of a perfectionist and would take the time to consider all matters thoroughly. Lillis wrote on February 25, 1973, George "comes home depressed because meetings drag on so long. He feels there is a lot of wasted time." Very often his Sunday meeting with the high council would last in excess of 4 hours. He would miss meals with the family, returning home after 10 PM. It is possible that the other men did not have the additional constraints on their time that George had with work and study.

George identified his frequent assignments to speak in church as an important part of his duty. He felt that to speak well he needed to reflect on a topic for about a week before putting pen to paper. He said that public speaking was taxing and he could not do it without divine help and preparation. His intention was to write new specific text for each audience and occasion. Thus he never filed away old speeches to use again (but some notes do survive). He was under no illusion that he held everyone's interest, and in fact, sometimes he addressed only a segment of the audience. But even then his remarks were purposed for the occasion. He avoided long quotations and long passages of scripture. He was not averse to quoting current relevant thinkers; as an example he quoted Bob Dylan over the pulpit. He sought out criticisms of his rhetoric, content, and delivery. He adjusted his cadence to speak more quickly based on such criticism. Another criticism, which he felt was valid, was that his eye contact was poor. He tried to improve that, but balanced with staying on schedule and on topic. He rehearsed his speeches to the point that he knew within a minute how long his remarks would take. He rarely deviated from his prepared notes.

There is evidence that he was a successful public speaker because people frequently asked for copies of his talks, which he never gave out. He excused himself by not preparing written texts, preferring to speak from detailed notes. Also, he was frequently asked to speak, such as at graduation ceremonies in the public school system and at funerals and other occasions.

On stake conference Sundays, Lillis would ask George to save her a seat near the front by placing a book or coat on the pew. Other men in stake leadership who had meetings prior to stake conference would do just that but George refused. It was an example of something that he and Lillis disagreed on, but not strongly; it just rubbed him the wrong way.

It was customary on the weekend of stake conference for members of the presidency to invite the visiting General Authority over for meals. Entertaining was Lillis's strong suit. Occasionally she would record the names of these men who ate at her table.

PARENTAL CONCERNS

Parents worry about their children. Some worries are common and predictable: will the children be healthy; will they go to war. Some parental worries are irrelevant, even annoying. George and Lillis worried whether their children would marry well. In their opinion a good marriage was not only a component of a proper life, but it was also a sacrament. Their fixation with marriage seemed at times anguished, impatient, and disproportionate to the risk. The children, like all children, had their own agendas and worries. Yet they seemed to bend to the tug of their parents' concerns.

Rem entered school at the University of Utah in the fall of 1971 to study biology with the hope of entering medical school. But medical school was competitive; in 1974 there were 2,200 applications for 100 openings at the U. Rem applied to several schools year after year, through 1979. He even considered foreign schools. This was another worry. George worried in his diary that Rem was putting all his eggs in one basket, and wished that Rem would give up on medical school. George and Lillis gave Rem a weekend vacation at a condominium in Cache Valley in 1976 because he seemed distraught over school and a troubled romance. Lillis wrote in February 1979, "Rem can't get his mind off med school. I feel bad he can't seem to adjust better to other jobs. He seems so un-objective; it is of concern to me. I feel a bit discouraged with it all tonight." Then, just like a fable instructing children to ignore their parents, Rem was accepted to medical school in 1979.

Leslie finished her nursing studies in 1975 and soon took a job as a nurse at a boys summer camp. When she returned she was in love with one of the camp counselors. For all of his nobility, he was not LDS—and that was a deal-breaker. Over the next several years she went from one unhappy romance to another. Lillis and George suffered fear, despair, and disappointment with Leslie at every turn over several years. Their concerns may have been counterproductive.

In October 1978, Leslie was considering serving a mission, almost a cliché for single Mormon women without hope. In February 1979, Leslie decided she should move out of her parents' house and "try it on her own," in Lillis's words. "I can't see that it is necessary or right but [I] have refrained from saying so. . . . It made me feel sick inside. . . . I know . . . how very much she should like to be married." After a day of moving furniture, the extended family had a dinner party, then went their separate ways. Lillis wrote, "I feel very depressed tonight. I'm glad there is no one here to experience it with me. I asked Geo while we were driving home how he felt. He said 'I'm very tired and also a bit depressed.'"

All the while Lillis noted in her diary the friends and cousins who were getting married or having babies. In 1975, for example, Shari Casper, Myrna Tolley, Bill Leslie and Kim Nelson, Kim Remington, Donna Quick, Allen Andersen, and Dave Goddard—friends of Leslie—were married. It's safe to say it was a preoccupation for Lillis.

Rem was living his own drama at the same time. He broke an engagement in June 1977 after the formalities of planning the wedding, holding a bridal shower, and the parents meeting for dinner. The difficult decision was made more uncomfortable as the former fiancée or her father would stalk and corner Lillis or Rem, unannounced, at work or at home, to persuade or to shame.

Later, Rem married Carolyn English in March 1978. Dean married Lorraine Hyer in August of the same year, 10 days before they left for Tehran.

Dean's fellowship to Tehran University was another source of anxiety for George and Lillis. Lillis wrote, "Dean and Lorraine came for a while and we discussed . . . their departure. . . . They both seem calm in spite of the fact that they have no place to live in Tehran nor a promise of a job [for Lorraine]." In October 1978, 6 weeks after they arrived, there was an earthquake in Iran which killed 25,000 people. But the more frightening news was the Islamic Revolution which began on September 8, just 2 days after their arrival in country. Telephone and postal service were poor. On two occasions people traveling to the US delivered mail to the Brooks family. But several weeks at a time would pass with no personal communication, only news of strikes and killings. The family finally learned that Dean and Lorraine were on their way home when they called Salt Lake City from New York on January 16, 1979, the same day that the Shah abdicated.

Even as late as October 1979—both Rem and Dean were married, both had full-time employment, both had mortgages—Lillis wrote, "I continue to be concerned over Rem and Dean not being finished with school and not having a clear vision of a definite goal."

WINNIFRED PARRY BROOKS, 1892–1977

On her birthday in 1970 Lillis wrote, "For the first time in my married life Mother Brooks came by on my birthday and gave me $5.00 and a bottle of jam. We visited for a while." Lillis was 47 years old; Winnifred was 78. As Winnifred got older she became more respectful and kind to Lillis. Winnifred had close relationships with her own daughters and relied on them. But as she became more frail she may have understood a need for Lillis's particular insights. More importantly, she may have recognized Lillis's willingness to have a relationship.

Winnifred had colorectal surgery and surgery for breast cancer in 1970. She fell and hurt her face in 1972. Winnifred suffered from gout all her life. During an attack in 1973 Lillis gave her shots of Demerol, stocked her fridge, checked in on her at bedtime, bathed her, and did her laundry. Lillis took her to her doctor appointments and helped her interpret her test results. Lillis administered Demerol again during a gout attack in 1974, sometimes responding to Winnifred's phone calls in the middle of the night. In 1975, Winnifred came to Lillis and George, frantic over a conversation with one of her daughters who had suggested she should sell her house and move out. She had tachycardia in early 1976 and by late 1976 her cancer had metastasized. Over the years she had been "offish" (George's word) with George. But she was now relying more on him as well. He responded to calls to fix frozen pipes, replace a toilet, and to re-shingle her house.

In 1976, George started to visit or telephone her daily. On one such occasion, Saturday, November 13, George broke into her house to find her lying on the floor, entangled in a fire screen. Apparently she had suffered a stroke the day before. She was cold and her face was cut and bruised. Winnifred made some improvements quickly, speaking and moving her left leg on the first day. But she had lost her hearing aid and therefore appeared bewildered or even unresponsive. She continued to make incremental improvements in a care facility, but died June 25, 1977.

George tried to make sense of his relationship with her, both before her stroke and after her death. He remembered his life with her, her aspirations, her pride, and character. He summarized the end of her life noting that her edge had softened.

> She remained always quite mentally lucid. . . . She spoke to me with far more real affection, she even liked Lillis much more. . . . She died . . . a sweet, faithful, expressive old lady who had learned to suffer without complaining and had learned to sublimate many feelings which in her healthier days would have been tense, even explosive.

Winnifred's house was sold and her trinkets divided, some of which may have had value. With some relief and a bit perplexed, George wrote:

> I have all but lost contact with [my sisters] Beverly and Bobby. It is as though we were not related. I cannot fully explain why there is such a poor relationship between me and them. I suppose it is more accurately described as a non-relationship, occasionally manifesting itself in mistrust and mild hostility. Probably jealousy is part of the motivation, maybe even guilt. I am probably wrong in feeling some relief at this final breaking off of familial relationships with them. Fortunately I still maintain a very good communication with [my brother] Sam which I fondly hope will continue.

STAKE PRESIDENT 1979–1985

Gordon Hinckley, an apostle of the church, visited the Sugar House Stake during conference in October 1978 and advised George that he would be asked to serve as the next stake president. By way of context, during this time Rem was trying to get into medical school, Dean and Lorraine were living in Iran, Leslie was fretting about her boyfriend who was not a member of the church, and Nyman was on a mission in Taiwan. To his credit, President Hinckley was generous with his time and spoke personally with the members of the family who were available and present. He very generously spoke with Leslie alone, in private for a half-hour or so, and reassured her that falling in love was not a mistake. It is hard to say whether George and Lillis were persuaded by Hinckley's calm regard of the Brooks children.

Though George had served in the presidency for 9 years, he was still surprised by the new demands on his time. He felt that he was of service and felt rewarded in the work, particularly when helping people work through personal problems.

George reorganized the stake in the summer of 1979. The inner-city demographics were changing and the population had shrunk. The neighborhood had long been elderly. Forest Elementary School and Irving Junior High had closed and South High School would close a few years later. By September, George consolidated the nine wards in the Sugar House Stake into five. The reorganization was an urgent necessity with many components to address. But the transition went smoothly, with four new wards up and running on the same Sunday in September.

In March of 1980 the church transitioned to the "block meeting schedule," reducing weekly meetings from about 7 hours to 3 and moving all meetings to Sunday. Two weeks after the new meeting schedule was implemented George wrote that it "seems to have had a miraculous effect already, increasing meeting attendance dramatically."

In May 1980 George wondered whether:

> . . .it is normal or good to feel quite inadequate as a stake president. I see very little empirical improvement in the stake in the past year and a half. I enjoy many things about the calling and am frustrated about many other things.... We have a good spirit at our meetings. Some things seem to decline, however. Almost all of objective evidences slowly decline—home teaching, tithing participation, sacrament meeting attendance, etc.

His writing took on a tone of worry. He may have been caught in a trap of irrelevant metrics. Or he may have been caught in a trap of top-down priorities. The neighborhood was old and poor and no doubt had many problems. But he started to write and worry about formulaic problems of church attendance, doctrine, and sin.

WOODWORKING AND JOGGING

George wrote in May of 1976 that he went for a ride in the car with Lillis and her parents. It was a common pastime for Lillis to drive through the rich neighborhoods, inventing or imagining the back-stories of the residents, commenting on their taste and landscaping. George did not like it so much, and on this occasion actually found it depressing. Acknowledging his own house for what it was—albeit well-constructed, beautiful, well-furnished, it was small and in a neighborhood which was increasingly "neglected and ugly with ugly people." In this mood he wondered:

> . . . where we might have made our home if we had had the foresight and money to have taken a nicer place, one with more space, another bathroom, a greater assortment of children and youth for our children to have grown up with.

George was by nature happy and amusing, but occasionally moody. The pressures of work, the legal trials, the undependability of his coworkers, worry over his children, his mother's declining health, all combined to make him "tense and often depressed."

> I worry about the security of my job. I worry about my relationships with the Supt. and board members. I worry about the effectiveness of the personnel office. I have come to be a worrier and consequently my life of late has not been as pleasant to me as it used to be. I also worry about bringing disappointment, even embarrassment to my family if I should fail or appear to fail in this job. I also worry about my children, especially as they approach the age they should be married.

In these days of much pressure and little free time George took up woodworking and jogging. He bought a table saw and a router in 1974 and built some simple bookcases. As his skills improved he built the case for a granddaughter clock in 1976 which stood about 5 feet high. He purchased plans for that piece, and also purchased some of the milled trim. It turned out to be a beautiful, refined piece of furniture. Feeling more confident, he drew his own plans and routed his own trim for a china cabinet or display case which echoed the lines of the clock but with glass on all sides. By late 1978 he had made several schoolhouse wall clocks. These had an octagonal face with a pendulum case on the bottom. He also made the faces for some with pen and ink. And of course he did the finishing and staining on everything he built. He also made several copies of a Shaker step stool, laptop desks, china cabinets, bookcases, and toys. He gave most away to friends, coworkers, and relatives. He was quite prolific.

Jogging was first mentioned in Lillis's diary in 1972 when George and Lillis ran together. Certainly by 1979 or so it was George's preferred exercise routine. He started out running 1.5 miles, three times a week, and running a mile in 8:30. He won a first-place ribbon (his first ribbon ever) in a 10K on Thanksgiving Day 1982. By 1984 (58 years old) he was running 3 to 10 miles, three times a week and could run a single mile in 6:30. He ran a 10K in under 48 minutes, and a half marathon in under 2 hours. He ran his first marathon that year but the details are lost.

By looking through a disorganized folder where George kept some of his ribbons and the number placards that he pinned to his shirt during a race, it would seem that he ran about 30 races between 1980 and 1986, winning ribbons in about half. In one multi-stage, multi-distance event— the Grand Prix of 1983—he won 5th in the series, and was thus ranked 5th in the state in his age group. He ran all distances. In some events the distance was optional; Lillis would occasionally run a shorter distance such as 5 miles (with her bad back and arthritis), while George would run a longer distance such as a half marathon. As much as anything, George enjoyed beating his brother-in-law Don Remington. Don, like George, was a serious amateur. He was a good weight, and 5 years younger than George. George once confided that he could hear Don's footsteps and recognize Don's breathing behind him, so he could make an effort to keep ahead of Don without looking over his shoulder or disclosing his intention.

By 1984 George had lost 30 pounds, never to be regained. And he had a resting pulse rate below 50 bpm. He was not a health faddist, but would not set butter or salt on the table.

LILLIS AND HER CONCERNS

It might seem symmetrical at this point to dwell on Lillis's many church assignments or her professional life. But in truth, she lived the life of a mid-century Mormon woman. Women's professional positions or positions in church did not usually provide comparable institutional prestige. If one can enumerate without patronizing, she became ward Relief Society president in July 1971. She was in charge of the LDSH Nurses Alumni Association party that autumn. She was appointed to a 1-year term as president of the Aurora Club in 1976. These reveal little about who she was.

Lillis quit nursing in 1970, and then hired on again in the LDSH recovery room in 1974. It's possible she felt she needed employment and more money as her children went on missions and to college. Over the next couple of years she took a series of work-related classes, some of which were held at the University of Utah. She studied EKG and cardiac issues in 1974; heart and pulmonary pathology in 1975 (her nursing school classmate and friend in Hawaii, Jean Langdorf, also attended that class); the infant nervous system (Leslie also attended that class), moni-toring, and blood transfusions in 1976.

In March 1973, Lillis went in to have a scabbing freckle removed which turned out to be cancerous. In a follow-up she had lumps removed from her hands, arms, chest, and face. She and her sister Lois and her sister-in-law Marilyn had hysterectomies that year. There was no malig-nancy with Lillis's hysterectomy. She was 49. Lillis complained in September 1976 of pain in her back and down her right leg, which she thought might be arthritis, although she also admitted to an unspecified disc problem. Other than that, her health was good.

Lillis spent a lot of time with her parents from 1972 through 1977, helping them collect, tape-record, and write their histories. She also spent time quilting with her mother. That task was important for Edith. They made quilts for most if not all of Edith's grandchildren and great-grandchil-dren—maybe two dozen individual pieces of folk art in the 1970s. Many of them included pieces of Fuller's old suits from his days as a salesman.

On a day-to-day basis, Lillis was an important and dependable friend. She continued to visit Marion Carver, who suffered painful spasms related to multiple sclerosis. Lillis's neighbor around the corner, Beth Tolley, was diagnosed with cancer in the summer of 1971. Her disease progressed quickly and she died in the fall of that year. Lillis was often at her bed-side to change dressings or administer medication, even responding in the middle of the night. She invited the children over to Thanksgiving that year and continued to watch them and their father. The widower, Wallace, had served with George in the bishopric. He suffered depression for years. In January 16, 1979, she wrote:

> Today was cold and stormy. . . . Wallace is very ill with depres-sion and neurosis. Geo and I have spent some time with him during his most restless and depressed days. He is so terribly upset, wringing his hands and crying, refusing drugs or com-mitment. He has been under the care of a psychiatrist with little relief. It is so tragic to see his suffering . . . and so difficult for his two young daughters at home.

She gave prescription injections to her neighbor Dorothy Tuddenham. She also bathed, changed the bed, and cared for another neighbor, Howard Updegraff, as he lay dying in 1972. She frequently gave rides to Dora Lewis to doctor appointments. Certainly there were many others, including her own parents.

Lillis's diaries and letters reveal additional heartbreak and worry over her brothers and sisters, some of whom suffered stress or collapse of their marriages in the 1970s. And she tried to shield her parents from the details of the news.

TAIWAN AND HONG KONG

George, Lillis, and Leslie traveled to Taiwan in March of 1979 to meet Nyman after his mission, and to tour in Taiwan and Hong Kong. They were abroad for 2 weeks. Lillis wrote nightly and filled 40 pages, 8½ by 11 inches. Lillis's travelogues reveal an appreciation for the genius and diversity of humanity. She wrote about the natural beauty of the land-scape and the moods of the weather, the food, the shrines and monks and thousands of statues of the Buddha, the smells of the cities, the poverty, the press of the crowd and the individuals going about their daily tasks. She also wrote about confronting her cultural biases and her exhaustion at the end of each day.

They visited a night market where Lillis described a vendor selling drinks of the blood and fluid of living snakes, some were cobras, hanging from a line, writhing as their bellies were cut open, then left there alive for the next customer.

> It was a most horrifying and shocking performance. . . . The snake was still alive twisting and turning. We turned in silence and walked slowly on the other side of the street only to come upon another area where we could have witnessed the same thing. . . . Everyone around us looked so well dressed, fine looking, and civilized . . .

They traveled off the beaten tourist path, taking advantage of Nyman's understanding of the language, culture, and landscape. Occasionally they would draw a crowd as if the locals had never seen Caucasians before. Then the trip ended:

> The ride to the airport was very interesting thru the crowded early-morning streets. We rode mostly in silence with our own thoughts. It was a beautiful morning and I thought of the many things I should liked to have done but did not have time for. And I wondered if I'd ever be back again and if so, how soon and under what circumstances. I thought of . . . the people in the shops we had been friendly with, the happy faces, the sad, and the tragic faces I could see individually in my mind. The airport was large, clean efficient and beautiful. . . . We finally boarded our DC-10, a large plane with nearly 400 passengers aboard. . . . It was only moments until we watched our past two and half weeks slip behind us and disappear over water and clouds.

They flew the great circle over Japan, Alaska, Seattle, and to Oakland. Her brother Earl picked them up and they stayed a day at Earl's and Karol's beautiful home in San Ramon. Lillis noted that Nyman hesitated to enter their house with his shoes on. He hesitated again at Karol's generous steak supper. The next day on the road he asked the question, "How much wealth should one person have and still be just?"

A SEA CHANGE

There is no question that Lillis returned from her trip humbled, renewed, and enlightened. About this time there were a lot of refugees trying to get out of Southeast Asia, fleeing the camps in Thailand, and the fighting in Laos, Cambodia, and Vietnam. Sometimes they were collectively called *boat people*. It was an enormous crisis. With Nyman recently returned home, no doubt whispering his exceptional views, George and Lillis were persuaded to help.

George and Lillis sponsored a married couple who had survived the Khmer Rouge; Dean and Lorraine sponsored another family with an infant daughter. They all arrived in Salt Lake City in June with nothing more than a pack of cigarettes and the clothing they were wearing. These five Cambodian nationals had been acquainted with each other in a Thai camp. But, as subtleties were revealed, they did not really like each other. George and Lillis sponsored Tong Tea (*Tea* was the surname) and his wife Jenye (alternatively, *Jenya, Jenyea,* or *Jenny*; she spelled her own name *Khien Hiek*) who were ethnic Chinese and formerly wealthy. Dean and Lorraine sponsored the Boun family who were native Khmer, and not of the privileged class. The Bouns spoke no English and so their first weeks in Dean's home were lonely. Tong spoke several languages including English, and Nyman could speak to him or Jenye in Chinese. Occasionally Tong was asked to translate for the Boun family which he willingly condescended to do.

The experience enriched particularly Lillis's life and demanded the full measure of her time and compassion. Her life became involved with doctor appointments, driving lessons, job interviews, furnishing apartments, legal problems, first days at school, and so many other tasks. Refugees who were strangers to the Brookses would occasionally show up on Lillis's doorstep looking for Tong or Lillis as they gained notoriety in their community for being helpful. The refugees had problems of all sorts. Landlords and employers were often in dispute with the refugees. It seemed that all the refugees were always trying to locate relatives who were either left behind or had taken refuge in a number of countries around the world; they needed help with bureaucracies and language barriers. Even when things were going well they could suffer from depression. Once Lillis bought shoes and winter clothes for a Vietnamese refugee who stepped off the plane barefoot in the winter. They were frightened by the fireworks on the Fourth of July; they were frightened by the costumes on Halloween. Jenye was invited to a Christmas party where she was frightened by a dwarf who was dressed like an elf. (Admittedly, that one was unseemly by any measure.) Sinh Thuch Boun was too malnourished to produce milk for her infant daughter. And it soon became apparent that she was pregnant again. She suffered from morning sickness and could hardly get out of bed. Tong Tea passed a worm in his stool; he always looked frail. Nyman used to enjoy speaking Chinese with Jenye, and sometimes would tease her. Once he got her laughing and she commented, "This is the first time I have laughed since the Communists took over 5 years ago."

Tong once commented that he had been rich, but was no longer concerned with money. He just wanted to enjoy the peace of a normal life. That was easier said than done. He was an architect in his former life, and so he got work as a draftsman with Frank Ferguson who helped design Abravanel Symphony Hall in Salt Lake City. The company gave Tong tickets to the concert on opening night. But he gave them to Dean because he was humiliated to be merely a draftsman. This illustrates the impossibility of comprehending someone else's struggle.

George and Lillis Together

George and Lillis loved being together. They would carpool to work or meet for lunch as a way to spend time together in a busy schedule. They continued to socialize with their lifelong friends in their study group. They had season tickets to the symphony, the theater, the opera, and the ballet. Because of their busy lives they gave many tickets away. They went on long drives, such as to the Trappist monastery in Huntsville, UT, to hear the monks sing or buy a loaf of their bread. Sometimes in her diary she would break from her matter-of-fact writing style to tell about George. These brief, occasional vignettes beg to summarize her writing:

Friday, January 12, 1979. I went shopping today at Auerbach's downtown. . . . Geo met me at noon and we had lunch together. I enjoy being with George more than anyone else. He has always been the right one for me. It never ceases to amaze me how lucky and blessed I am to have him. I'm always excited to see him walking towards me in a crowd. It thrills me to hear his voice on the phone or to know he will be spending the evening at home with me. I find great warmth and comfort and security each night as I go to bed with him or waken at night to find him by my side. He is fun, loving, and honest in his relationship with me. He is a constant support and reinforcement for me. Even though he has always carried heavy responsibilities and pressures at work and in the church he always has found time for his children and me.

XXIV

Clean Breaks
1980–1986

ENGLISH

English, the first grandchild, was born in September 1979. Lillis babysat him until Rem moved the family to Hartford in 1985. Along the way she chronicled English's milestones in her diary. He sat in a chair March 24, 1980, walked in August, and talked in October. English was good-natured and always amusing. She enjoyed taking him on errands if only to show him off to her friends. In July, Rem and Carolyn traveled to San Diego and left English with Lillis for 3 days. On their return, English was content to play with Leslie (who had helped in his care), disregarding his parents, which made his mother, Carolyn, cry. When little sister Cate was born, the precocious and verbal English announced, "I saw her extension cord."

STRANGERS WITHIN THE GATE

There were neighbors and friends that Lillis checked in on and helped routinely. A subset of these included the Asian refugees or immigrants. They are difficult to count because sometimes their names are not recorded well. For example, she often drove a group of girls to English class whom she just referred to as "the Korean girls."

There was a teenager, Qui Hua, who was bringing up her siblings, Long and Loan. (*Qui* is alternatively spelled in Lillis's diary and letters as *Quie*, *Kuei*, or *Kwi*; Lillis pronounced it *kui* to rhyme with *we*.) They were ethnic Chinese refugees from Vietnam. In 1980, Nyman and Lillis helped Qui get a Canadian visa to visit relatives who had been separated in the refugee camp. It sounds easy enough but it was a difficult, multi-week transaction with the Canadian consulate. Qui could not have resolved it by herself. In the summer of 1982, Qui's 5-year-old nephew visiting from Canada fell from a chair onto concrete and broke his eye orbit. Lillis took him to Primary Children's Hospital for treatment. In 1985, they were still helping her with immigration papers for family members living in Canada to visit the US.

There was a fellow named Minh Tran who scalded his face and arm while working on his car radiator. Leslie took him to the hospital for treatment and Lillis changed his bandages twice daily for a week. Leslie and Nyman were also deeply involved with the refugee community. There were always cars to register or insure, landlords to deal with, sickness or accidents, school registration, children to help with schoolwork, English classes, documents to translate, and many other unscheduled urgencies. Some brought Lillis cash and she would mail her personal checks to pay their bills. On a very few occasions they came without cash.

One refugee came to George distraught that his wife had become pregnant by another man. A few letters survive from this episode in which the husband recounts how his wife saved his life while he was sick and enslaved by the Khmer Rouge. Ironically, he wanted children but was probably sterile because of sickness or injuries he received in the camps. An illegitimate child was a catastrophe. George calmed him, saying that in America the husband was free to accept the child and go on with his life, that nobody really cared. That was the path that the husband chose. He continued for years to send letters to George and Lillis, sending pictures and writing endearingly of his new baby son.

Emblematic of Lillis's and also George's involvement with refugees was their experience with a young Vietnamese woman (we'll call her Maili), and her three children, beginning in 1980.

Lillis wrote that Maili had probably lost 19 lbs. over a few months after arriving in the US, down to from 105 to 86. Among the many doctors and dentists that Lillis took her and her children to visit, Dr. Kwong diagnosed Maili with stress and anxiety. It is remarkable that he could make any diagnosis given that Maili spoke almost no English. But she spoke enough that Lillis knew a little about her. This poorly nourished mother of three had a husband missing in action in the Vietnam war; she did not know the whereabouts of her extended family; she had thought she would lose her child to disease as they drifted in a boat on the South China Sea looking for refuge; she had no money, no job, no friends, did not recognize the food in the stores; her landlord cheated her; and her children were not adjusting well to school. Maili barely trusted Lillis. But then, what choice did she have? Lillis felt that what Maili needed most was some adult friendship and conversation; she was completely alone. Lillis recognized that she could never be a close friend because they couldn't talk to each other. Sometimes when they were together Maili would begin to weep, and Lillis would just stand by with no capacity to respond.

Little by little, first things first, Lillis moved Maili and her family into a new apartment. She got the phone and the gas turned on, and George fixed the appliances; she took Maili and the kids to countless dental and medical appointments, paying for some. She enrolled Maili in English classes. George drove Maili across town to class at the Horace Mann Jr. High on 2nd West and 1st North, taking a different route each time to teach her the layout of the city. Then he rode the bus with her and taught her how to transfer. Lillis took her shopping, and took her and her children to family parties or picnics or fireworks on the Fourth of July. Lillis enrolled Maili in welfare and took her to a rehabilitation program. She took her to apply for jobs. She took the kids to museums, parks, drove them to the ski resorts to watch skiers (they had never seen snow). Family lore has it that Maili tried prostitution for a while to make ends meet. Rumor also has it that she became pregnant and Lillis took her to an abortion clinic. Maili dutifully submitted to listening to the LDS missionaries. After weeks of lessons and church services she said thanks, said she believed it all, but was not ready to go further.

Three years later, Lillis could see a change in Maili. Her teeth were now repaired or replaced. She had a nice smile. She had gained a little weight. Her hair was curled, and she wore a flowered velvet jacket which she had bought in Chinatown in Los Angeles while visiting a sister. She was calm. She laughed freely and complained fluently in English about the weather as though she were a local. "I couldn't help but feel a renewed faith in all people to be able to adjust, change, and overcome." "She trusts me on one level. But on another, we don't know each other; I will never comprehend her struggle."

In 1984, Maili had enough money that she took George and Lillis out to eat in celebration of Chinese New Year. In 1985, she bought baby gifts for Leslie's daughter Carly, and for Rem's daughter Cate.

EDITH AND FULLER

George reminisced about his mother-in-law, Edith Remington, in his diary:

> . . . I have become increasingly fond of her. I cannot imagine that she will ever be old. When I close my eyes I see her hands opening a jar or dusted with flour as she works in her kitchen. I hear her voice as it relaxes into her rural Utah dialect and grammar. She has a remarkable intuition and forewarns us of bad fortune and good, even across the miles. Her shyness makes it difficult to compliment her. She turns away, dismissing it all with some final comment. She enjoys a good joke and laughs heartily.

Edith was diagnosed with melanoma on her heel in January 1978. Over the next years she was occasionally treated with surgeries and chemotherapy. Sometimes she needed special attention at home, not only for her wounds and tubes, but also for meals and housework. Fuller was always cheerful and attentive to his wife. But he was old and had his own limitations. In February 1979, Fuller suffered and quickly recovered from a slight stroke. By December he was having trouble buttoning his shirt because he had lost tactical acuity.

Edith had a perfusion in her leg in November 1979. Her recovery at home from that procedure lasted into January 1980. Then she was admitted to the hospital again to treat an infection.

Subtly a family dysfunction became apparent. It fell to Lillis to care for Edith and Fuller. With very few exceptions, it was Lillis who took Edith to her many medical appointments, or showed up early to make breakfast for her father. Lois, Don, and Ted also lived in the city. The parents did not drive, so Lillis would take them grocery shopping. In the fall of 1980 she asked her brothers and sisters to contribute $20 monthly for their parents' groceries and household expenses. All the Remington siblings could easily afford that nominal amount, but strangely, one balked.

Edith was 83 and Fuller was 89. But they were so well groomed, so alert and independent, that it was easy to forget their age. Mention of Edith's illness seems muted in Lillis's diary in 1980, almost as if Edith might be cured. In the fall of 1980, Lillis commented that Edith seemed cancer-free. There were good days when Lillis would go shopping with her mother while her father worked in the garden. In February 1980, Carl Hadlock died, leaving Edith as the last survivor of the eight children in her family.

The cancer came back in 1981. While bathing her mother, Lillis saw spots of melanoma from her leg to her shoulder. The two of them fell into a tearful conversation about the end game and Fuller's life alone. Edith increasingly feared the pain and dreaded the expense of her many treatments, drainage tubes, excisions, and short stays in the hospital. Sometimes George and Lillis had to coax her to go to the hospital. In March 1981, Lillis wrote:

> I find myself fatigued from my concern for Mother. Really find myself suffering more from Mother's illness than I thought I would. Find myself on the edge of tears most of the time. Can't seem to get on top of it. It pains me to look at Dad so fragile, this once proud, independent man becoming so dependent because of his declining physical health.

Lillis's routine was changed. She started cleaning her parents' house, taking in their laundry, doing their shopping, and cooking their meals. She resigned from her job at the hospital in June 1981 (though often she was called in when the hospital was short-staffed). All the while she tried to keep up with her club meetings and church work. She was still involved with Salt Lake Council of Women's charitable work. She was a visiting teacher for six elderly widows in the ward. She attended the monthly meetings of the Aurora club and remained active in the LDS Hospital Nurses Alumni Association.

George and Lillis took a trip to the East Coast in December 1981 to visit Dean's family in Maryland. Rem called them and told them to hurry home. They dawdled, touring the Madison and Jefferson plantations at

Montpelier and Monticello, Virginia. Rem spoke to them on the phone the next day and again told them to hurry home. Edith had a bowel obstruction and was refusing treatment, food, and water. So they drove straight home, stopping only for gas. Lillis wrote:

> Mother was very alert when I went to see her. She told me how terrible she felt that night I left [on my trip to Maryland] and she worried for fear she would never see me again. She also told me how much she loved me, had always loved me, how grateful she was for all I had done for her. She told me I had brought her great joy from the time I was a little girl until now. She said she had wanted to tell me for a long time but she knew how sad it would make me and I would only cry. She told me she hated to leave me. . . .
>
> Mother lived another week without food or drink. She . . . remained alert and coherent until the day before she died. She visited [talked] with everyone in her family. Talked to her grand-children out of town by phone. She showed great courage and sense of humor and patience. . . .
>
> She died New Year's morning at 1:30 AM. . . .
>
> As I stood with the large family, surrounding her open grave . . . I couldn't help but think how quickly life ends, how surely the end does come. How well she had met her challenges. . . . I looked at my own children and thought how very soon this occasion would be repeated. . . . I remembered back to my grandmother's funeral when my mother stood by me. . . . I felt sorrow and sympathy for my aged and fragile father, 90 years old, left with so many challenges to meet.

Fuller was distraught after his wife's death. He was not quite coor-dinated enough to cook for himself. He had stayed for a short time at Don's house, but he scalded himself with tap water and flooded a bath-room floor. After that he was *persona non grata* at the homes of his chil-dren. They all had stairs in their homes. Fuller was over 6 feet tall and maybe his children were afraid they were not strong enough to deal with him. But in retrospect it really seems that someone could have taken him in. The Remington family for the most part was well-off. With the exception of Ted and Lillis, they had spacious homes and their children were grown. One thing should have persuaded them: They all knew that Fuller would have made any sacrifice for them. For good reasons or not, the Remington siblings decided to move Fuller into a care facility. Fuller became angry, sullen, and started to suffer moments of disorientation. People who had known him for a long time were surprised at his quick decline; he had been so strong and reliable. As George noted, he had been so generous in his life that it was always a riddle how much money he had actually made, and where it had all gone. He had been known to be insistent when imposing a favor or a loan on someone. Though he was genteel and well groomed he was not adverse to physical labor for long hours. He could forego sleep or meals if someone were sick and needed attention. He was patient and gentle with children. Decades later in 2012, when Leah Cook was 90 years old, she had one salient memory to recount: She remembered her Uncle Fuller's generosity. And she regretted leaving Fuller, her protector and benefactor in childhood, in a nursing home in the last months of his life.

Family members would visit their father and grandfather, or take him on short outings. But there were limits to their charity; they all had busy lives. Lillis commented that she did not invite Fuller to dinner one Sunday because it was Fast Sunday (one Sunday a month when Mormons skip meals), a shallow excuse, which might indicate that she was fatigued.

In fairness, 1981 and 1982 had been so frenzied that it would almost excuse the neglect of Fuller.

Lillis had an appendectomy in July 1981. She was treated for a chronic bladder infection in August which had had bothered her for years. She was still complaining about it in November.

In October, while Lillis was fretting over Edith's last months of treatment, George was hosting about 400 guests to the convention for the American Association of School Personnel Administrators, which lasted a week. George wanted to show the city off in a good light for his national colleagues. Lillis had to make some semi-official appearances at dinner parties during the convention. She broke a cap off one of her teeth and didn't have time to fix it until the convention was over.

That summer the tenants moved out of George's and Lillis's rental property, stealing appliances and vandalizing the house to the degree that it could not be rented for many weeks. Lillis and George did most of the repairs and cleanup themselves. They also filed a suit to recover expenses.

The exceptional and enormous distraction that year was Leslie's star-crossed engagement to be married. It was a long, tortured, time-consuming entanglement for George and Lillis as well as for Leslie which need not be recounted here. But certainly George and Lillis worried far more over Leslie than they did over Fuller and Edith.

But back to Fuller: he didn't survive Edith even a year. He died October 22, 1982, after suffering from pneumonia for 10 days. Coincidentally, Lillis and George were again visiting Dean's family in Maryland; their new granddaughter Ashley was a bit more than a year old. This time they did not hurry back. They completed their plans to visit their grandchildren, and to visit Nyman who was now studying in Boston. Lillis regretted missing the funeral. But she had weighed the contingencies and committed to the trip even prior to leaving Salt Lake City. She advised her sisters that if her father were to die they should not to delay a funeral for her return.

MISGIVINGS

In her diary Lillis tried to come to terms with her regrets. "I tried to analyze why I felt so grief-stricken. He was 91½ years old. Ill in health, unable to do for himself, sad and lonely in his life at the nursing home . . ." Though she had borne her parents' burden in the heat of the day, she continued to second-guess her decision to miss the funeral, even years later. Maybe she was befuddled by criticism from her sisters for not attending the funeral. As the funeral rolled over in her mind she never criticized or scrutinized her siblings' inattention to Edith and Fuller during their lives. She tried to work it out in her diary:

> I felt if my father was aware of my shortcomings he is also aware of my love for him and I am sure of his love for his children regardless of his mistakes or any misjudgments in his relationships with us. There was more I could have done to make his life better but I'm sure he knows I did the best I could at the time. A parent has no right to hold a child too tight or to make one feel guilty for being different or not walking to his drum beat. I must learn this with my own children. . . . I have always felt

some guilt when doing things differently than my parents would do them. They were good parents, were never mean and always giving to me.

In the months following Fuller's death, another family drama played out. One of the Remington children objected to an equal distribution of the inheritance; he believed that his brother had borrowed or received a gift from Fuller prior to his death, and that amount should be factored into the shares. Fuller and Edith had only their house which would not have been worth more than $40,000; hardly enough to make a substantial difference in anyone's life when divided seven ways. Fuller had no disposable cash or anything else of value; as was noted above, Fuller had been living off a small allowance from his children for the past two years. So whatever money he had given away to one child, it was certainly a small amount.

Rather than pay one brother less, the siblings came up with a formula to pay the other brother more and thereby soothe an alleged injustice.

NYMAN

Nyman graduated from the University of Utah in June 1982. School seemed effortless for him. Of course, it is never effortless for anybody. Lillis noted in 1980 that Nyman would break out in hives under pressure during his finals. But by any measure he was an unusual intellect.

As an undergraduate, Nyman wrote a history of milling in Utah that was so well received that one of his professors, Dean May, persuaded him to apply to Fletcher School of Law and Diplomacy at Tufts University in Medford, Massachusetts. He was accepted for the fall of 1982. It sounded like a life-changing opportunity.

To state the obvious, Tufts was different from the U in many ways; first of all, it was more expensive. Tuition at the U was only a few hundred per quarter. A student could pay his own way to the U with part-time or summer jobs.

Things changed for Nyman in graduate school. He needed money from his parents to attend Tufts. George and Lillis paid a first installment of $6,000 in June 1982 for tuition and housing; they were caught off-guard by the costs. George and Lillis visited Nyman in Boston in October 1982 shortly after Fuller died. Nyman had spent the previous night walking along the Charles River, mourning his grandfather's death.

George and Lillis were shocked at how poor Nyman's living arrangements were. Lillis said, "I have given much better [furniture] to the Deseret Industries [charity]." They were also shocked at the excessive drinking and marijuana use among his classmates, though they felt confident that these things would not tempt Nyman. They were also worried about the academic pressures. Fletcher only accepted about 50 students each year; the cadre was drawn from the best and brightest.

Nyman magnified the pressure on himself. In his mind he was no longer just spending his own money; he felt he had to answer to his parents for every dollar spent and every *A* not achieved. Unwittingly he and his parents set up a dynamic where he would understate his needs and they would never offer more.

The problem was not just money and grades; it was also parental criticism and control. Lillis was judgmental and insulting about his living arrangements. Many students tried to economize by moving off campus into a variety of substandard arrangements. Nyman moved into a room in a boarding house. A woman lived in the same house; once she answered the phone when Lillis called. She told Lillis, "Nyman is asleep; I'll go wake him." By the time Nyman came to the phone Lillis was upset. Nyman couldn't see the difference between a boarding house and the college's coed dorms. And he was acting in good conscience to keep to a budget. He ended the conversation by saying, "You are 2,000 miles away and not in a position to manage my problems." Nyman went on to live in other boarding houses; in each instance a woman also rented a room.

Nyman tried panhandling in Boston with some success. He ate peanut butter and pasta for days at a time. Pressure and bad diet broke him down. He became so distraught that he stopped making meaningful headway on his degree. He may have been suicidal. In the summer of 1984, he called home and said he was out of money and felt he must come home. Lillis was cold to him on the phone, no doubt thinking about the money she had spent on Nyman's counterculture lifestyle. He returned home by bus in September, tired and dirty. Lillis wrote in her diary that she had sent him a plane ticket. But Nyman remembered it differently; he had used his skimpy allowance to get home the best way he could.

By chance, George discovered that Nyman had stiffed his roommate for the last month's rent. George sent a check to cover Nyman's debt. He also offered to pay for psychological counseling, which Nyman refused.

Maybe George or Lillis would have given any amount to keep Nyman in school if only Nyman could have framed the request. After all, they were generous in other situations. For their own different reasons, both parents failed to understand Nyman's needs.

Nyman never returned to Tufts and did not complete his degree. Lillis continued to worry and nag about his indolence at home. Nyman watched a lot of TV and was ineffective making up his schoolwork or writing his papers, but he was not completely idle. He substitute-taught in Granite School district, and he was deeply involved with the Indo-Chinese refugees, their schoolwork, and their many other problems. When he earned a little money, Lillis criticized him for giving some to a beggar on the street. Lillis found it easier to worry about Nyman sleeping late than to explore the causes or note his many accomplishments. Nyman had a girlfriend; that romance foundered, likely due to the greater issue of his stress. They broke up just before Christmas.

There is no documentation or memory to indicate that Lillis or George scrutinized their roles in Nyman's crisis. Given another opportunity, it is possible they would have done better, been more alert, been more nuanced in their thinking, provided better support or guidance. The wisdom to act contrary to one's inclination requires experience; it is the paradox of knowing the path before the journey.

Nyman's problems were resolved and his life moved on when he was given a job at CIA in Langley, Virginia, in September 1985.

TRAVEL

Every year, usually in July, George and Lillis would vacation with Lillis's brothers and sisters. The group would sometimes take a long weekend to attend the plays at the Cedar City Shakespeare Festival. Others might tag along such as George's jogging buddy John Bell and his wife, Jeanie. Sometimes they travel long distances to run. More than once they ran in the St. George Marathon; they ran the Bay to Breakers in San Francisco; they ran races in Moab; and in the Salt Lake metro area. They all had some disposable income, and they were starting to decompress from their busy lives.

George and Lillis took a trip to Hawaii in 1983. They traveled with Lillis's siblings and in-laws: Don and Marilyn, Lois and Harvey, Earl and Karol, Leslie, Jill Remington, and John Hirschi. The next year, 1984, roughly the same group, plus Lillis's sister Cleo and her husband Lee Atkin, took a trip to New Zealand and Australia. In 1985, George and Lillis toured the Mediterranean by themselves.

Characteristically, Don and George continued to run, even on vacation. A morning run in Australia took them from their hotel over the Sydney Harbor Bridge to the Opera House and back.

Both Don and his father, Fuller, had served church missions in New Zealand, so reminiscence of Fuller was a big part of their conversation. It had taken Fuller many weeks to travel to New Zealand in 1912. He took a stagecoach from Vernal to the mines in Dragon; then narrow gauge rail to Mack, Colorado; another train to Salt Lake City; another train to Vancouver, Canada; and finally 22 days onboard ship to New Zealand.

Lillis had her spine checked again in April 1985.

> Went to see Dr. Momberger. He took many X-rays of my spine. Said my scoliosis is very severe. I have lost 2½ inches of my height in the last ten years. . . . I am to return in six months to see if my height and scoliosis have stabilized. I have been having trouble with my back when I sit down my ribs rest on my hip-bones. I have been able to hide my deformity quite well with the clothes I buy. I feel I have done well in spite of the severity of it.

This little insight is a reminder that outwardly Lillis was very capable and self-assured while suffering and hiding a bad back. She was also insecure about her looks. She did not like her freckles and would sit with her palms upwards, exposing the white, unfreckled side of her arms. And she sometimes dropped little clues that she had not liked the color of her hair since her earliest memories.

On another day that spring she walked 2 miles to the Salt Lake Clinic on 3rd South and 9th East to have blemishes removed from her arm and some small tumors removed from her breast; then walked home.

George and Lillis started their 1985 Mediterranean tour in the fall, about a week after the *MS Achille Lauro* was hijacked off the coast of Egypt. The intrepid travelers took little notice of that event. In her diary, Lillis effused in great detail about the sweep of history and the rise of western culture. There was a marathon being run in Athens on the day they arrived. George quickly changed into his running clothes and crashed the last 10 miles of the race which finished with a lap around the Olympic Stadium. Then he bought a race T-shirt for himself and one to take home to Don.

Their visit to Israel was more reverent, like a pilgrimage. While they were traveling in a bus to the Sea of Galilee the tour guide asked if anyone knew a song about Galilee. George's seemingly endless repertoire included a song from the old *Deseret Sunday School Songs*. And he was pleased to sing a solo for the tourists:

> Each cooing dove and sighing bough
> That makes the eve so blest to me
> Has something far diviner now
> It bears me back to Galilee.
> O Galilee! Sweet Galilee!
> Where Jesus loved so much to be;
> O Galilee! Blue Galilee!
> Come, sing thy song again to me.

Then the tour guide sang a love song in Hebrew; it was just those two who shared their songs.

RETIREMENT 1986

As the years passed there were increasing responsibilities, pressures, and demands on George's time—weekly school board meetings lasting late into the evening, annual contract negotiations lasting months, seminars and conventions. In 1980, Chicano (the preferred self-identification) teachers brought a suit against the school board, alleging hiring discrimination. It fell to George to gather data that the federal prosecutors requested. Also that year, George fired a teacher accused of felony fraud and theft; that teacher sued George's office to get his job back. In the spring of 1981, George fired a bus driver; a week later someone broke out all the windows on George's car and started to make harassing phone calls. In the autumn, George hosted the American Association of School Personnel Administrators. At least that went very well; he received many personal compliments and also written recognition from the AASPA Executive Director, Arch Brown, and from Salt Lake Superintendent Don Thomas. The week-long convention took a lot of time to plan. It

George, 1984, about the time he was appointed Superintendent of Schools.

included banquets, meetings, and lodging for 400 attendees, also daily field trips and evening entertainment. Through it all, George would occasionally be forced to slip away to attend to church matters.

In August 1984, Superintendent Thomas announced that he would take a new job out of state, and Wayne Evans would serve as superintendent for a year or so while the board looked for a permanent replacement. Evans had no professional or scholastic background in education. He had used his elected position on the school board to vote himself into a high-paying job. It was an example of unethical mismanagement.

In September, the Utah Board of Education ruled that Evans was not qualified and was ineligible to serve. The Salt Lake Board met in an emergency session and unanimously appointed George. George accepted but stipulated that he was not a candidate and would only serve until a permanent superintendent could be found. For the next several months, George kept desks in his personnel office and in the superintendent's office.

George assisted with the search for the new superintendent. The board settled on John Bennion in January 1985. Dr. Bennion was from a prominent family of Utah educators, and was serving as superintendent in Provo. He was well respected and his selection seemed to please everyone. He started work in March 1985.

In time, Bennion came to the conclusion that he should "refresh" (George's word). He offered a cash incentive to encourage some of the older administrators and principals to retire. Before Christmas of 1985, George announced that he would take the incentive on June 30, 1986.

> Whether Supt. Bennion achieved what he wanted to achieve, only he could answer. I suspect there were some administrators who did not take the offer that he wished had, and vice versa. I am of the opinion that he would have preferred me to stay. He said so convincingly but I am sure that it was the right thing for me to do. I have been in the personnel office since summer of 1969. Before that I had served as elementary principal at Forest School (4 years), Jackson Elem School (7 years), teacher at Garfield School (3 years); totaling 31 years with the SL Sch. Dist. [with an additional 4 years in other districts].

George continued to work into July to finish up with annual salary and contract negotiations. But then it was over; he never looked back.

George had an acquaintance at the board office who summed up George's tenure as interim superintendent in a farewell letter. Rob Wakefield was not an educator; he handled some PR matters for the board office. He said that Don Thomas was energetic and brash with a knack for PR, but that George was actually more successful in his short term:

> The stage for effective public relations is set when you act responsibly as an organization and allow for two-way communication with the constituency you serve. You did that better than any of the three superintendents I've known. . . . You accepted my input, no matter that I didn't have a degree in education. . . . While you were superintendent, the atmosphere among employees and the community was more serene, and morale was higher, than any other time since I've been here. Your influence on the district was indeed calming.

Also in the summer of 1986, George and Lillis moved into a new house in Bountiful which forced the church to release George as stake president in Sugar House. This made an enormous impact on his free time. He had served as stake president for more than 7 years. Prior to that he had served 9 years as counselor to the stake president. Before that he was a bishop. For more than 20 years he had spent all his Sundays in meetings or private interviews. Saturdays and Wednesday evenings were also largely encumbered. Spare time was often used to write speeches or letters to church members. Additionally, he attended many church social functions, campouts, seminary graduations, and the like.

The weeks leading up to June 30 were a blur of tightly scheduled church and school social engagements, dinner parties, farewells, gifts and mementos (including a silver tray from the school board and a silver bowl from the PTA), kind letters, speaking engagements—people well-wishing and reminiscing as George and Lillis were trying to move on. Lillis wrote that it was a relief when the social engagements came to an end.

> Everyone was warm and well-wishing . . . saying how much they will miss us, etc. It is wonderful to know we will be missed and

we feel nostalgic but I'm glad the parties, dinners, and receptions
are coming to an end. . . . It can be too much.

Additionally, there were the transactions to sell their house and their
rental property, and to buy and build the new house.

Lillis had quit her volunteer work at the Church History Museum.
And by August, George had retired from the board office, been released
from the stake presidency, and had even abandoned the neighborhood
where he had grown up and lived all his life. One might reasonably ask
why they ever allowed their previous exhausting schedule, particularly
when so many of their daily tasks were voluntary. Now Lillis and George
were free to sit together in church for the first time in decades. It seemed
George's only responsibility was to teach a Sunday school class to his new
friends in Bountiful.

XXV

Kenya, England, Zimbabwe
1989–1990

George and Lillis had presumed or planned for a long while that they would go on a mission. They spoke about it even prior to George's retirement. Lillis asserted that George's decision to retire, their decision to move out of their house on Wilson Avenue, and even some of the financial sacrifices were made in anticipation of serving a mission.

LIFE IN BOUNTIFUL 1986–1989

Along the path toward that goal, they furnished their new house at 538 West 2900 South in Bountiful. Lillis also planted a flower garden in the yard. She commented frequently on the views of the sun setting over the Great Salt Lake, or the fruit trees which had been planted in pioneer times and now scattered fruit over the sidewalks in her neighborhood in such abundance that she would gather it and take it home to preserve. The house was well laid out to accommodate their children and grandchildren when they would visit. For example, Rem and his family stayed with George and Lillis for a month in 1988 while Rem completed an organ transplant rotation at LDS Hospital. George and Lillis also travelled roughly each year to the East Coast to visit Rem and his family in Connecticut, Dean and his family in Maryland, and Nyman in Virginia. Nyman was not yet married, which continued to cause anxiety for Lillis.

She frequently asked Nyman about his social life, as if it were one more loose end to tie up before their mission.

Leslie and her husband Cy bought a house in April 1987 which needed extensive repair and updating; George and Lillis added home repairs to their routine. George installed shutters, cabinets, new wiring, new plumbing, repaired the garage and patio. He would sometimes work at Leslie's house two or three days a week; Lillis helped with drapes and decorating. George and Lillis were also happy to babysit Carly and her baby sister Brooks while Leslie went to work.

George and Lillis kept up their social life, not limited to a rich association with Lillis's brother and sister-in-law, Don and Marilyn. They still attended their study group with the friends from their youth in Lincoln Ward; the group had started to diversify their lessons from the classics to include lessons on financial planning for retirement or church history. In 1988, George and Lillis took assignments as guides on Temple Square, memorizing a lengthy set of scripts, word for word; they worked at Temple Square two evenings each week.

MISSION CALL

It was George's attitude that if he had to live out his life going to the theater, picnicking in the canyons, running foot races, and working in his wood shop, he would certainly go crazy. He wanted purpose. It would be fair to say that George was the motivator for going on a mission, and Lillis was a willing follower.

George's friends advised him that he could and should take an active role to help determine where he would serve, to ensure a pleasant and interesting assignment without a lot of vaccinations. Friends would argue, "Do you think you are needed in one place and not another?" Or, "Do you think the church leaders pray over every assignment?" It was George's simplistic opinion that he should not make his service conditional, but should accept an assignment where there was a need; and if he alone were to pray about it, that would be sufficient.

In contrast, Lillis was apprehensive. When contemplating a mission, she spoke wistfully about leaving the new, nicely appointed house and garden. She didn't want to leave her friends and social clubs, and particularly she said she would miss her close ties with Leslie's children. She worried about leaving Leslie alone with her brothers far away. She worried about leaving Nyman while he was still unmarried. She feared that no matter how a mission played out, her life might never return to how it was. Late in March, she sat down with George and enumerated all her misgivings; George listened. They went for a long walk. Then George called the Church missionary department and asked if he could come and pick up the official calling rather than waiting for the mail.

When they learned that they were called to serve in Kenya, Lillis's attitude abruptly changed. She felt it was meant to be. She started to look forward. She studied up on Kenya and commented that she felt a bond with the people, although it is doubtful that Kenya had ever crossed her mind before. Later, when they met Robert Sackley and Alexander Morrison of the Church area presidency over that part of the world, Sackley said, "Your application was an answer to our prayers. We wanted someone just like you." George took them at their word. The Church operated without official recognition in Kenya. George and Lillis would be the senior leadership in the country.

In the interim, they took a final vacation trip to India and Nepal in February and March of 1989. They described their trip as a bewildering landscape of charming waiters and dirty tablecloths, of shrines, palaces, stupas, monkeys, innumerable gods, mountains, and magnificent sunrises. They gasped in wonder at the Taj Mahal. Characteristically, they also occasionally ditched their guided tour to wander the streets alone. George described an excavation being dug by hand for the construction of a high-rise. The pit was probably 40 feet deep. It appeared that families—men, women, and children—were in the bottom, removing the dirt one basket at a time. The poverty of children always caught Lillis off guard. There would be plenty of poverty in Africa.

They had visited the Atlantic states recently in November 1988 to see their new baby granddaughter, Natalie. But now, with the mission departure close at hand, they went back east again in April to say good-bye to their sons and grandchildren. Natalie was now 5 months old. The grandparents insisted that the baby should sleep in their room to give Lorraine a little rest. Lillis had chills, pain, and nausea from recent typhoid and tetanus vaccinations; she could not lift Natalie, so it fell to George to get up in the night with the baby. They brought trinkets from India and Nepal, and George told his boys he wanted to take them hiking in the Himalayas.

They attended formal training at the Missionary Training Center (MTC) in Provo from April 26 to May 12. To avoid a daily commute, they stayed in the dormitories on the BYU campus. The MTC had a monastic spirit about it: the spartan dormitory, restrictions on phone calls, living with few possessions, rigid daily routine of study and prayer, all under the umbrella of a religious hierarchy. Lillis felt boxed in and admitted that she was out of her comfort zone. Some of the classes required role-play, which she dreaded. Some of her classmates were on their fourth or fifth missions and so she projected on them a skill-level or fitness that intimidated her. She felt inadequate for the task and relied on George to lead the way. She grew weary of the constant personal attention and positive reinforcement. And there were more vaccines: polio, yellow fever, cholera, and gamma globulin. At least the food service was good, and she and George kept up their practice of long daily walks.

One psychological drag on their mission planning was their unlucky investment in a rental condominium on Redwood Road. Proving foresight may be vain, the Savings and Loan Crisis of the 1980s and a housing bubble came at the moment they were trying to cash out. It was a protracted downturn during which they could neither rent nor sell. As the months passed their losses increased to about half the value of the house—about $20,000. In a strange and tragic turn of events, they accepted an offer on the house just prior to leaving on their mission in April 1989, but the buyer was murdered, leaving a family of small children. In the end they left the property in the care of Cy and Leslie, who persuaded them to take a short sale. The condominium finally sold in July after they had arrived in Kenya. Lillis wrote in her diary that it was "a difficult loss but nothing that can be done about it at this point." Throughout their time abroad, in Kenya, England, and in Zimbabwe, Lillis and George were indebted to Leslie and Cy for taking care of the many loose ends, caring for their house, monitoring bank accounts, filing taxes, or receiving mail.

Tom English, Rem's father-in-law, died in May of a heart attack while George and Lillis were at the MTC. Tom was in his 50s. Rem and the family returned to Utah for the funeral; George and Lillis also attended and enjoyed one last moment with Rem and his family. The MTC training ended on Friday; George and Lillis had dinner with Leslie, Rem, and their families on Saturday. Then they flew out on Tuesday, May 16.

KENYA, MAY – AUGUST 1989

The first leg of their journey was an overnight flight, arriving in London in the morning. They had a 9-hour layover in London—essentially all day. The sun was up on a new day, though for a traveler it felt like late last night—too early to go to bed. They cancelled their hotel reservation and spent the day touring London. That evening they took another overnight flight to Nairobi, flying over Kilimanjaro, and Mount Kenya, silhouetted against the scarlet morning sun. They were tired and finally ready to sleep.

As they waited at the airport to pick up their bags, they heard a ruckus in the next room—a man shouting angrily. That was their introduction to Marvin Bowden; George and Lillis were to replace Elder Marvin and Sister Elva Bowden. Marvin was shouting at someone because he was not allowed to pass backwards through the customs area at the airport to check on the Brookses in the baggage area.

The Bowdens drove the Brookses through the crowded and chaotic streets of Nairobi, talking all the way, briefing the blurry-eyed Brookses and stopping along the way to run a few errands. The first stop was the post office.

Nairobi, with a population of over a million, had only one post office and no mail delivery. It was necessary to go to the post office frequently to pick up the mail. The church had a P.O. box (actually a large bin on the floor), which many church members also shared. If the mail were not collected in a timely way, it would be thrown out when the P.O. box became full. They walked up five flights of stairs to pick up a parcel, then downstairs to pick up mail, then upstairs to buy stamps. To enhance the Kafkaesque spirit of the place, the post office was packed with people standing in long lines to pay bills and conduct other transactions.

The next stop was to buy groceries; Elva suggested they might want to buy food or other personal things. Lillis asked, "Like what would you suggest?" Elva said, "Whatever you want."

Even after they arrived at their house the orientation briefing continued until Lillis and George fell asleep in their chairs. They awoke to find the Bowdens sitting and waiting quietly. They finally went to bed and awoke the next day, Friday, at 9 AM. They bathed and changed the clothes that they had been wearing since Tuesday. After the long sleep they were ready to start their work.

Their term overlapped with the Bowdens until mid June. During that time they traveled over much of Kenya and visited two remote branches. George became more confident driving on the left side of the road through the mostly unregulated streets of Nairobi. They transferred title of the cars, and completed many other transactions, all of which seemed much more time-consuming and tortuous than necessary.

Marvin Bowden demonstrated over time that he had a quick temper. He had a tendency for aggressive driving, even road rage. He treated his servants—all of whom were members of the church—with a colonial arrogance. There were several employees—gate guards, groundskeepers, drivers—and there were always others in the queue asking, "Do you need a house boy?" Marvin would make extravagant promises, and would give extravagant gifts—appliances, food, money, tuition—to his favorites among the impoverished members of the church. He would often remind people what he had done for them while in actuality he was giving away church money. He justified these misappropriations saying, "I can't help it; I've always had a big heart;" or, "Church leaders never pay attention to these expenses." He also traded money on the black market. When his term ended in mid June he carried off some of the church's financial files which had been kept in a locked cabinet, and he would not let George see them. The Bowdens had provided an invaluable service setting up the Brookses. On the other hand, the Brookses were glad to see the end of Marvin's strutting, bragging, and temper.

Cleaning up the church records and bringing closure to some of Marvin's unfulfilled promises proved to be time-consuming tasks which distracted George and Lillis from more important goals, such as establishing a humanitarian program on behalf of the church and securing legal registration for the church. Without registration it was illegal for the church to proselytize or operate in Kenya. So, for example, cars and property had to be titled to individuals rather than the church. This weighed heavy on the minds of church leadership; they were still smarting from the very abrupt deportation of missionaries and expulsion of the church from Ghana where they had tried to operate under similar legal restrictions.

George relied heavily on Isaac Musembi to help sort out the church records. Isaac was one of the local church leaders and also the groundskeeper who worked at the house where George and Lillis lived.

He was that reliable friend and advisor that every bewildered expatriate hopes to find. He instructed the Brookses at length in the subtleties of culture. Isaac alerted George to the jealousies that Marvin had fostered, even though he himself was a beneficiary. Isaac also would occasionally accompany George and Lillis when they would travel over dirt tracks to distant villages, or he would interpret for George when George had to give a lesson. George described him this way:

> Isaac Musembi is probably one of the most seasoned church members in Kenya. He is thoughtful, sensitive and very insight-ful often giving me sound advice when it comes to dealing with the native people; He knows them well and understands their tribal cultures and mine. . . . [In his gardening tasks] . . . He whistles and sings to himself native music on a scale of strange intervals, in unintelligible language, usually in high falsetto.

There was much that needed interpretation, much that was surpris-ing or difficult to comprehend. Once a young woman asked Lillis how many children she had, and how she practiced contraception. Kenya had one of the highest birth rates in the world. This young woman said her husband preferred the rhythm method, and she seemed completely igno-rant of other options. Lillis coincidentally had a magazine article with her on contraception, complete with illustrations, which she shared. Lillis wrote in a letter:

> I found it interesting that a rather shy, quiet girl . . . would talk so openly with me. She was baptized a week ago and I met her for the first time then. She seemed very interested in my family. Asked all about each of you and how many children you have.

One night George and Lillis witnessed a raging fire in a shantytown. People who had almost nothing lost everything and were left homeless in an instant. There was screaming and moaning; the sounds and sights were terrifying. They saw street children, some as young as 5 years old, abandoned. One child, bewildered and frightened with tears running down his dirty cheeks, seemed to be trying to run with his older brother, but was too small to keep up. Lillis wrote in her diary, "I shudder to think what has happened to him. Not knowing the law or custom, we did nothing for him. The passing locals paid little heed. It is difficult to be happy in this country."

The chaos of everyday life in Kenya did take a toll on George and Lillis. The child of a Mormon US diplomat was assaulted, slightly injured, and had some jewelry stolen. There were also the half-day trips to the post office, the many impediments to getting a phone line, the worrisome bug bites, the poverty, the boiling of drinking water, the anti-malaria pills, the guards at the garden gate, and the traffic. The traffic was an ever-present irritation. Police didn't care so much about accidents, injury, or liability; they just wanted the traffic to move, and occasionally they wanted a bribe.

George and Lillis finally recognized that they could not continue to live with constant fear and apprehension. They prayed for a way forward, and happily, their resolve became a successful turning point and the beginning of peace of mind. They began to enjoy the culture, the landscape, and their lives.

They had not been involved in a traffic accident before that point. After that, Mike Coleman, a wealthy Mormon expatriate, was run off the road. He smashed his car and bled a lot, but had no broken bones. About the same time, George and Lillis were side-swiped in a roundabout and lost their rearview mirror. Lillis called the other driver a jackass, but regretted it later, saying that she unjustly blamed him for all the bad traffic in Kenya.

But their focus moved on to their rich relationships with their new African friends and the beauty of the country. They sometimes traveled with other missionaries and church leadership to distant villages. Once they set out at 4:30 AM in the mission's four-wheel-drive truck. Lillis and others rode in the back under the shell while George drove and others sat in the cab. They crawled over the rutted roads and crossed shallow rivers. Lillis recalled:

It was more than rewarding. A magnificent giraffe gracefully sauntered across the road. Rhinos could be seen feeding beneath the umbrella trees in the distance. Large groups of ostriches were along the roadside. When we crossed the railroad tracks there sat a large baboon with his arms folded as though he were waiting for us. I waved but he ignored us. We bounced over small boulders, washed out roads, dry riverbeds, leaving clouds of red dust behind us. Women and children carrying heavy loads of water . . . could be seen walking the long distances between wells and home. The tall slender Maasai were herding their cattle along the roadside. Their small mud houses with thatched roofs sat in small villages along the way. Emanuel and George traded off driving. Emanuel drove all the way home . . . which was a terrible road and it was getting dark. We drove the steep mountain road home. It was narrow with hundred-foot drop-offs. Emanuel is young, an excellent driver, very alert. We were most grateful for him. Isaac Musembi also went with us. . . It had been a rewarding but very tiring day.

At the end of the day their backs and legs ached from the constant bouncing and jarring. "As I washed the dusty day from my tired body that night I felt renewed and rewarded."

The dynamism of the country captivated them. There were probably more than 100 people in Kenya who were acquainted with the church through friends or family and who wanted to be baptized. George and Lillis were teaching the discussions many times each week, sometimes teaching two or three of the prescribed and sequential lessons in a single session. Several people would be baptized each week. It seemed that everyone in the country was thinking about religion. The rapid growth of the church was actually a cause for concern because there were not enough seasoned local leaders in the three Nairobi branches, much less in the small and distant congregations in the linguistically diverse counties which were difficult to support.

Joseph and Gladys Sitati were among the seasoned and reliable leaders. Joseph was president of one of the three branches in Nairobi. Lillis had several occasions to chat with Gladys and always found her engaging. They ate at the Sitati home; Gladys was a generous hostess. Gladys would bring them a basin and a pitcher of hot water to wash their hands before the meal.

The primary concern for George and Lillis was to secure legal status for the church. They had a Kenyan lawyer who was completely ineffective and usually unresponsive. The next level of church leadership was the Area Presidency over the UK, Ireland, and Africa, located in Solihull, England. The president was Jack Goaslind; his two counselors were Alexander Morrison and Robert Sackley. Morrison visited Kenya in July to confer about the church's legal status. He gave instructions to minimize overt proselyting, baptisms, and to comply with national law as far as was practical. There was another missionary couple in Kenya who resisted these instructions; the church abruptly reassigned them to serve out their term in England.

Robert Sackley visited Kenya in August. He and Joseph Sitati met with the US Ambassador to Kenya to seek his support. They also tried to track down $25,000 that the church had donated to the Rotary Club to fight polio. Apparently the money was lost, illustrating the abstruse difficulty of business in Kenya. It was soon decided that the church would close its efforts in Kenya until it could achieve legal status. The members were instructed to meet in private homes in small groups. George and Lillis said their good-byes, took steps to secure property, and packed their bags. They ate supper with Sackley in the evening of August 7 and conversed amiably with him for almost 3 hours before taking him to the airport for his night flight to Heathrow. The Brookses flew out the next day. It was difficult for Lillis to go to sleep that night. She wondered whether she would ever return. She thought about the beauty of Kenya and the personal fulfillment she had enjoyed.

ENGLAND, AUGUST 1989 – JANUARY 1990

George and Lillis were transferred at least temporarily to Nottingham, England. They arrived in the UK on August 9. Almost immediately they suspected that they would never return to Kenya, however, the uncertainty made it difficult for them to settle in. They had 15 months remaining in their mission term; they were in limbo.

There was no denying that England had some benefits. George said the countryside was hypnotically beautiful and restful. Green was everywhere with tranquil sheep among the hedgerows and stone fences, tall ancient trees, Norman churches, half-timbered gables supporting slate or thatched roofs, wavy glass windows, and small doors as if for small people. It was so lovely, he said, that it would leave an indelible impression and change him forever. Within a month or two he decided to stop taking pictures because he was afraid his inadequate photos would distort his memory. Any drive through the countryside to a zone conference or to visit a distant member would evoke such feelings as to fill pages in their letters or diaries.

In a way it was like coming home. The language and the culture were easier to understand. The oppression of poverty was not visible and crime was of little worry. On their first day off they drove to North Wales and visited George's ancestral homeland where his great-grandfather Samuel Brookes had tended a lighthouse at the mouth of the Dee.

But it was not home, and it was not Kenya. Lillis said she had never been homesick while in Kenya, but she became homesick for Kenya while living in England. The work had seemed more meaningful and fulfilling in Kenya. Though the situation had been stressful and hectic, people were more interesting. There seemed to be a religious awakening. In England people were disinterested in religion if not atheists. The English also seemed to have a less approachable demeanor.

Their assignment in England was to track down people who had been baptized many years earlier, but who had lost contact with the church. The program was officially called *Lost Sheep;* George called it *Wild Goose.* Their days were spent knocking on doors using outdated address lists. Most of the people were long gone and forgotten by their neighbors. The work took them into old working-class neighborhoods, sometimes overtaken by immigrants from the former colonies. George described neighborhoods of row houses in long featureless blocks like slices of bread, often three storied, and only a little wider than the front door, so he felt like he had to shrug his shoulders to get in. The combination of the reserved affect of the English, the dreary streetscape, the cold and rain, the indifference to religion, the monotony of the work, all seemed to merge into a dystopian tableau in black and white. George and Lillis professed that the work was important, but they started to slack off a little early on many days to tour castles or stone churches or museums. There was no shortage of historical sites.

Occasionally they would find someone, but probably never actually brought anyone back into the fold. In December, a few weeks before they would depart, they did turn up a member—a woman who had lost contact with the church for a decade or two. She was about 50 years old, and was caring for her invalid husband. He had fled Lithuania and the Bolsheviks to avoid one of the many now-forgotten post-war waves of atrocities. He went to England on a program which promised him freedom to live and work where he wanted if he would first work in the coal mines. He was a refugee, the last survivor of his family and friends, and now suffering from silicosis.

He was a quiet, polite man who had nothing good to say about Russians or Germans. She was gentle but had been estranged from her family because she married a foreigner who was Orthodox. They had no children and so they were alone in a crowded country.

The four of them talked for a long while. They listened to the stories of his childhood. Lillis suggested that he should write his life story. He responded, "No one would read it; my family is dead and I have no children." George asked if he could remember any songs from his childhood. He looked surprised and said, "It has been a long time and I have no breath." But they pressed him a bit. He sat quietly for a moment, then began to sing with labored breath a folk song in his native language about two little girls. Lillis commented in a letter, "How different his life should have been. He was a hard worker and a kind husband."

As they parted he said, "If your rules were different I would like to have a brandy or a coffee with you." This story, and Lillis's need to write it, reflects a bit of humanity far outside the framework of commonplace interactions.

In late summer there was an area conference in Birmingham where George and Lillis met with Neal Maxwell, an apostle from Salt Lake City. Maxwell was a friend of George since the 1940s when they served together as missionaries in French Canada. He reported news from Kenya that President Daniel arap Moi was becoming suspicious of all expatriates and willing to blame them for his political problems. It was apparent that missionaries would not return quickly. Soon thereafter George and Lillis decided to secure their own apartment and settle in; they had been renting a single bedroom in a member's home, Sister Jean Flinn. They bought winter clothing; Lillis had been borrowing warm clothing from Jean. They enjoyed their new privacy. And they enjoyed setting their own thermostat. One of the quirky things in England was the practice of keeping houses cold and wearing coats indoors, even while cooking or watching TV.

In the fall, after the church's general conference, Maxwell called to ask George, without being specific, if he would be willing to serve as a mission president. George and Lillis came to the same resolution, again by different paths. George wrote, "Lillis and I have always felt impelled to readily accept such calls; they have always been a blessing to us." Lillis did the math and noted in her diary that a mission president's term of 3 years would not end until she was 70.

> We have noticed the toll the stress has taken on our mission pres and his wife and they are 20 years younger than we are. The thought of not seeing children or grandchildren for three years is almost more than I can bear to think about but we have been greatly blessed in all our calls during our lifetime.

George and Lillis served an unofficial function as surrogate parents to some of the younger missionaries, and invited them to dinner, particularly on holidays. They had 20 guests for Thanksgiving. One of the missionaries was from Finland, some from Germany, others from the UK and the United States. Guests who entered their apartment always commented, "It's so warm and cozy in your house." On Christmas, George read passages from the short novel *The Story of the Other Wise Man* by Henry van Dyke to his guests, which had been his tradition with his own children. They talked of home and loved ones, and opened gifts that Lillis had bought them.

The call to serve as mission president was official with a phone call from the apostle Thomas Monson in December. They returned to the US in January and were finally informed of the specific mission, Zimbabwe, in March.

TIME IN BOUNTIFUL

Leslie stocked her parents' refrigerator for their return. Betty Minor, their next-door neighbor, put out "welcome home" signs. Lois and Harvey met them at the airport. The night of January 18, Lillis and George slept in their own bed. It was very easy to slip into their old routine. Soon they were babysitting Carly and Brooks. They were taking their long walks. George repaired Leslie's garage door. Lillis attended a luncheon with the Aurora club, and trimmed the roses in her garden. Qui came by with her new baby, Silvia, and talked about her failing marriage. Qui looked thin and Lillis invited her to live in her house but Qui had arranged to live with her mother.

The study group met again; the Hibberds had retired and moved to St. George but they came up in May to attend the study group and see the Brookses. Jesse Davis had had a heart attack; both he and Sterling Workman had had heart surgery since they last met. Rex Moulton was wearing a hearing aid. Audrey Davis had arthritis. Lillis had had cataract surgery a year or two earlier; she joked that now she could see more clearly how old she had become. All were in their 60s and showing age.

They took a trip back east in April to reacquaint themselves with Rem's children and Dean's children, and to see Nyman. Lillis continued to fret about Nyman's marital status in her diary.

In May, George had a transurethral resection to treat a benign obstruction, and spent a night in the hospital. They both had chest X-rays to get their visas. George had a root canal and a crown repaired. Lillis became ill with pain in her back. She thought it might be arthritis, but it turned out to be shingles. The disease progressed and stayed with her through the spring and summer. George had a coincident bout with cold sores which he blamed on stress. Also in May, Lillis had 25 spots burned off her face and arms. In June they started to get their shots—gamma globulin, meningitis, cholera.

All the while there were many documents to read, video and audio tapes to review, seminars, meetings in the church offices, people to meet related to the mission call. They actually entered the Mission Training Center in Provo on June 18.

The accommodations and program for mission presidents at the MTC were a bit different than for other missionaries. They had an apartment with their own bathroom. Chocolates were left in the room. Meal tables were set and were away from the other missionaries. Pastries and treats were always available at break times. Every lecture or class was presented by some member of the church's general leadership, often apostles. Lillis was in pain with shingles and found it difficult to sit in class all day.

ZIMBABWE, JUNE – JULY 1990

George's brother Sam and Sam's wife Carolyn were at the airport. So were Lois and Harvey, Don and Marilyn, Allen Price, Siv Boun and his family (the Cambodian refugee family that Dean and Lorraine had sponsored), and some neighbors from Bountiful. Cy was away on a business trip, but Leslie came with her children. She was pregnant and had morning sickness and some early contractions. Five-year-old Carly Castle gave Lillis her favorite hand puppet as a going-away gift. It was a tearful good-bye, with a hint of foreboding. Leslie said, "I feel I will never see you again." George said, "You know that isn't how it works."

They flew out on June 25. The trip would take 8 days with stop-overs for further consultations at area headquarters in Solihull, England; Nairobi; and Johannesburg—often in the company of other mission presidents assigned to Africa. They would spend 30 hours in the air and take 7 airplanes. Joseph Sitati met them at the airport in Nairobi. They laughed and hugged each other, and then had a sweet reception with many of their Kenyan friends. Sitati took them back to the airport the following day. On the way a policeman stopped them and demanded a bribe. Sitati refused and requested a court date, but was released without delay. They visited Johannesburg on Sunday, July 1, a very cold winter day. They arrived in Harare on July 3 and overlapped only 3 days with the outgoing mission president, Joseph Hamstead and his wife, Margaret.

They seemed to settle in a little easier than in Kenya. Lillis was pleased with the abundance and variety of fresh fruit and vegetables in the market. She was pleased with the house and the caretaker, Tikey Jambo, who endorsed his paycheck with an *X.* He was delighted when Lillis taught him to write his name; he kept saying, "My name! Is that my name?" She started practicing writing with him every day.

There were 20 young missionaries—all African—and 20 older missionary couples from the US and Canada, scattered about 300 miles apart. It was George's and Lillis's first priority to find, meet, and inter-view these isolated missionaries. Contact with the distant branches and missionaries had been neglected over a long period of time. Now there was evidence of fractures and factions in the church organization. They set out on a 600-mile round trip to visit five cities—Kadoma, Kwekwe, Gweru, Bulawayo, and Masvingo—to meet about half the missionaries and to plan for a zone conference. About that time there was news that 18 people had been killed in demonstrations in Kenya. The drive was exotic and beautiful. Lillis commented that the sunsets were indescrib-able. They found themselves driving at night to keep their schedule, and

Probably the last picture taken of George and Lillis together, Zimbabwe, July 1990.

Lillis noted the curious practice of people driving the highways without headlights at night.

The zone conference was held in Harare on Thursday, July 19. George was happy with how well things came together, how well the staff in the mission office worked, and how well the missionaries responded to their individual assignments to conduct the conference, and how well the branches seemed to be operating. On Friday, they relaxed and visited a lion reserve and the zoo. One missionary couple stayed over with the Brookses a couple of days. Elder Anderson was in pain and wanted to see a doctor in Harare. George and Lillis drove the Andersons home to Bindura on Saturday and Lillis planted flowers in her garden that evening.

On Monday, July 23, Lillis complains a bit about her shipping consignment still hung up in customs. It contained adult literacy materials and household items. They had been in country 20 days.

She resumed writing in her diary on the same line and on the same page, but a year later, 1991. As she finished telling about the events of 1990, her handwriting was now dramatically changed to the shaky handwriting of a quadriplegic.

It was actually on Thursday, July 26, 1990, that George and Lillis were attending another zone conference in Kwekwe. Again, everything had gone well. They had met all the missionaries. George had interviewed the local church leadership, and reorganized a branch. They were waiting around to set apart a branch president who was very late for the appointment. The church leadership in Salt Lake City had given George and Lillis a list of tasks which they thought would be difficult and time consuming—mostly contacting all church units, and reorganizing a few; interviewing all the missionaries (some missionaries had never been interviewed nor received instructions from the prior mission president); holding two zone conferences; fixing the financial records, and establishing accounting guidelines. They finished it all in 3 weeks, a demonstration of their priorities, leadership style, and effectiveness.

Driving home that night, after dark, George ran into a truck which had lost a wheel and was lying on its axle, unable to move off the road, without lights or reflectors. One of the missionaries, Sara May, said that neither George nor Lillis saw what they ran into. Writing a year later, when her hands had recovered a bit, Lillis wrote:

George was killed instantly without a mark on him that I could see. I had several scalp wounds broken teeth, broken glasses, a bone poking out of my left arm, compound fracture near the wrist, broken neck, broken ribs. Both our seat belts were fastened but the girders [carried on the truck] had come through our windshield. Blood gushed over my glasses into my lap. The pain in my arms and chest made breathing difficult. I felt so all alone, so deserted, I envied George's death but knew at that moment that I would not die. I had to face whatever was ahead.

Among the trivial thoughts that clogged her mind as she suffered alone in the wrecked car, she was disappointed that she would not complete the assignment, and sorry for the loss of the car which was so difficult to acquire in Zimbabwe, and the expense to the church. But then she realized that she was alone in a foreign land on a dark and empty highway.

Fear and panic filled my mind. Moments later a feeling of comfort and peace quieted my soul. The thought came to me that everything was alright; it didn't matter the things that were terrorizing me. I felt more calm and even the pain seemed more bearable.

In a little while some people chanced upon the scene. One was Brother Tembo, the newly designated branch president from Kadoma. He rushed back to Kwekwe to get an ambulance for the 3-hour drive to Harare. There was no spine board and no care to immobilize her head. There is anecdotal evidence that she had feeling and function in her legs and may have transferred herself from car to gurney. There is also some evidence that she rode in a private car back to Kwekwe before being taken to Harare by ambulance.

The ride to Harare hosp. was touch and go. Bright lights, moving from stretchers to table to bed, voices discomfort, strangers, difficult breathing, chest tubes, NG tube, needle pokes, blood being drawn, X-rays, the doctor ignored my questions of where Geo was and how he was. The next day I asked Sis [Alma] Whiting if Geo was dead and she told me yes. The pain from that news was almost unbearable even though I had known the answer before I had asked.

She would survive another 10 years, a widow and a quadriplegic, a mother and grandmother. That her injuries may have been aggravated after the fact was something she never dwelt on.

XXVI

Lillis as a Patient
1990–1992

Neal Maxwell, one of the apostles of the church, called Rem on the telephone Thursday, July 26, the same day as the accident. Rem was working on a medical residency in St. Louis, about 8 hours behind Zimbabwe time. Maxwell wanted Rem to go to Africa to see what needed to be done. A new passport was fast-tracked for him. Rem and Nyman flew out to Harare via London on Sunday evening, July 29.

Lillis had been taken to a hospital in Harare where she was put on a ventilator and had emergency surgery on her neck. There she suffered pulmonary arrest and so she was airlifted to Johannesburg. Her condition and injuries were beyond the capabilities available in Harare. Truth be told, she might have been a candidate for benign neglect anywhere on the continent.

Rem and Nyman changed their plane reservations in London to arrive in Johannesburg Tuesday morning. Lillis was alert but unable to talk because of her airway.

There were no records—not a single note—from Harare nor from her short time in Johannesburg. Her physician was said to be an intensivist but he did not have trauma training and he had put no thought or time into her care. In one of her undated manuscripts Lillis wrote:

I hadn't been seen as yet by a doctor and no treatment of any kind had been ordered. Rem was furious. He called the American Embassy and the consulate came immediately. I don't know the details of events but the doctor was soon there and in my hearing I heard him say, "This patient is too old and too seriously injured to save. We have too many younger patients who need our attention." He apologized for being so long coming but said he had that too many other patients to see. Rem kept pressure on them and so did the embassy. My little Pentecostal black nurses were kind and overworked but told me they were praying for me. The doctor took my halo off and tossed it across the room and said it was put on wrong and had not stabilized my neck. He immediately took me and put a tracheotomy tube in place which allowed me to breathe somewhat better.

The gloves were off; there was little courtesy between Rem and the negligent, undertrained, and arrogant South African doctor. Africa was going through an unchecked AIDS epidemic and Rem flatly refused to allow the ICU to transfuse four units of blood. He demanded that the blood be brought in from the US. The embassy stepped up and donated the blood from their staff. Both Nyman and Rem asked the hospital staff to address her diarrhea and to nourish her through an IV or a Miller tube. The surly doctor responded, "I'm the doctor; you're not." Nyman responded, "You are our employee and you will do what you are told." But Lillis was not fed in the 12 days from the time of her accident until she returned to Salt Lake City. She lost 30 lbs., complicating her recovery.

The Trip Home

The church leadership, including apostles, were more polite but equally obtuse. In fairness, it is likely the church had never confronted such decisions before. Certainly many missionaries had died in the field. But what seemed to stymie the church on this occasion was the neglect Lillis faced in Africa, and the huge, completely unforeseen cost to bring her home. Injuries such as Lillis's would not necessarily be fatal in the United States, where one could expect more sophisticated care. Those were some of the factors that they had to come to terms with. They were in over their heads and so were their physician experts, some of whom were also priesthood leaders, but not trauma specialists. In the end they had to trust Rem's assessments.

In the conference calls over the next days, Rem first struggled to convince the church that Lillis would not survive in a South African hospital.

Then he had to convince them that she needed an air ambulance. The church preferred a commercial airliner, unaware that an airliner would not have allowed her onboard. Rem walked them through the complexity of layovers, transfers, and moving respirators and equipment through airports. Of course there were no direct flights from Johannesburg. The church even considered borrowing an airplane from Jon Huntsman, the rich industrialist who was chummy with church leadership. It was difficult for them to come around to the idea that a new problem would require a new solution. And the clock was ticking.

The air ambulance that had taken Lillis to Johannesburg was a Zimbabwean plane. It was large, well equipped, and well staffed. By the time the church came around to hiring that plane, it was no longer available. The story goes that the church wanted to hire it, but a secretary in Salt Lake City had misplaced or ignored the order until it was too late.

An ambulance plane was hired out of Georgia. It turned out to be a small Lear jet which was barely adequate. Indeed, the respirator took up a quarter of the cabin space. The airplane would require multiple fuel stops to cross the continents and the ocean. There was an FAA requirement to swap out pilots en route; three pilots would take off and there would be a total of five pilots with shift changes. Rem made a list of the essential crew and supplies. They would need a nurse, a pulmonary technician, and a doctor familiar with trauma management. The flight was scheduled for the first week of August.

A day before the flight, Rem learned that the flight doctor was not immediately available. Lillis's condition was deteriorating so quickly that Rem saw no other option than to step up and do the job himself. The South African doctor seized one last opportunity to complicate Lillis's care. He refused to put in a multiport central venous catheter to facilitate IVs during the flight. He cited policy and law, but in reality he was simply being obstructionist. Rem had had it by this point and said, "You don't understand. I don't care about what is appropriate, policy, or legal. Mom will have a central line if I have to break into your supply cupboard, steal a catheter, and put it in myself. Then you can deport me." The doctor installed the line.

Lillis needed constant attention during the flight. She would later recall:

> Rem sat on the floor by my head all the way home. . . . We stopped in the Ivory Coast for fuel and the heat and humidity was so stifling and oppressive. Rem fanned me all the time we were on the ground and gave me iced pop to sip even though it was suctioned back as soon as I swallowed it, but it was refreshing. He turned me, kept the suction going, changed the IVs, quad coughed me, and kept me from choking. He changed my line and emptied my down drain bag. I would have died without him.

The plane had not been supplied correctly. Rem had to ration atropine and substitute an isuprel drip at landings and takeoffs when Lillis's heart rate would drop into the 30s. Rem had to fabricate a suction using plastic bottles from the trash to reinflate her collapsed lung; inexplicably there was a respirator on board, but no suction. The crew had failed to supply Valium and so Lillis was in discomfort for 28 hours—until a stop in Bermuda. The IV solutions had the wrong ratios of sodium, potassium, dextrose, and lactated Ringer's, so what they carried had to be mixed and measured.

Perhaps it is a detail in Lillis's story, but Rem's skill, loyalty, tenacity, and endurance over those 10 days were essential for Lillis to survive. There were many who had some responsibility for her—Church headquarters, the hospital, the ambulance at the scene. But among those, Rem was the only one with honest intentions, the correct set of tools, and the temperament to save her. Additionally, Nyman, the embassy, and the Pentecostal nurses demonstrated sincerity of purpose. The flight made six refueling stops—Namibia, Ivory Coast, the Canaries, the Azores, Bermuda, and Tennessee—before landing in Salt Lake City. Rem was awake during those 36 hours.

When the plane landed on August 8, Lillis saw Neal Maxwell through her window at some distance in the morning sun. He waved to her.

It was a welcome relief to land early that morning just as the sun was coming over the mountain. I could see Neal Maxwell on the tarmac waiting for us. . . . It was the morning of George's funeral, to be held in Granite Stake House. Rem turned me over to the care of the hosp. and rushed to change and attend the funeral. . . . The nurses and technicians at LDS Hosp were as efficient as machines. I knew immediately my chance for dying was over. It would never happen here.

FUNERAL

Meanwhile, George's body had returned home a day and a half earlier. George's brother, Samuel Jr., and Leslie received the body at the Salt Lake City Airport. The six-sided coffin fit him snugly. It had abstract African designs burned into the sides. It had a window above his face so that Leslie could see his mission nametag in his pocket, and she could tell that a stranger had tied his tie. The suit, the nametag, and the coffin were discarded and he was dressed in temple clothes for a more traditional Mormon presentation.

He had commented before leaving on his mission that if he should die abroad he preferred to be buried in the mission field. This may have reflected frugality, a commitment to his calling, or a nonchalant faith in the restoration of things after death. Regardless, it seems prescient that he would express a preference. The church paid for his repatriation and persuaded the family to ignore his wishes.

Those attending the funeral, 2,000 or so, filled the Granite Tabernacle. The service was beautiful, with choral music provided by his aged friends from the Toronto Mission (including Neal Maxwell and Allen Price), and a choir from the Samoan Ward. Bishop Ed Collard of the Val Verda Ward in Bountiful spoke. He recalled a temple recommend interview when he asked George if he supported the church leadership. George had responded, "Yes, and that includes you, Bishop." Don Remington reminisced on his association with George. Neal Maxwell spoke on life, mortality, and God's love for his children.

Recovery

One might guess that loneliness would be a big problem for a patient like Lillis. But quite the opposite was true. Her life and consciousness were oppressed by routines, shift changes, and even visitors who disturbed her sleep both day and night. Routines began as early as 4:30 AM, and she spent the rest of the day looking to catch up on lost sleep. When she could hold a pen again, she recalled that she never had time alone to think.

> The hours, days, weeks and months that were to follow were so filled with treatments, procedures, distractions, discomforts, doctors, nurses, people, machines, noises, it left me little strength, concentration, or effort to think about my great pain: the loss of George. There were those moments at night I would find myself alone with the clicking of machines and the beeping of the IVs when for minutes the whole reality of my loss would rush in on me and I would weep bitterly and uncontrollably but quickly it was time to be suctioned, tubes to be checked, breathing to be stimulated, IVs to be added, turning to be done, medications given, and feeding started, computers updated, blood drawn, X-rays taken, no time for mourning or meditating, little time for prayer; only time for submitting and enduring.

The stabilization part of her recovery took about 9 months. But even a year later she was still having broken teeth repaired. She arrived at LDS Hospital with a ventilator. She couldn't talk, cough, or blow her nose. A respiratory therapist sat near the head of her bed for the first 6 weeks. She couldn't swallow without choking. She couldn't open her hands, lift her arms, or turn her head. She had her neck stabilized at LDS Hospital. Her left hand was also reset there, but because of injury and paralysis it was never very functional. She had bedsores on her back and heels. Her veins were bruised and of little use for IVs. She had spasms in her legs. Glass was removed from her arms and face.

Nyman kept a vigil near her bed during those months, patiently communicating with her by means of an alphabet board. He lived in her house, ran errands, and brought her mail. He learned how to perform the common tasks of lifting her, assisting her to cough, and monitoring her drainage. He bought her first wheelchair. The CIA, his employer in Virginia, graciously gave him a lengthy leave of absence, but he never returned to work for them.

Leslie would relieve Nyman daily, and Nyman would retire to tend her children. This was during Leslie's difficult pregnancy. She had started to suffer gestational diabetes on the day she got word that her father had died. When her baby became somnolent, the delivery was induced. Baby Bronwynne was born in early November and Leslie stayed home to recover with her baby. Nyman continued his daily visits alone.

During her months of recovery and for the rest of her life, Lillis fought intermittent pneumonia, urinary tract infections, cystitis, and allergies to antibiotics. One of her problems was uncontrolled diarrhea. In December 1990, she had a bowel resection:

> Dec. 31, 1991 Tues. . . . As I reflect over the past yr, I remember how terribly ill I was a yr ago tonight when I was rushed to surgery for a bowel problem. Dr. Larry Stevens removed part of my colon and the cecum. . . . I awoke on a ventilator. I returned to my ICU room to find the New Year in [January 1, 1991] and balloons hanging on my wall. I was so miserable and uncomfortable. Nyman spent many hrs with me for the next many days until I was more physically stable.

Months into her recovery and no one had really talked about end-of-life issues; the cascade of more immediate problems had always gotten in the way. She grew in strength but there were setbacks in efforts to take her off the ventilator, an essential milestone for leaving the ICU. At one point the doctors thought they may have ruptured her trachea, which would have been a catastrophe. Also about this time a nurse had noticed that Lillis's pupil did not respond to light, an indication of brain damage. Because Lillis was intubated she could not explain that her eye had been injured during a cataract repair years earlier, in 1986, and her iris had stayed open ever since. This fact was noted in her voluminous chart but had been overlooked by most—let's say everybody—until Leslie pointed it out. It was about this time that L. Stephen Richards approached Leslie and asked, "Why are you trying to save her?" The question had never been put to her before. Richards was an MD (though not involved in Lillis's care), and a friend of George from their time together in French Canada.

Leslie consulted with Lillis's doctors James Pearl and Larry Stevens; it was their opinion that Lillis was far from any end-of-life decisions. All her treatments were the appropriate ethical standard of care, nothing more. At least a door was now open for conversation.

These stories illustrate, if nothing else, how vital it is for a patient to have a friend and advocate; even a layperson to witness, to bring some supplemental, contrasting, and expansive thinking into the noisy, distracted, compartmentalized hospital. This was the value that Nyman, Leslie, and Rem added.

Leslie, Lillis's most trusted agent, soon went to her mother and asked, "Do you want to die?" Lillis, in a conspiratorial tone said, "Yeah. What's our plan?"—an example of her glib, sometimes irreverent humor.

REHABILITATION AT LIFE CARE

Getting off the respirator was the essential step for getting out of the ICU, for any serious rehabilitation, or for life at all. Lillis recalled, "Part of my life was returned to me after my tracheotomy tube and later my respirator were removed and my voice was back." Also, her chest tube, NG (nasal-gastric) tube, feeding tube, and IVs were gradually removed. She was in and out of the ICU over about 5 months, and another 4 months at LDS Rehabilitation. Costs mounted quickly, and after 9 months there was pressure to move her out. She was released from LDS Hospital to Life Care, an inpatient rehabilitation center in Bountiful. It's fair to say that physically she was barely ready for the transition.

As Lillis was preparing to leave LDS for Life Care, the family started to think about where Lillis would ultimately live long-term; customarily, such patients live with family. Leslie took the initiative to look for a new house to buy, one with a yard big enough that an addition could be built for Lillis. She actually took an opportunity to bid on a house before her old one was sold, confident that the pieces would come together. This was the summer of 1991. In September, Leslie took a job with the University of Utah Medical Center so that she could learn about the care of people with spinal cord injuries.

Lillis had incomplete injuries to her spinal cord; at C_{3-4} on the left and at C_{4-5} on the right; and other injuries. The term *incomplete* acknowledges some function or feeling below the injury. She had, for example, the function of an opposing thumb on her right hand, and use of her triceps on both arms, but not the use of her diaphragm.

At Life Care she was too weak to press her call light, so the nurse would place it near her cheek so she could trigger it by rolling her face on it. She could not grasp a Kleenex. She continued her physical therapy and occupational therapy. By July 1991—a year after her accident—she was beginning to write in her diary again with a ballpoint pen strapped to a brace fitted into her hand. Among the first things she wrote, she tried to recall and list all the people who had visited her over the past year. She came up with about 270 names, most of whom had visited multiple times.

Not surprisingly, some of her writing complained about the care facility, which Leslie began to call *Life Scare*. Life Care was so poorly staffed that occasionally they missed her morning bowel care, and there would be no one willing to do it on the next shift. She bonded with and admired some of the nurses, but there were others who smelled of alcohol and cigarettes, used profanity, or had dirty uniforms. Some did not know how to use the automated thermometer or blood pressure cuff. One nurse contaminated her catheter. "I didn't make an issue because the damage was already done. She held my leg with her gloved hand and then took hold of the end of the catheter." It happened too fast for Lillis to intervene.

The food was terrible: fried, starchy, sugary, processed, unimaginative, rarely anything fresh. "It is ugly to look at, poorly prepared, poor quality, really quite disgraceful in a land of plenty." Once for breakfast they offered her a bowl of raisin bran without milk. On that occasion Leslie castigated them until they sent a nurse to the grocery store to buy milk.

Lillis said the place was noisy in the day, like a barnyard.

Many patients wander aimlessly up and down the halls in and out of our rooms babbling, swearing, crying, drooling, some in wheelchairs, some walking. It is continuous from early morning until night. It causes one to wonder what these poor souls were like in younger and healthier days and if they are suffering as greatly as their groans and gruntings would indicate.

In November 1991, a confused patient named George Kato came into Lillis's room and became violent. He hit her with his fist, shook her bed, grabbed her phone out of her hand, and peed on the floor.

She enjoyed the actual PT sessions; the therapists were all refined and smart. Sessions lasted 2 hours 30 minutes in the morning and 90 minutes in the afternoon. She would lie prone on a mat and exercises her triceps; she would lift weights, some weighing 10 lbs.; exercise with pulleys; exercise hands, legs, and arms.

> I rather enjoy physical therapy because most of the patients who come there have their wits about them. We are all in the same small room at the same time—five or six plus the therapists— and it becomes a social hr. where we exchange complaints about the atrocious food and unbalanced diets and the shortage of nursing care. We all air our complaints with one another since it falls on deaf ears with any of the management. Our therapists agree with us.

UNIVERSITY MEDICAL CENTER

After a year and a half in therapy it was still very difficult for her to sit in a chair. All the exercises at Life Care had been done lying on the floor. Her progress was therefore limited.

Lillis had three general problems: When she tried to raise her head above a certain level she suffered orthostatic hypotension—a sudden drop in blood pressure. She also suffered from dysreflexia, a sudden onset of excessively high blood pressure which can be lethal. Dysreflexia is associated with any number of reflexes or stimuli below a spinal injury. She also suffered spasms, another autonomic response typical in persons with spinal injuries.

By September 1991, Leslie had started her new job at the U Med Center. And the Castles had bought a house on St. Mary's Drive. Leslie used some of Lillis's money to build an attached apartment designed specifically to Lillis's needs. Leslie had met Dr. John Speed, a spinal cord specialist, and had begun planning a way forward for Lillis's care. The apartment was ready in December 1991. Lillis moved in a day or two before Christmas.

Rem, Dean, and Nyman thought it was a terrible idea for Lillis to live in Leslie's house. They thought that Leslie could not raise her family while being a nurse to Lillis. Lillis could be rigid and difficult. If they couldn't get along, then the costly investment to build the apartment, from Lillis's savings, would be irretrievable. Cy was always supportive of Leslie, but he also understood the financial risk. He made his foresight clear, saying:

> I don't mind building an apartment on my property, but the house is mine and it cannot be subdivided; if this arrangement fails I will not reimburse Lillis; the brick has to match; she is not my mother.

In retrospect his foresight was astute and his terms were generous.

Meanwhile, Dr. Speed at the U Med Center was confident he could address Lillis's symptoms more effectively than had been done at LDSH or Life Care. He suggested Lillis be admitted to the U after the holidays in January 1992 for a thorough evaluation and a sort of boot camp rehabilitation. Lillis stayed 2 months at the Med Center, until the end of February. Dr. Speed addressed her spasms by prescribing a dose of baclofen far greater than LDS Hospital was willing to prescribe. When her symptoms subsided, he titrated the dose downwards. In general, he felt it was best to accept a risk to achieve a necessary outcome. He treated the orthostatic symptoms with long practice sessions, raising her head a bit and lowering it, until finally her body learned again how to sit up. Soon she was sitting for hours at a time. When she was able to sit, she was able to use a motorized wheelchair. He addressed her dysreflexia by discovering the several triggers and relieving those as part of her daily care routine.

So, to state it again, Leslie had a comprehensive understanding early on, and took the initiative to address Lillis's many health and lifestyle issues. She took a job at the U so that she could learn about spinal cord injury and offer better advice in Lillis's recovery. She did that while caring for a new baby, moving into a new house, and modifying it to suit Lillis's needs against her brothers' advice.

Lillis had her own bundle of fears:

Today [February 29, 1992] I am to be discharged from University Hospital where I have been for the past 2 months. After spending the past 19 mos in hospital it is like losing my security blanket to leave and be on my own, responsible for hiring my own help and in charge of my life. I have to face my inabilities in a way I have never had to before.. . . My greatest reservation is the responsibility I'm placing on Leslie. Nyman has carried a heavy burden of being with me nearly every day for the past 1½ yrs while in hospital, running errands, the stress of dealing with the church over expenses and who should pay the bills. It has been a most unpleasant task that seemed never to end.. . . Leslie has been untiring in her efforts to help me plan and make my life less stressful and easier. I worry about her burning out. . . . She carries a heavy load, and hopefully I'll be able to carry a little of it now.

I feel I've made improvement here this past 2 months. I've learned to remove my shirt and undergarment, pull myself to a sitting position, lift weights from my original 15 lbs., now 72 lbs., and many other small tasks. I feel more independent and secure about being alone.

She had a general anxiety over many things besides imposing on Leslie's family. She was moving to a new congregation where she had no acquaintances and a diminished ability to socialize. She was panicky whenever Leslie would get sick. Soon she would have to hire her aides and pay them. She was by no means unskilled, but George had balanced the checkbook and filed the taxes most of the time. Now she would have to hire an accountant to figure Social Security for her aides.

When Lillis returned to her apartment at the Castle house, she found it decorated with her own books, keepsakes, and furniture, including the granddaughter clock that George had made. It was intelligently designed and could be divided into two private rooms; one had a fold-out couch so someone could stay overnight, or she could have a moment of privacy from guests. Through her window she could see squirrels and quail and the change of seasons in Leslie's backyard. The apartment was spacious and beautiful.

XXVII

Money among Friends

Lillis's medical expenses were huge. The plane flight home cost in the neighborhood of $100,000 all by itself. The shock of large and open-ended expenses could be offered as an excuse for the shenanigans employed by church leaders and bureaucrats to avoid any commitment to pay.

Neal Maxwell was the first to broach the topic of medical insurance and care for Lillis. Maxwell was an apostle, one of only twelve in the senior quorum of leadership in the Mormon Church. He was also George's friend from their missionary days in Canada in the 1940s. One would think he had the power and motive to do the right thing. It was in August 1990 that Maxwell and Dean crossed paths at LDS Hospital just after Lillis had returned home. They gave her a blessing. Maxwell anointed Lillis with oil and Dean blessed her, saying in part, "You are not yet as Job; your friends and family stand by you."

On this occasion, without prodding, Maxwell volunteered that the church would take care of Lillis, and then went on to specify: the church will pay for her hospitalization, pay to modify her house, pay for in-home nursing care, pay for wheelchairs, vans with lifts, or other appliances that she may need, and that her private insurance (which had a lifetime cap) would not be spent for these purposes but would be preserved for health-care unrelated to the accident. Then he said to contact Burton "Buzz" Tingey at church headquarters who would facilitate payments.

Within days, Sue Campbell, George's secretary at the school board, alerted the family that Buzz Tingey was representing himself as the agent for Lillis Brooks and was seeking personal and confidential information about George's pension, finances, and insurance policies. Sue had refused to help him. Tingey had also contacted banks and insurance companies around town with the same pretense. Soon the Brookses received a letter from Tingey listing all the family resources that he could find but offering no financial help from the church. Of course, this was of no help to Lillis; it was information she already knew. Though Dean protested to Maxwell and to Tingey, Tingey's report continued to circulate among church authorities from then on.

Neal Maxwell never spoke to Dean again, never acknowledged Dean's letters, never ran interference of any kind, and never spoke to anyone in the Brooks family again about expenses. It seems very possible that when Maxwell got back to his office in August 1990, his colleagues or bureaucrats told him to stop making promises, and he acquiesced. Over the years he continued to visit Lillis; he and his wife, Colleen, would bring cookies, they would chat amiably and ask about each other's children.

Lillis was so committed to the church, so enfolded in the community, so dependent, and so very fragile both emotionally and physically that she could not involve herself in finances for the first years. She never spoke about finances to Maxwell, for example, though he visited her frequently. She abdicated that to her children without a whisper of instruction. So it was the children who decided on which wheelchair to buy (at $15,000), which van to buy and how to modify it (a total cost of $18,000), and so on. Nyman did much of the work to sell Lillis's house while Leslie designed her apartment. Lillis was too compromised and too weak to think about money, much less confront her erstwhile friends at the church.

INSURANCE

In the orientation for mission presidents, George and Lillis were instructed that the church was self-insured and would cover injuries for the mission president and his dependents. It is a fine point, but technically Lillis was not a dependent; she was a missionary in her own right. Nonsensical as it might seem, the church asserted that their obligation to Lillis ended when George died, because she was merely the wife of the mission president. George had the presence of mind to mention the insurance policy to his children before he left the US. The church tried to deny the existence of that insurance. Then the church refused to define the limits of the coverage. So the primary concerns for the family were: the meaning of "self-insurance"; the terms of that policy; and whether the church would continue to cover for injuries sustained in the mission field after the missionary was released.

Dwayne Liddell, the director of the church risk management office, finally acknowledged in a letter that the church was self-insured and that payouts would come from the general tithing fund. In contrast, the apostle L. Tom Perry said that payments would come from the church fast offerings program (local-level welfare). He was essentially proposing that the local leadership could choose to offer or to refuse a discretionary gift while the corporate headquarters could disengage.

It was customary with fast offerings that the beneficiary would have to impoverish herself before she could receive assistance. And customarily the church requested financial participation from the extended family before the church would pay. Obviously those provisions are not conditions of normal insurance, and would not be in the spirit of Maxwell's promise. But those were the miserly provisions that Perry asserted, and the probable motivation behind Buzz Tingey's research. Perry said, with no sense of irony, that church funds "were sacred, like the widow's mite" (see Mark 12:41–44) and thus needed protection. Perry tried to persuade the Brookses with religious platitudes, once saying, "The family will be blessed to the extent they were willing to sacrifice. And the children would receive testimony of the rightness of her call." He was promising a spiritual reward in exchange for greenbacks. On that occasion, Rem asked Perry to clarify "sacrifice," pointing out that each of the Brooks boys, including Cy Castle, had interrupted or terminated their careers, three of them had relocated across the continent, Rem had given up his residency, Nyman had walked away from his job in Virginia, and the Castles were enlarging their house to take Lillis in.

Bargaining Posture

When the Brooks family wrote letters to correct minutes or to ask for clarification between contrasting instructions or agreements, they would get no response. Church office managers would deny that mail had been received. Registered mail did not help. Finally the family started to courier correspondence in person, and to demand a signed receipt from the secretary on duty. Even so, the church's default was simply to not respond.

The Brooks children (Rem, Leslie, and Nyman) met several times with L. Tom Perry, his staff members, church welfare officers, people from the missionary department, accountants, and risk managers, together and individually. It seemed to emerge that the church wanted two things: they wanted to avoid paying the extraordinary costs, and they wanted to avoid precedent and documentation. Leslie pointed that out to Buzz Tingey. Once when a meeting with him went longer than anticipated, Leslie said, "I've got to go and put money in the parking meter or I will get a ticket." Tingey said, "Don't worry, we can pay for the ticket." Leslie responded, "You are happy to pay for things that are not your responsibility if they are cheap, but you refuse to pay for things that are your responsibility if they are costly. Your motive is not justice; it is money." The paper trail showed Tingey to be a caricature of an officious low-level bureaucrat who had difficulty understanding the subtleties of a problem. He once made the unintelligible argument: "If we had an African missionary serving here in the US and he became injured we would not send him to Africa to be treated. And if we had an African missionary serving in Africa we would not bring him here to be treated." He also told a rambling story about a bishop who had been murdered and stuffed into the trunk of his own car while he was visiting members of his ward. The point Tingey was trying to make was that the church had no financial liability in any of these scenarios. It says something about the priorities and motivations of an organization, and the individuals who constitute that organization.

A breakthrough of sorts came when Bishop Jay Horrocks got involved. Horrocks was bishop of the Monument Park 9th Ward, Leslie's ward, where Lillis would live. Horrocks was also president of Beneficial Life, a church-owned insurance company.

In his spacious presidential office at Beneficial Life, he assured the Brooks family, verbally, that he would provide Lillis with all the necessary resources, as her bishop, through fast offerings. One by one he addressed their fears. He would not inquire about the assets of the extended family. He would not ask Lillis to spend down her savings. He would not require the monthly bishop's interview to determine Lillis's worthiness. He would not question her requests. He said, "I'm the bishop and I can manage her correctly in my own way." Leslie offered Lillis's health insurance policy, valued at $100,000, if the church would guarantee payment through her life. But the Church refused to put anything in writing. So that insurance benefit was never used. Horrocks said, "There are some risks you have to take. Let's move forward. I will pay her bills. The longer I serve as bishop, the more likely my successor will be to continue to keep faith." The Brookses accepted fast offerings—discretionary welfare at the parish level—based on a realization that life involves risk; based on a belief that this solution was cheaper, quicker, and less risky than a law suit; but also based on trust in Horrocks's integrity.

IMPLICATIONS AND IRONIES

It was informally projected that Lillis would hire unskilled labor at $10 per hour, 4 hours on, 4 hours off every day, at the cost of $44,000 per year. Plus there would be expenses for incidentals such as handrails or occasional hospitalization (which would be covered by Medicare). That cost of home care would be less than half of the price of continued residence at Life Care. That may have been part of the motivation for the church to pay for home care without acknowledging their insurance obligation. They may have been keen to break their continuity of institutional care. The church had taken care of Lillis since her hospitalization in Africa, and they may have been looking for a logical break to hand her off to informal home care.

Medicare and the church paid for 9 months at LDS Hospital, 8 months at Life Care, and 2 months at the University of Utah Medical Center. So all the while that the church leaders were bickering and mis¬behaving, they were also paying. For the same price, the church could have been honest and dignified, which was their pretense. In the end the only lesson the church learned was to stop promising health insurance to mission presidents.

Lillis was humiliated by the agreement. For the rest of her life she had to send an hour sheet to the bishop, who would write individual checks to her aides. The bishops who succeeded Horrocks did indeed continue to pay, but they gave in to pressure from the stake president and started to send memos to her in the mail each month, reminding her that members of her congregation were making a financial sacrifice to pay for her needs.

Fast offerings are supposed to be paid into a common fund based on individuals' inclination to donate. There is no prescribed assessment, only the suggestion that the amount should equal or exceed the value of a skipped meal during the fast. The funds are distributed based on an individual's confidential need. One congregation might be paying into the common fund to support members in a different congregation. As L. Tom Perry artlessly said in a meeting in November 1991, the welfare fund is "very large and definitely adequate for" Lillis's needs.

But in Lillis's case, the stake broke the rules of confidentiality and consulted with a few wealthy members; Lillis's expenses were disclosed to them, and they were asked to pay a specific assessment. This was done for the silliest of reasons. The stake pesident's pride would not allow him to draw more money from the fast offering fund than his stake took in. And the monthly memos to her indicate that he felt it was proper to demean someone on welfare. The Brooks children had tried to protect her from priesthood chicanery, but failed in the end.

Lillis had always felt that donating to church funds and charities was a form of worship. But it became an irony and an embarrassment for her to donate because she was never sure who in the congregation might scrutinize or discredit her devotion. In that way, even her own money was not her money. She was so embarrassed by her dependence on welfare that over 10 years she never raised the wages for her aides, never allowed for overtime or bonuses, and sometimes dismissed aides before their shift had ended and docked their pay. There is some indication that she had a hard time retaining employees. There were days when she went without care, and short-staffing created friction between Lillis and Leslie.

She said that the church had taken away her insurance and shamed her even though she, her ancestors, and everyone in her extended family had paid full tithing and fast offerings since before anyone could remember.

XXVIII

Getting On with Life

TEMPLE TRIP

Lillis attended a temple session in September of 1991. This was very early in her recovery, before her rehabilitation at the University Medical Center, and before moving into her apartment at the Castle home. She was still very weak and filled with anxiety when leaving her bed.

> Diane Rindlisbacher, my excellent primary care nurse in LDS Hosp Rehab, who has continued to visit me since I left LDSH, called and invited me to go to the temple with her. I hesitated to go but told her I would. She came and lifted me and drove me to the Jordan River Temple. It was a beautiful day. I never remember enjoying a session more. I felt a peace and comfort I haven't felt before since my accident. Lois was serving there that day and helped me all the way thru. Diane was also by my side. . . . Diane was efficient in her handling and lifting of me. I appreciate all she has done for me this past year. The flowers around the temple grounds were beautiful, the mountains so majestic in the distance making such an awesome backdrop for this valley that holds such happy memories. . . . It was a tiring day.

Plans for any outing were complicated. Even grocery shopping could be cancelled at the last minute by little things such as a spike in blood pressure. Parking and transport were always problems. Temple sessions were just long enough that special attention had to be paid to when she first sat up in the morning and who would drive her; a trip to the temple would be longer than an aide's shift. That is why she only attended maybe four more temple sessions in her life. But she kept her temple recommend current.

Temple recommends—the authorization to enter a temple—are renewed annually after interviews with the bishop and stake president. In one such interview, the stake president thoughtlessly asked her one of the prescribed questions, "Do you wear your temple garments day and night?" Chagrined, Lillis had to explain life with a catheter and other difficulties in the life of a quadriplegic. The stake president tried to wave off his embarrassment with a patronizing, "Oh, you don't have to explain; I understand, Sister Brooks." To which she responded, "The hell you do."

After one temple session Leslie asked how it went, and whether she saw George or felt his presence there. Lillis responded, "No, but you have to understand, your dad never really liked going to the temple." This droll rejoinder was typical of her humor throughout her life. But sometimes she seemed honestly bewildered that she had no spiritual manifestations related to her mission or George's death. Many of her friends and acquaintances with analogous life experiences often bore testimony of spiritual experiences. Some people would propose their own spiritual insight, as if Lillis's experience were a blank wall inviting graffiti from any passerby. Some claimed, for example, that there was a purpose in the accident or a foreshadowing. But Lillis described to Leslie the moments preceding the accident: "There was no warning. We were not distracted. We were fasting. We were talking about how much we loved being in Africa. We were in tune. If God had only whispered we would have heard him. There was no warning." The reality for her was not that George was present; it was that he was gone, which she mourned and mentioned frequently for the rest of her life.

She was likewise annoyed when people would assert that she was fighting hard, being courageous, or had made a sacrifice. She dismissed these as meaningless clichés, saying privately to her children, "I just haven't died yet. How have I been brave? What could I have done differently?"

Rehabilitation at the University Medical Center

After moving in to her apartment at the Castle house, she continued to go to physical therapy sessions at the U Med Center twice a week through 1992. She learned to ride Flextrans, UTA's non-emergency handicap transport. On her therapy days she fell into the routine of meeting Rem for lunch at her apartment; he always brought her some special kind of take-out, such as Greek or Chinese.

Flextrans gave her a measure of independence, but each ride required her to face down the fear, helplessness, and the disorder in her life. If the driver came late or dropped her off at the wrong curb, she might have difficulty crossing through traffic, or she might miss part of her session, or miss her ride home and her lunch with Rem. Once the driver let her out as a helicopter was preparing to take off from the hospital, and she was chilled in the downdraft. Once a truck was parked in front of Leslie's drive, which made getting to the curb difficult. Flextrans might pick up other passengers on the way out or the way back, requiring a long and unexpected route through the city. She often wrote about the beauty of the day that she observed during her rides—spring blossoms or fall colors, or trees that had matured since she and George had lived on campus.

As soon as she was capable of sitting for long periods, she took up the task of reviewing and disposing of the paper files that she and George had collected over the years—correspondence, financial records, things they had collected in their travels. She also gave away her furniture, books, china, and art. "They seemed to have value then, but now they are a burden." There were so many files and other belongings that they filled the Castles' two-car garage. She recognized the clutter as an imposition on Leslie, and hurried to dispose of it. Still, it took many weeks. Fortunately her diaries, letters, photos, and scrapbooks survived the cull.

She had friends and professional acquaintances at the hospital and even knew some patients there. She would often check in on them after her therapy. In September 1992, she was surprised to find that her nephew's son, Brett Remington, had been admitted and was in the same room and bed she had occupied. "He looked fragile and nervous his first day there. I enjoyed the visit. He is a handsome boy with a lot of challenges ahead of him. My heart aches for him. I tried to be positive and encouraging." Brett had injured his spinal cord in a motorcycle accident; he was 17 years old.

Lillis's sympathy was authentic, not just for Brett but for the many people she met along the way of her recovery. She once said:

> I am more surprised than sad about what has happened to me; and I am ashamed of my surprise. What was I thinking, all those years when I wheeled patients through the halls, patients who were so ill and so injured? I thought I was being compassionate. But I thought this was an experience for them and not for me.

She felt that her suffering illuminated for her the commonality of human struggle. When people would express sympathy for Lillis, she might dismiss it by reminding them that she had friends who were worse off, with a higher injury, or more pain, or fewer resources. Indeed, her diaries are filled with detailed chronologies of her friends' illnesses and life challenges.

SOCIAL GROUPS

Her new routine started to echo her old routine. She kept up with most of all of her former social contacts as best she could. These included her monthly study group; an annual reunion with her aged friends from the Lincoln Ward Gleaners (a young women's organization); an annual reunion with the Parry cousins (George's family); Remington parties on Pioneer Day, Thanksgiving, and Christmas; Zimbabwe Mission reunions; LDS Hospital Nurses Alumni; Aurora Club meetings; correspondence; and church. In December 1992, she took Flextrans to attend the LDSH Nurses Alumni Christmas party. The party was held in a mansion called the Colonial House which was owned by the hospital and located on a steep hill in the Avenues neighborhood. The streets were clogged with snow and as she struggled to motor her chair up the drive, some of her old colleagues came out to meet her to push her the last few yards. "The home was beautifully decorated with two lovely trees. The buffet table was elegant and the program fun. It was a delightful afternoon visiting and renewing acquaintances."

There were weekly trips grocery shopping where she would sometimes run into ward members or neighbors. There were occasional outings such as to see a movie. Priscilla Anderson, one of her aides, made a point of taking Lillis for rides in her van. They might visit the capitol grounds or a park to look at the flowers or autumn leaves. Nyman, Leslie, or others might also take her out for a drive as far as Park City or Heber.

An important part of her routine was writing letters to friends, grandchildren, nieces, and nephews. For example, between 1999 and 2000 she wrote about 40 multi-page letters to Kristal Hirschi—the daughter of her nephew Stephen Hirschi—while Kristal served as a missionary. Kristal was just one of her pen pals. She also wrote almost weekly to Dean or Dean's children. Conservatively estimated, she wrote well over 1,000 letters with a ballpoint pen as a quadriplegic. She also kept up her journal.

She had a surprising number of friends, which she carefully maintained. Her relatives were among the most faithful. Her brother-in-law Harvey Hirschi, Lois's husband, spent time with her every week. Lillis said, "He's more like a brother." Her classmate from nursing school, Anna Kurata Kato, sometimes came to visit though she lived in Boston. She kept in touch with Dick and Jane Sardella from Syracuse, New York, whom she had met at Bowling Green State University in Ohio. She had friends from high school in Vernal, from Lincoln Ward in Sugar House, from the Indian School in Brigham City, from the school board office, Dr. Joyce Johnson and Liz Child from LDS Hospital, many friends from Richards II Ward, from Africa, and from England.

CHURCH

Possibly the most important part of her social life was attending church. Getting ready for church and getting to the church on time was a challenge from the beginning. In June 1992 she recounted riding her chair to attend stake conference alone:

> . . . my 2nd Father's Day since George's death, also 2nd wedding anniversary, our 43rd. The pain seems to be more bearable this yr. I have allowed myself the luxury of thinking about him this year. As I have grown stronger physically I've dared to think about the great void that his death has left in my life. Yesterday I attended Stake Conference. It was very stressful for me because of the huge crowd, the uneven sidewalks, many cars, concern over the building [accessibility] I was unfamiliar with.

Jon Huntsman was released as stake pres. A great amount of back-slapping, praises, flattering, inside jokes, etc. I was sorry more time was not given to introduce the new stake pres. Elders [apostles] Marvin Ashton, [David] Haight, [Melvin Russell] Ballard were all there and spoke. . . . I was glad to be home again without any serious happening.

There in a few words she gives a good sense of how she experienced the world. A month or two later she attended a mission homecoming sacrament meeting at her ward. Her response was:

Why do I feel such failure because we served for such a short time? . . . It is hard for me to share in the joy of others' successes when we fell so short. These are the wrong feelings I struggle with.

There was another Sunday that she was too sick with a respiratory infection to attend church, and Nyman came up to "quad cough" her (quadriplegics need assistance to cough). And another Sunday when the weather was warm and she was ready on time. Cy drove her in her van to church, but after two meetings she started to feel ill, and she left church early:

A beautiful spring day. Koco came early and helped me. . . . I wheeled home alone in my wheelchair. Leslie had offered to drive me home but I didn't want her to be late for her Sunday school class. I insisted on coming home alone. It was very frightening for me. The parking lot was uneven and made me feel like I would turn over in my wheelchair. As I wheeled up the steep hill it felt like I was losing power. I worried my battery would give out and leave me stranded in the middle of the road. The street seemed more level than the sidewalks so I stayed in the street but I had to cross from one side to another twice and the gutters were deep for my chair to run smoothly. . . . I was delighted to find myself safely wheeling up my own driveway. Carly let me in the house.

Very often Sundays turned out to be a day of rest. Most of her would-be visitors were busy with church and so she discovered she had hours to herself on Sunday mornings. She enjoyed that time, catching up on her correspondence, reading the newspaper, and listening to the Tabernacle Choir on the radio.

She also liked to listen to the multi-day sessions of the church's General Conference which were broadcast on the radio in April and October. There were many Mormons who regarded General Conference as a holiday from normal church services and they would take advantage of the free time to visit Lillis during conference. Those interruptions annoyed her because she actually enjoyed listening to conference. If guests were not careful they would come without appointment or agenda. Some brought gifts that she could not store, use, or give away. She wrote:

> Much of the time I feel I have little control of my life. People run in and out any time they choose. Many visitors come without calling. I love seeing them but it unnerves me never being able to know who and when they will interrupt perineal care, exercise, when I'm eating, or just dropping off for a greatly needed nap. I'm awake at 4:45 AM. each morning for morning chores, dressed and in my wheelchair by 5:45 AM. I'm awakened to be turned during the night and am prone from 12 midnight until 12:30 AM. Also take baclofen and drink a large amount of fluid after my prone posture and turned after that, leaving me 3½ hrs sleep at most during any one night. I have few periods of time during the day when I can make up that greatly needed rest. I have been on a schedule similar to this ever since my accident 2½ yrs ago. I believe this is the cause of the great stress I feel most of the time.

Visitors with a friendly greeting might interrupt the Castle family as well; it grew to an irritation that continued day after day, year after year. Even well-mannered visitors might not recognize that they were imposing as they walked through the Castles' house to get to Lillis's apartment.

She started to make new friends at the ward. Among the first were her assigned visiting teachers, Barbara Moench and Eileen McKean. The three of them were born within a year of each other and they got along like sisters. They were playful raconteurs, maybe even gossips. Eileen had something else in common with Lillis; they both had recently lost their husbands while serving as missionaries; they understood each other's grief. Eileen moved out of the ward to a retirement community in 1998 but continued to bring Barbara along to visit until Lillis died.

The rotating shift of her aides presented a problem for regular church attendance. Those shifts, 4 hours on, 4 hours off, did not always match up with the church schedule. Here are two typical complaints:

> March 6, 1994 I didn't attend church today. It is so difficult to get there. It costs $30 for an aide to take me and bring me home, which would be $120 more each month I enjoy going and miss it terribly when I don't go but I need someone to drive me over. I hate to ask Nyman to do it every Sunday.

> November 27, 1994 It snowed several inches last night. I should love to attend church but I have no one to drive me over in my van. It's difficult for me to wheel in the snow. It has been months since I partook of the sacrament . . . about eight months ago. . . . The time schedule makes it quite difficult for me to attend.

These are veiled, personal criticisms of Leslie. The complaints are unfair and misdirected because Cy and Leslie drove her to church many times. Her aides also drove her without extra charge *if* they were on duty. On a few occasions she went to church in her motorized chair, with a granddaughter or a friend walking by her side. The real obstruction was getting Lillis up and ready at the right time. Getting Lillis out of bed, fixing her breakfast, exercising her, dressing and grooming her, tending to her catheter, and other morning chores could take a couple of hours. These were exactly the tasks that the aides were hired to do. Indeed, they did them every day. But they did them at the wrong time on Sundays.

Leslie saw herself as a failsafe for her mother's care and safety. And thus she would most often refuse to do work that the aides were paid to do, such as dressing Lillis for church. As often as not, Leslie was getting her children ready for church or preparing a lesson for Sunday school and had no time to spare. The little drama replayed every week. Lillis was willing to make demands of Leslie and willing to feel sorry for missing church, but she was unwilling to manage the schedule of her employees. After decades of telling children what to do, it was difficult or impossible for Lillis to comprehend a child telling her *no*.

XXIX

Another Obstacle

FRICTION

Lillis tried to assert her herself in little ways. She began paying Leslie "rent," arguing that she should pay her share of utilities. Leslie accepted the money but had never required it. The money failed to make Leslie more submissive.

Lillis would summon Leslie to serve a glass of lemonade to one of her guests—even if that guest were Leslie's brother. Lillis might refuse to be lifted in bed by one of her sons, preferring to call Leslie into her room. Once she was chilled because she could not turn off her air conditioner. She made some phone calls around town looking for Leslie. One call was to Rem's house; Rem's wife Carolyn answered and offered to come and turn off the air conditioner. But Lillis refused that help.

Lillis asked Leslie to cook for her, saying, "Just bring me what your family is eating." Leslie would take her at her word and bring her a cheese sandwich and a bowl of soup. Then Lillis would criticize her for her irregular meal schedule and lack of attention to nutrition and presentation. In general, Leslie did not care about routine or presentation as much as Lillis did.

Lillis would be bothered by any little disorder in her apartment, but Leslie was wary and resistant to being responsible for straightening up. So if a sock were lying on the floor, it would taunt Lillis until the next shift when an aide would come to pick it up.

A couple of times Lillis bought flowers or shrubs, and had her aides plant them in Leslie's backyard. And then she grumbled because Leslie did not maintain them, or her dog dug them up.

Lillis loaned out her van, for example when Nyman needed it to do landscaping, or maybe her brother Ted wanted to take his paintings to a gallery. But if Leslie were to borrow the van, Lillis would snipe at her. The van was underutilized, rarely driven more than 50 miles in a week. When Leslie or Cy needed it they rarely asked permission; after all, they were the chauffeurs, they held the keys, they did the maintenance, and they resented the hulking monstrosity parked in front of their house.

Sometimes Rem would visit and bring his children. At one point Carolyn would direct her children to go play with their cousins, maybe conscious on some level that the Castles were busy. Leslie would send them back to Lillis's apartment. Then Carolyn would say, "Well, I guess we are bothering Leslie; it's time to go home." Then Lillis would scold Leslie, saying, "You make them feel so unwelcome." Leslie's children could also play proxy, and often invaded Lillis's privacy.

When Lillis's brother came to visit he would tease Leslie's dog and provoke it to bark. Sometimes he would hit the dog in the face with the gate, then brag about it as if it were a comedy routine.

Lillis was often sick, easily tipped off-balance by some visitor who had a cold, or dirty hands. Leslie stayed with her and cared for her during those frequent emergencies. Sometimes Lillis was so sick that Leslie could not even leave her alone with an aide. Once in the middle of the night Leslie had to go out in a snowstorm to get some vancomycin, an IV anti-biotic, to hang for Lillis. Leslie was dressed in old sweatpants and as she was getting ready to leave, Lillis was so very sick, but had the energy to say, "Well, you're not going out dressed like that." Leslie responded, "Yes I am; and I'm going to tell everyone that you are my mother."

It sounds amusing now. But in the moment it was like a classical tragedy. The heroic protagonist who was so admirable and sympathetic continued to cause herself pain, completely unaware of her flaw, and seemingly powerless to change. Parenthetically, it should be noted, Leslie was exhausted by the demands of her own children, by her employment, and by her mother. In the secrecy of her diary, Lillis acknowledged, "I have far more comforts and interests than I have earned. . . . Leslie has made my life full and meaningful by taking me from institutional care and giving me the freedom and comforts of my own home."

THE DARK DAYS

The crisis came to a head in July 1995. Lillis asserted that Leslie was evicting her. Lillis had had some success in her life with taking a stand and offering ultimatums; that strategy may have been a component of the impasse. If so, she overplayed her hand. As the days passed, Lillis lamented the money she had spent building the apartment and she worried about where she would move. Embarrassment must have been a component in her thinking, and also whether the next bishop would continue to pay for her expenses. But she never mentioned those factors.

> Monday 7/10/95 I have been so sad and stressed today. Feel like I would have a heart attack and wish I could. The thought of having to pack up and move to who-knows-where, change all my addresses again, new checks, phone numbers, I worry about being [*Two pages are torn out here, and she resumes in a different color of ink, apparently on a different day.*] left alone with little money to take care of myself. I shouldn't feel this way because my children have always been supportive of me and have been willing to do anything they thought would be of help. My brothers and sisters and nieces and nephews and my cousins have also. I am so dependent when it comes to any sort of an emergency. My one hand is capable of many things but not being able to lie down when I'm tired or get myself into the chair is terribly worrisome. I feel very vulnerable and helpless at times. Sometimes I feel not strong enough for another challenge. But there seems to always be another hurdle or mountain to climb and today I feel such an unwanted burden to everyone.

It is heartbreaking to read through that period and contemplate her despair. Over the years she had railed against Leslie in her diary for perceived insults. Some pages are blotted out with felt-tip marker or torn out. Many others remain legible; certainly she would not want those quoted here. To give perspective, she also took turns, over the years, criticizing Rem, Nyman, and many other loved ones—to their faces or in her diary. Dean lived on the other side of the Rockies and largely escaped her reproaches. She complained about Rem's beard and derisively congratulated him when he shaved it. She excoriated Nyman in her diary as shallow, lazy, and light-minded when he refused to talk about attending church or paying tithing. She criticized her youngest brother Ted when he showed up to visit her in his running shorts, sweaty, midway through his long-distance runs. But Leslie was her closest and most frequent target.

The Brooks brothers tried to intervene but were ineffective if not inept. They informally engaged Dean's father-in-law, Grant Hyer, who was a social worker at LDS Hospital. He stated the obvious: that some distance, geographical or emotional, needed to be put between Leslie and Lillis.

Nyman had two houses and offered one to Lillis. It was rented out but could be made available. That was probably more of a bluff than a solution. The house was a small historic house on Marmalade Hill near the capitol, on one of the steepest, narrowest streets in the city. It was inconceivable that a room or door would have been big enough for her heavy hospital bed. Moving to Dean's house in Colorado was never seriously considered. And (no criticism implied) Rem's wife, Carolyn, didn't want her.

Finally, Lillis defused the situation in July with a declaration that belied any eviction notice. She wrote in her diary, "I've decided to remain here at Leslie's and not move. We had a long talk." That was on a Sunday; she also noted that her aide Gretchen Lund had dressed her and driven her to church. And there were additional indications of her new resolve. About this time, Lillis started to have her aides cook her meals in her apartment. Lillis started to see a counselor in August, Joan Anderson, in Bountiful; they had three sessions. Three sessions seems like too few to be effective, but given her self-reliant personality, it is remarkable she submitted to any at all. Leslie had also gone in for counseling, before and after this crisis. In early October, Lillis had an exterior door installed in her apartment. The lack of her own exterior door was a glaring oversight in the original house design. This account is abridged; her problems and behaviors were not all fixed in a couple of months; many persisted. But July 1995 and her decision to remain in her apartment at Leslie's house seemed to mark an important transition.

SELF-WORTH

Lillis had many acquaintances who knew her to be a good conversationalist with thoughtful insights. As a result she was often invited to speak in church or at firesides or at one of her many social clubs. But public speaking was difficult for her. Her one-on-one skills did not transfer easily to speaking in public. If she were given 2 or 3 weeks to prepare, she would spend that time fretting, and would come up with remarks that were formulaic and labored. At a late moment she would sometimes seek help from Leslie or Nyman who might encourage big structural changes.

In November 1995, Bob Miner asked her to speak at a Christmas worship service on December 24. Miner was the Sugar House stake president, and had been one of George's counselors when George was stake president. When the day came, Lillis recorded:

Sunday, 12/24/95 Had to speak today in Sugar House Stake and I feel badly about how jerky my voice was and short of breath I was. I felt I did poorly. I never intend to do it again. Nyman drove me. I don't think he was too happy to do it for me. He was later coming than he said he would be, which caused me stress and then he took the long way there and became angry when I suggested a shorter and better road that wasn't bumpy. He slammed on his brakes and nearly threw me out of my chair and told me he was tired of me giving him orders. I felt bad I had upset him. I'm realizing more and more what a burden I am. My leg bag was not turned off when it was emptied and it leaked on the carpet in the church. I feel so terrible I could die and never have to socialize with anyone again. It is very humiliating for me. This is the most depressed I have ever been.

Monday, Christmas day 1995 This is the most sad Christmas I can ever remember. I can see no purpose in my being here. . . . I bore my children; I long for serious conversation with them.

This story is one example of her self-worth collapsing during the drawn-out gloom of 1995. In such moments she was far too critical of herself. It may be that she never truly appreciated her successes, the strength of her own character, or the admiration of her friends. This passage does not display practical or effective self-examination. She was not suicidal but had periods of situational depression caused by physical pain, by conflict with her children, or by grief over George's death, which was never far from her mind. On those occasions, she would say that her life was a drag on her family and the greater society; her death would bring her closer to George and would be of no consequence to anyone else.

This episode contrasts with the many times she spoke successfully in public, lifted spirits, told exotic and compelling stories, and introduced people to new ideas. Fortunately, she continued to socialize and to accept speaking engagements. She had said that she was not strong enough for another challenge. But in fact she continued to face down her fears and manage her daily problems. She did not give up. Discipline was the flip side of what some might call rigidity. She got up and dressed most every day of her life; that is extraordinary for any spinal patient. She was self-directed, managed her medical care, exercised daily, maintained humor, laughed at herself, and took responsibility for her employees.

XXX

Growing Old

Besides being confined to a wheelchair, Lillis was also growing older, like anyone else. Many of her friends were coming to the ends of their lives. Her cousin Morris Cook died September 1992. Cousin Mable Young died April 1993. Glen Cahoon, who was stake president after George, died at age 65 in September 1994. Al Hibberd, a member of her study group, died in June 1995. Neal Maxwell came down with leukemia in 1996. Cousin Jennie Brown (Hattie's sister) died February 1997. Melvin Hodgkinson, her high school sweetheart, died of lymphoma in January 1998, and his brother Reed Hodgkinson died that same year in April. Another high school friend, Garth Atwood, was caring for his wife who was disabled with Alzheimer's. Marjorie Atwood finally died in August 1999, and Garth continued to call and visit Lillis to talk about his loneliness. At her study group, Lillis noticed that Rex Moulton's hands were shaking, but she commented that he looked good after his bypass surgery.

Hattie Hadlock Lee announced in September 1998 that she had liver cancer. Hattie was her cousin and about her same age. They had been close friends since childhood. Hattie was the street-smart girl who had taught Lillis how to ride the streetcar and open revolving doors in Salt Lake City when they were children. Lillis saw Hattie frequently and wrote, "I had not an inkling of how ill she is. We have been such good friends since childhood. I shall miss her terribly. It makes me very sad." It was a shock when Hattie died the very next month. A few days later, Hattie's children visited Lillis, brought her flowers and news from the funeral.

Lillis turned 75 in October 1998, and in her diary she reminisced about her grandmother Edith Ann Hadlock who had died at 75. Edith Ann was crippled from polio. Lillis as a child had shared a bedroom with her grandmother and was responsible for lifting her into bed. Lillis wrote, "She seemed very old to me at the time." On June 22, 1999, Lillis noted her 50th wedding anniversary in her diary: "How terribly I miss George. How different my life would be were he here. I feel blessed to have had him as long as I did."

Lillis was sick as often as every month or two with respiratory infections, urinary tract infections, and other infections common to people with spinal injuries. Rem made it a habit to bring his stethoscope whenever he visited, and sometimes he would leave the visit to go get antibiotics. Then her antibiotics would bring on bouts of diarrhea. When she got sick she would resist going to a doctor because she was too uncomfortable to contemplate the task of getting dressed and getting into the van. Her dedicated doctors were kind to her; Dr. Jim Pearl, her respiratory doctor, even made house calls, recognizing that she was not stubborn so much as incapable of getting out of bed. Even when she was healthy she was never comfortable. She complained about being in bed until she sat in her chair; then she complained about being uncomfortable in a chair.

CANCER

It was difficult to remember which pains were new and which were old. So it is unclear when she came down with cancer. She mentioned pain in her hips and knees in December 1996, in her "long bones" in March 1997, and in her scapula in August 1997. She shrugged it off as related to her scoliosis or to lying in one position too long. Aspirin helped. In August 1998, her midnight aide Laurie came and showered her, dried her off, and wrapped her in towels, then wheeled her outside to see the full moon. "It was so beautiful, the sky so clear and blue. We also heard an owl hoot. It was the first time in 8 yrs I had seen a full moon. My room is on the north and I don't see the moon."

She discovered a large lump in her right breast in November 1998. The lump was difficult to biopsy and didn't show up well on a mammogram, but intuition told her that it was cancerous and well advanced. She had a mastectomy in December 1998. She did not announce her hospitalization to her brothers and sisters until the surgery was over. Her drainage

Lillis at 68 years old with her granddaughter Lindsey.

tubes were removed in January 1999 and she was on the road to recovery. Some people speculate that she typically recovered quickly from all her illnesses because of her clinical insights and her discipline as a patient.

For the next year she went in for follow-up appointments, had her lymph nodes checked, and her bones scanned. Other than that, little changed for her daily routines. She attended a temple session in March. She went to her study group. She sometimes attended all church sessions—3 hours at a time—to return home a bit surprised that she was so exhausted. She attended the Remington Christmas party at the home of her niece, Jill Remington Love. They opened a time capsule from 16 years earlier that they had assembled for the new millennium. George had contributed a letter and a *Time* magazine; he was the only one who had been present before but was not present now.

She discovered a new lump in March 2000, again on the right side. After a long talk with her oncologist, John Ward, she decided to refuse treatment, but in June when the lump became painful, she had it removed.

All the while she continued to worry and sympathize with her friends who were suffering their own trials. She worried about Lee Atkin, her sister Cleo's husband, who had prostate cancer. Cousin Carmel's two daughters were ill, one with MS, the other with breast cancer. She was pleased that Neal Maxwell's hair was growing back after the end of his chemotherapy. One of her aides, Jessica, had a crisis and missed a shift; Lillis worried about her, knowing that Jessica needed the money; she told her she could work whenever she was able. And she continued to attend church.

But there was a change. Over these weeks her diary entries became shorter and less frequent, and her handwriting became difficult to read. It was not so much that she was in denial; more probably events just caught up and overtook her. Nyman took her in for a bone scan on June 6, which confirmed metastasis. Soon after that she went on hospice.

She wrote on June 16:

Lois came early this morning and gave me a permanent. She drove in alone thru heavy morning traffic. . . . I was in so much pain and she tried to hurry. She was so patient with me. She gave me a good permanent. She also brought a huge breakfast roll and delicious cheese. She never comes empty-handed.

Her hospice physician, Greg Miller, asked her what things she had left unfinished. Typically, she had a long list. The salient item was she wanted to attend the mission homecoming of her grandson English. Miller pointed out that it might be possible, but there would be a price to pay in medical intervention. She thought for a moment and said, "I think it would be OK for me to miss it." Then he prescribed morphine for the pain she had been ignoring, and some caffeinated water to help her stay alert while on morphine. She accepted the morphine but refused the caffeine because of her Mormon sensibilities.

She survived about 6 weeks on hospice, long enough to speak again with each of her many friends and relatives. She was gracious with her doctors, thanking them for allowing her to be acquainted over the past 10 years with her grandchildren, including the youngest, Aidan and Malcolm. She died at home on July 20, 2000, at 76 years of age.

It seems like yesterday.

XXXI

Coda

George liked to read *The Story of the Other Wise Man* by Henry van Dyke to his family each year at Christmastime. In the preface of that story the author asked, "What does life mean? If the meaning could be put into a sentence there would be no need of telling the story."

There is value in a story if it allows one to see or maybe even understand, through the example of others, that which is impossible to assess in oneself. These stories of George and Lillis have been told with a minimum of interpretation. The reader must bear some of the burden to understand.

However, a few assertions seem to emerge: We all proceed without knowing the risks. Good people struggle all their lives with no assurance of success. Patterns are easier to see in retrospect. Regardless, in the end it may not be clear whether we are justified. We are subject to the whims of fate, birth, economy, health, war, and other forces we have yet to identify. Children need generous parents all their lives. Parents and grandparents also need a bit of clemency. People need friends. We imagine our ancestors as heroic, but that is likely a willful distortion.

George was patient with people. He was curious about language, religion, art, music, poetry, and the milestones of human thought and culture. In these he was largely self-schooled. The more he looked out in all directions at the circular horizon the less inclined he was to see himself as the center. It could be said, he did not seek his own—not his own opinions, not his own culture, not his own comfort. He sought understanding.

Lillis was disciplined, perceptive, rational, industrious, and fiercely loyal; those are the qualities that she was born with. What she became was broad-minded, liberal, forgiving, and patient. She relaxed method while maintaining discipline. She helped people as a healer, confidant, and provider. For whatever motive, she saved these stories, allowing us to see that ordinary people live wondrous lives.

By introspection and effort they got better with age. The French proverb "To understand all is to forgive all" seems to have been a component of their thought. Maybe it should be a component of ours as we consider them.

Finally, George and Lillis were kind to each other, and devoted.

Index

Page numbers in *italics* refer to images.